Classics in Linguistics

Chief Editors: Martin Haspelmath, Stefan Müller

In this series:

1. Lehmann, Christian. Thoughts on grammaticalization

2. Schütze, Carson T. The empirical base of linguistics: Grammaticality judgments and linguistic methodology

3. Bickerton, Derek. Roots of language

ISSN: 2366-374X

The empirical base of linguistics

Grammaticality judgments and linguistic methodology

Carson T. Schütze

language
science
press

Carson T. Schütze. 2016. *The empirical base of linguistics: Grammaticality judgments and linguistic methodology* (Classics in Linguistics 2). Berlin: Language Science Press.

This title can be downloaded at:
http://langsci-press.org/catalog/book/89
ISBN: 978-3-946234-02-9 (Digital)
      978-3-946234-03-6 (Hardcover)
      978-3-946234-04-3 (Softcover)
      978-1-523743-32-2 (Softcover US)
ISSN: 2366-374X
DOI:10.17169/langsci.b89.100

Cover and concept of design: Ulrike Harbort
Typesetting: Felix Kopecky, Sebastian Nordhoff, Carson T. Schütze
Fonts: Linux Libertine, Arimo, DejaVu Sans Mono
Typesetting software: XƎLATEX

Language Science Press
Habelschwerdter Allee 45
14195 Berlin, Germany
langsci-press.org

Storage and cataloguing done by FU Berlin

Freie Universität Berlin

For my mother, Dorly Schütze,

and the memory of my father, Ted Schütze

It is simultaneously the greatest virtue and failing of linguistic theory that sequence acceptability judgments are used as the basic data.

(Bever 1970b)

Contents

Contents

Preface (2016)

Since the original version of this book (University of Chicago Press, 1996) went out of print in the 2000s, I have continued to receive inquiries from people asking how they can obtain a copy. I am therefore thrilled that Language Science Press has offered to make the title available again, as part of their Classics in Linguistics series. I would like to thank series editors Stefan Müller and Martin Haspelmath, as well as Sebastian Nordhoff and Felix Kopecky, for their help in making this happen.

The content of this new printing is identical to the first printing, with the following exceptions:

- I have altered the wording in a few places where I found it insufficiently clear or terminologically outdated;

- my uses of the term *informant(s)* have been replaced with *consultant(s)* or *speaker(s)*, in keeping with current practice (of course, the former term still appears in some quoted passages);

- I have updated the reference information for a couple of works that had not been published at the time of the original printing, particularly Cowart (1997);

- the original index has been split into name and subject indexes, and both are now more comprehensive.

In terms of presentation, the following things have changed:

- the format of citations and references has been adapted to LangSci house style, as have other minor typographical choices;

- full given names have been added to references whenever available;

- since the text has been freshly typeset, the page numbers do not match those of the original printing; however, the (sub)section numbers are unchanged: I suggest using those if it is necessary to specify a location within a chapter. Example numbers are also unchanged.

Importantly, I have *not* attempted to update the content in light of subsequent relevant research, since this would undoubtedly have compelled me to try to write a whole new book. Of course, linguistics and psycholinguistics have changed a great deal in the 20 years since I completed the original manuscript; e.g., "theoretical" linguistics has notably become more "experimental." Also, some of my own views on the issues have evolved over those two decades. There are passages in the book that I would have omitted or altered, *if* I had allowed myself to make any substantive revisions. Instead, I have chosen to restrict all follow-up discussion to this preface. In what follows I try to point readers to works that should allow them to "get up to speed" on intervening developments.

For collections that are comprised mainly of papers on topics that are important in the book, see McNair et al. (1996), Penke & Rosenbach (2004), Kepser & Reis (2005), Borsley (2005), Featherston (2007) and replies in the same journal issue, Featherston & Sternefeld (2007), Featherston & Winkler (2009), and Winkler & Featherston (2009). My more recent views can be found in the following surveys: Schütze (2006; 2011) and Schütze & Sprouse (2013).

There have been (at least) four major developments involving the empirical base of linguistics that anyone interested in the topic should be aware of.

1. The adaptation of the magnitude estimation task from psychophysics to judgment collection (Bard, Robertson & Sorace 1996). This was touted as having numerous potential advantages over the traditional Likert scale task, most or all of which have been subsequently refuted (see Weskott & Fanselow 2011 and Sprouse, Schütze & Almeida 2013).

2. The use of World Wide Web searches to establish attestation, and infer acceptability, of certain sentence/construction types. I discuss the limitations of this approach in Schütze (2009).

3. The use of Amazon Mechanical Turk (AMT) and potentially other crowd-sourcing platforms as sources of subjects for acceptability judgment and many other psycholinguistic experiments (so far, in only a handful of languages). For an empirical investigation of how AMT results compare with judgments collected in the lab (on a small range of constructions in English), see Sprouse (2011).

4. Detailed empirical challenges to – and defenses of – the proposal, advocated in Section 7.2 in the book, that Subjacency effects could be reduced to processing factors. See Yoshida et al. (2014) as well as the Stanford/Maryland debate (Hofmeister & Sag (2010); Hofmeister, Staum Casasanto

& Sag (2012a,b); Sprouse, Wagers & Phillips (2012a,b), and many of the contributions in Sprouse & Hornstein 2014).

Finally, there is a statement by Chomsky, which I attribute in the book (p. 195) to a popular press source, about which I have often been questioned, wherein Chomsky calls it a truism that genetically based Universal Grammar (UG) is subject to *some* individual variation. For those who have asked whether Chomsky's position can be confirmed in any academic publications, I offer the following quotes:

> Putting aside genetic variation (an interesting but marginal phenomenon in the case of language) and conceivable but unknown epigenetic effects, the principles of UG, whatever they are, are invariant. (Chomsky 2013: 35)

> It is hardly controversial that [the faculty of language] is a common human possession apart from pathology, to an approximation so close that we can ignore variation. (Chomsky 2008: 138)

I am aware of no empirical evidence that would indicate how much UG can vary across individuals.

Carson T. Schütze   December 2015

References

Bard, Ellen Gurman, Dan Robertson & Antonella Sorace. 1996. Magnitude estimation of linguistic acceptability. *Language* 72. 32–68.

Borsley, Robert D. (ed.). 2005. Data in theoretical linguistics. Special issue. *Lingua* 115(11).

Chomsky, Noam. 2008. On phases. In Robert Freidin, Carlos P. Otero & Maria Luisa Zubizarreta (eds.), *Foundational issues in linguistic theory: Essays in honor of Jean-Roger Vergnaud*, 133–166. Cambridge, MA: MIT Press.

Chomsky, Noam. 2013. Problems of projection. *Lingua* 130. 33–49.

Cowart, Wayne. 1997. *Experimental syntax: Applying objective methods to sentence judgments*. Thousand Oaks, CA: SAGE Publications.

Featherston, Sam. 2007. Data in generative grammar: The stick and the carrot. *Theoretical Linguistics* 33(3). 269–318.

Featherston, Sam & Wolfgang Sternefeld (eds.). 2007. *Roots: Linguistics in search of its evidential base.* Berlin: Mouton de Gruyter.

Featherston, Sam & Susanne Winkler (eds.). 2009. *The fruits of empirical linguistics. Volume 1: Process.* Berlin: Mouton de Gruyter.

Hofmeister, Philip & Ivan A. Sag. 2010. Cognitive constraints and island effects. *Language* 86. 366–415.

Hofmeister, Philip, Laura Staum Casasanto & Ivan A. Sag. 2012a. How do individual cognitive differences relate to acceptability judgments? A reply to Sprouse, Wagers, and Phillips. *Language* 88. 390–400.

Hofmeister, Philip, Laura Staum Casasanto & Ivan A. Sag. 2012b. Misapplying working-memory tests: A reductio ad absurdum. *Language* 88. 408–409.

Kepser, Stephan & Marga Reis (eds.). 2005. *Linguistic evidence: Empirical, theoretical, and computational perspectives.* Berlin: Mouton de Gruyter.

McNair, Lisa, Kora Singer, Lise M. Dobrin & Michelle M. AuCoin (eds.). 1996. *Papers from the parasession on theory and data in linguistics* (CLS 32/2). Chicago: Chicago Linguistic Society.

Penke, Martina & Anette Rosenbach (eds.). 2004. What counts as evidence in linguistics? Special issue. *Studies in Language* 28(3).

Phillips, Colin. 2006. The real-time status of island phenomena. *Language* 82. 795–823.

Schütze, Carson T. 2006. Data and evidence. In Keith Brown (ed.), *Encyclopedia of language and linguistics*, 2nd edn., vol. 3, 356–363. Oxford: Elsevier.

Schütze, Carson T. 2009. Web searches should supplement judgements, not supplant them. *Zeitschrift für Sprachwissenschaft* 28. 151–156.

Schütze, Carson T. 2011. Linguistic evidence and grammatical theory. *Wiley Interdisciplinary Reviews: Cognitive Science* 2. 206–221.

Schütze, Carson T. & Jon Sprouse. 2013. Judgment data. In Robert J. Podesva & Devyani Sharma (eds.), *Research methods in linguistics*, 27–50. New York: Cambridge University Press.

Sprouse, Jon. 2011. A validation of Amazon Mechanical Turk for the collection of acceptability judgments in linguistic theory. *Behavior Research Methods* 43(1). 155–167.

Sprouse, Jon & Norbert Hornstein (eds.). 2014. *Experimental syntax and island effects.* Cambridge: Cambridge University Press.

Sprouse, Jon, Carson T. Schütze & Diogo Almeida. 2013. A comparison of informal and formal acceptability judgments using a random sample from *Linguistic Inquiry* 2001–2010. *Lingua* 134. 219–248.

Sprouse, Jon, Matt Wagers & Colin Phillips. 2012a. A test of the relation between working memory and syntactic island effects. *Language* 88. 82–123.

Sprouse, Jon, Matt Wagers & Colin Phillips. 2012b. Working-memory capacity and island effects: A reminder of the issues and the facts. *Language* 88. 401–407.

Weskott, Thomas & Gisbert Fanselow. 2011. On the informativity of different measures of linguistic acceptability. *Language* 87. 249–273.

Winkler, Susanne & Sam Featherston (eds.). 2009. *The fruits of empirical linguistics. Volume 2: Product.* Berlin: Mouton de Gruyter.

Yoshida, Masaya, Nina Kazanina, Leticia Pablos & Patrick Sturt. 2014. On the origin of islands. *Language* 29(7). 761–770.

Preface (1996)

The goal of this book is to demonstrate that the absence of methodology of grammaticality judgments in linguistics constitutes a serious obstacle to meaningful research, and to begin to propose suitable remedies for this problem. Throughout much of the history of linguistics, judgments of the grammaticality/acceptability of sentences (and other linguistic intuitions) have been the major source of evidence in constructing grammars. While this seems to have been an exceedingly fruitful approach, some skeptics have worried that theoretical linguists are in fact constructing grammars of intuition, which might not have much to do with the competence that underlies everyday production or comprehension of language. Also, in the pseudoexperimental procedure of judgment elicitation there is typically no attempt to impose any of the standard experimental controls, and often the only subject is the theorist himself or herself. Should we linguists be worried? I think so. I survey the way grammaticality judgments are currently used in theoretical syntax, and argue that such uses, together with the problems of intuition and experimental design, demand a careful examination of judgments, not as pure sources of data, but as instances of metalinguistic performance.

Several important issues arise when this view of grammaticality judgments is pursued, including which tasks one should use to elicit them, what people are doing when they give them, and what they can really tell us about linguistic competence. On the assumption that grammaticality judgments result from interactions among primary language faculties of the mind and general cognitive processes, I try to understand the process by identifying and analyzing its component parts. I review the psycholinguistic research that has examined ways in which the judgment process can vary with differences among subjects, experimental manipulations, and spurious features of the stimulus. Parallels with other cognitive behaviors are pointed out. After drawing together the substantive and methodological findings into a schematic picture of what the overall process of giving linguistic intuitions might look like, I propose strategies for collecting these intuitions that avoid the pitfalls of previous work and take account of the conditions that have been shown to influence such judgments. I suggest that we can actually strengthen the case for linguistic universals by giving empirical arguments that much of the variability in judgments can be explained without appealing to differences in Universal Grammar. Finally, I discuss how mainstream linguistic theory might be affected by the growing body of research in this area. I think we will increasingly feel not just a need but also a desire to tackle difficult data questions, particularly as theoretically sophisticated psycholinguistic research increases and we come to understand more about the ways in which linguistic competence is put to use in the mind.

Acknowledgments (1996)

*Just as the Navajo weavers pur-
posely make one error in a rug, to
let the soul out, so I cannily craft
errors into all of my papers.*

(Ross 1979)

This book is a substantially revised version of my University of Toronto M.A. Forum paper (Schütze 1991). It has benefited enormously in both content and style
from the contributions of several people. None of them bears any responsibility
for its remaining flaws, cannily crafted or otherwise; they are all the fault of that
little person who runs around inside my computer making it work. First and fore-
most, I would like to thank my supervisors at Toronto, Peter Reich and Graeme
Hirst, without whose comments and criticisms a far inferior product would have
resulted. Peter enthusiastically supported my academic work for several years,
and has supported this project in particular since August 1990, when we both discovered to our surprise and delight that there is a literature on the topic of grammaticality judgments. Graeme was invaluable in pointing out relevant work in
fields that I was unaware of, in tracking down current unpublished research, and
in his meticulous scrutiny of my prose. He was most generous with his time and
energy, despite innumerable other priorities. At MIT, Noam Chomsky provided
extensive comments on the penultimate version of the manuscript, adding important historical perspectives, especially for the first two chapters, and helping
me to see the big issues in a more critical light. For this I am very grateful.

Several other people have commented on part or all of the manuscript at various stages, including Tom Wasow, James McCawley, Wayne Cowart, Tom Bever,
and Jila Ghomeshi. At the University of Chicago Press, Geoffrey Huck encouraged me to turn the paper into a book, provided many helpful suggestions on
how to do so, and supported me every step of the way. I am indebted to him
for this wonderful opportunity. Karen Peterson edited the manuscript, vastly im-
proving its readability and lucidity, and cheerfully answered my incessant questions about the process. Thanks to Karen and Geoff, the publication process has
been a pleasure. David Braun, Colin Phillips, Jonathan Bobaljik, and Orin Percus
helped with the proofreading.

Acknowledgments (1996)

Much of the groundwork for this book was laid in the course of an M.A. Forum class at the University of Toronto, and I owe thanks to my fellow participants. Elan Dresher, our forum supervisor, supplied encouragement and skepticism in just the right doses to keep us working steadily. He also read drafts of several portions of the paper, providing a perspective that would otherwise have been lacking. His open-mindedness and sense of humor were a boon to us all. My fellow forum students, Amy Green, Päivi Koskinen, and Ana Palma dos Santos, commented on my work and, more importantly, provided camaraderie as we faced our tasks together.

Several other people have contributed in important ways to this book. I thank Elizabeth Cowper for useful discussions at the beginning of this project, and for her advice on portions of the book that deal with syntactic theory. Susanne Carroll brought to my attention one of the most important sources on this topic, Birdsong 1989. Charles Houpt at Cornell shared his thoughts and course papers with me and encouraged me to pursue this project. I would also like to acknowledge various USENET readers who contributed pointers to the literature.

The research reported in this book was financially supported by a postgraduate scholarship from the Natural Sciences and Engineering Research Council of Canada while I was at the University of Toronto. At MIT my research was supported by the Research Training Grant "Language: Acquisition and Computation" awarded by the National Science Foundation (US) to the Massachusetts Institute of Technology (DIR 9113607), by a doctoral fellowship from the Social Sciences and Humanities Research Council of Canada, and by an Imperial Oil Fulbright Scholarship. Their support of my research in cognitive science is gratefully acknowledged.

1 Introduction

Linguists have not formulated a "methodology of sentence judgments."

(van Riemsdijk & Williams 1986)

1.1 Goals

I aim to demonstrate in this book that grammaticality judgments and other sorts of linguistic intuition, while indispensable forms of data for linguistic theory, require new ways of being collected and used. A great deal is known about the instability and unreliability of judgments, but rather than propose that they be abandoned, I endeavor to explain the source of their shiftiness and how it can be minimized. I argue that if several simple steps are taken to remove obvious sources of bias, grammaticality judgments can provide an excellent source of information about people's grammars. Thus, I respond to two of the most widespread criticisms of generative grammar – namely, that it involves constructing theories of intuition rather than of language use, and that it is highly subjective and biased by the views of the linguist. This involves drawing from a wide range of literature and from linguistic theory (both pro- and antigenerative) and from the philosophy of language. Linguists can expect to take away from this book numerous practical suggestions on how to collect better and more useful data, and on how to respond to criticisms of such data. As I set out to review almost all the major psycholinguistic experiments that have been done to investigate the linguistic judgment process, psycholinguists should also find much of interest, including numerous suggestions for experimental work that they might wish to pursue.

Throughout much of the history of linguistics, linguistic intuitions have been the most important source of evidence in constructing grammars. Major types of intuition include canonical grammaticality judgments, intuitions about derivational morphological relationships among words, intuitions about correspondences among different utterance types (e.g., question/answer pairs), identifications of structural versus lexical ambiguity, and discriminations of the syntactic status of superficially similar word strings, among many others (Chomsky (1975)). While I most often talk about grammaticality judgments in this book, I treat this as a cover term, because these judgments have received much more attention than other kinds of linguistic intuition. It should be understood that wherever possible I intend the discussion to extend to other sorts of intuition, and I do not wish to imply that grammaticality judgments in the narrow sense have any special status.

It is not immediately obvious why a description of people's competence in understanding and producing language should be based on behavior in situations where they are doing neither but, rather, are reporting intuitions. There are four key reasons for the use of grammaticality judgments. First, by eliciting judgments, we can examine reactions to sentence types that might occur only very rarely in spontaneous speech or recorded corpora. This is a standard reason for performing experiments in social science – observational study does not always provide a high enough concentration of the phenomena we are most interested in.[1] A second, related reason for using grammaticality judgments is to obtain a form of information that scarcely exists within normal language use at all – namely, negative information, in the form of strings that are not part of the language. The third reason for using judgments is that when one is merely observing speech it is difficult to distinguish reliably slips, unfinished utterances, and so forth, from grammatical production. A fourth and more controversial reason is to minimize the extent to which the communicative and representational functions of language skill obscure our insight into its mental nature. Thus, we construct arbitrary situations for adults to deal with, which tap the structural properties of language without having any real function (Bever 1986). This last rationale presupposes a particular view of grammatical competence as cognitively separate from other facets of language knowledge and use, and hence its validity depends on one's theoretical stand on this issue. The first three reasons, however, are relatively theory-neutral. (See Grandy (1981) for these and other standard arguments in favor of the use of grammaticality judgments; see Newmeyer (1983: 62–63), for additional arguments against the use of alternative data sources.)

Such justifications seem sensible enough, perhaps even unavoidable, but that

---

[1] In principle, the conclusion does not automatically follow. One could in theory do experiments on the production and comprehension of sentences chosen by the researcher, without recourse to judgments. In practice, however, this is problematic. On the production side, it is difficult to induce a subject to produce precisely the sentence one wishes to study without actually exposing the subject to the sentence. On the comprehension side, it is hard to discover anything about the nature, or even the success or failure, of the comprehension process without eliciting some additional reaction, such as a judgment.

has not stopped some skeptics and critics from wanting to abandon the use of judgments altogether: "I ... regard the 'linguistic intuition of the native speaker' as extremely valuable heuristically, but too shifty and variable (both from speaker to speaker and from moment to moment) to be of any criterial value" (Householder 1965: 15). Gethin (1990) believes that grammaticality judgments are useless. Becker finds their very lack of communicative function problematic:

> And so the "modern" linguist spends his or her time starring or unstarring terse unlikely sentences like "John, Bill and Tom killed each other" (to pick one at random from a recent journal), which seethe with repressed frustration and are difficult to work into a conversation. These example sentences bear no discernible resemblance to the sentences which compose the text that purportedly explains them – yet the linguist's own sentences are also alleged (implicitly) to be drawn from the same English Language! (Becker 1975: 70)

In response to such attitudes, some philosophers of language have adopted positions that have gone farther in the opposite direction than most theoreticians would likely feel comfortable with. For example, Carr (1990) states:

> The arguments that intuitively accessed grammaticality judgments either are not sufficient or are not necessary as the evidential basis for linguistic theory cannot proceed, and the fact of theoretical linguistic practice shows that autonomous linguistics proceeds with such evidence being not only necessary but also sufficient for the testing of hypotheses. (p. 57)

As I make clear in this book, I do not believe that one can defend the sufficiency of judgments alone.

Regardless of what the critics say, it is clear that the use of grammaticality judgments is here to stay for the foreseeable future. Still, eliciting linguistic judgments is problematic in a number of respects. Not only is the elicitation situation artificial, raising the standard issues of ecological validity, but the subject is being asked for a sort of behavior that, at least on the face of it, is entirely different from everyday conversation.[2] This has led some to suggest that theoretical linguists

---

[2] Householder (1971; 1973) tried to find the closest conversational analogues to grammaticality judgments. He suggests that the following are some of the typical reactions one is inclined to have when a speaker utters something out of the ordinary: the listener is baffled ("I don't get it; come again"); the listener finds an inconsistency or implausibility ("You must mean X, don't you?"); the listener characterizes the speaker as being from another dialect area ("Aha, a southerner!"); the listener concludes that the speaker is quoting a proverb or poetry ("You mean 'figuratively speaking,' I suppose").

are in fact constructing grammars of linguistic intuitions or judgments, which need not be identical with grammars of the competence underlying production or comprehension (Bever 1970a; Birdsong 1989; Gleitman & Gleitman 1979). However, Wayne Cowart (personal communication) argues that linguistic judgments do play a fairly central role in our day-to-day lives, and cites the following examples. We might use judgments of other people's speech when we first meet them in forming opinions about them and categorizing them on various dimensions. We might assess other people's utterances with respect to our own grammar (and vice versa) in order to manipulate the extent to which we are perceived as belonging to the same community. Children growing up in a multilingual environment might judge the utterances they hear in order to assess which language they most closely resemble, allowing them to differentiate languages they are learning concurrently. The last of these three suggestions strikes me as the most compelling, but given how little we understand about multilingual acquisition, we cannot say with certainty that children's evaluations of utterances are similar to the explicit judgments of adults.

In addition to these problems, which are often found in psychology as well, there are important shortcomings that arise because linguistic elicitation does *not* follow the procedures of psychological experimentation. Unlike natural scientists, linguists are not trained in methods for getting reliable data and determining which of two conflicting data reports is more reliable. In the vast majority of cases in linguistics, there is not the slightest attempt to impose any of the standard experimental control techniques, such as random sampling of subjects and stimulus materials or counterbalancing for order effects. (See Derwing (1979) for a discussion of linguists' "blatantly informal" methods.) Perhaps worst of all, often the only subject in these pseudoexperiments is none other than the theorist himself or herself: "One of the unfortunate consequences of Chomsky's mentalist view of linguistics is that in recent years a number of younger linguists have indulged very heavily in arguments based on their intuitions about quirks of their personal idiolects"[3] (Sampson 1975: 74) (see also Newmeyer 1983 and Bradac et al. 1980). In the absence of anything approaching a rigorous methodology, we must seriously question whether the data gathered in this way are at all meaningful or useful to the linguistic enterprise. More than a few observers of linguistics have agreed with Labov's "painfully obvious conclusion ... that linguists cannot con-

---

[3] Such behavior is certainly not a consequence of the Chomskian view in the sense that he encourages or implicitly endorses it. If there is any causal link at all between the theory and such practices, it presumably arises from the mistaken belief that if the object of study (grammar) is in the mind of the individual, then the behavior of a single individual (e.g., oneself) constitutes the only data one need consult. I discuss throughout the book why this does not follow.

tinue to produce theory and data at the same time" (Labov 1972a: 199). What is to stop linguists from (knowingly or unknowingly) manipulating the introspection process to substantiate their own theories?[4]

The informal nature of judgment collection has long been acknowledged. Consider, for example, the following passages from Chomsky (1969):

> The gathering of data is informal; there has been very little use of experimental approaches (outside of phonetics) or of complex techniques of data collection and data analysis of a sort that can easily be devised, and that are widely used in the behavioral sciences. The arguments in favor of this informal procedure seem to me quite compelling; basically, they turn on the realization that for the theoretical problems that seem most critical today, it is not at all difficult to obtain a mass of crucial data without use of such techniques. Consequently, linguistic work, at what I believe to be its best, lacks many of the features of the behavioral sciences. (p. 56)

> I have no doubt that it would be possible to devise operational and experimental procedures that could replace the reliance on introspection with little loss, but it seems to me that in the present state of the field, this would simply be a waste of time and energy. (p. 81)

Derwing's response to this attitude is unequivocal.

> Such 'arguments' are not compelling at all. The choice here is between proven data-collection methods and the reliable 'hard' data to which they lead or inferior 'informal' methods and the 'soft' data which inevitably result. ... This is hardly a choice. In linguistics there is reason to believe that the choice is *available*, but has been ignored or neglected in the rush to theory. ... All that is necessary is 'to replace intuition by some more rigorous criterion' ([Chomsky 1962: 24]) and attempt to establish, under controlled experimental conditions, whether naive native speakers really can do all the things which Chomsky says that they can (such as make consistent judgments of grammaticality). (Derwing 1973: 250)

The conflict between these two positions is precisely what this book is about.

An additional rationalization for the use of grammaticality judgment data in some cases seems to have been related to Chomsky's competence/performance

---

[4] One possible answer is that competition among linguists will prevent such manipulation; see Chapter 4, fn. 19.

distinction (see Section 2.2 for a detailed discussion of this matter). Actual speech production and comprehension are supposedly fraught with errors of all kinds, such as false starts, and are subject to human memory limitations. These so-called performance variables serve to obscure a speaker's underlying competence. But what if we could relieve subjects of the "cognitive burden" of actual production or comprehension and present them with ready-made sentences such that the only task would be to judge their grammaticality? Would this not allow us to get much closer to people's true competence?[5] Unfortunately, there is ample evidence that it would not. While grammaticality judgments offer a *different* access path from language use to competence, they are themselves just another sort of performance (Birdsong 1989; Levelt et al. 1977; Bever 1970b; 1974; Bever & Langendoen 1971; Grandy 1981), and as such are subject to at least as many confounding factors as production, and likely even more.

The purpose of this chapter is to motivate the search for resolutions to the issues raised above and to outline the approach to be taken. The discussion will be mostly at an informal, conceptual level, with technical terminology and details left for subsequent chapters. The structure of the chapter is as follows. In Section 1.2, I use the problems raised above, along with others, to motivate the goals and approach of the remainder of the book. Before intuitions (or any other behavior) can really begin to tell us something about competence, we need at least to be aware of, and ideally to understand the effects of, the component psychological processes that intervene between the two. I propose that this understanding is achievable in principle if we construct a comprehensive model of the judgment process. This model would allow the extensive research already conducted by psycholinguists to be unified and integrated, and would allow contradictory results to be scrutinized. At the very least, a well-supported model of

---

[5] Sampson (1975) phrases the position as follows, although he goes on to reject it: "The part of our brain which makes conscious judgments about the English language perhaps has a 'hot line' to the part of our brain which controls our actual speaking, so that we know what we can and cannot say in English in the same direct, 'incorrigible' way that, say, I know I have toothache" (p. 72). I have not found many explicit examples of this reasoning in the theoretical linguistic literature, but the belief seems to have been very widely held, because there are numerous instances (cited in Birdsong (1989)) where Lasnik, Chomsky, and others attempt to curb this view. For example, Lasnik (1981: 20) states that "grammaticality judgments are often *incorrectly* considered as direct reflections of competence" (emphasis added). Certainly, many authors have wrongly accused Chomsky of claiming that people have a consistent ability to assess grammaticality (e.g., Nagata 1988). Gleitman & Gleitman (1970: 11) attribute to Chomsky the claim that *linguists'* judgments are free of contamination. The view might have stemmed in part from confusion of Chomsky's terms *intuition* and *judgment*, a matter that I take up in Section 2.2.

this type should raise the awareness of linguists to the vast complexities underlying the apparently simple task of deciding whether a sentence is grammatical. In Section 1.3, I further motivate the endeavor by describing some real examples of linguistic research that show how the approach I propose can work to benefit the field. Section 1.4 presents a working hypothesis concerning the source of extragrammatical influences on judgments that I assume in much of what follows. Finally, Section 1.5 sets out the scope and structure of the remainder of the book.

1.2 Approach

Linguistic intuitions became the royal way into an understanding of the competence which underlies all linguistic performance. However, if such a linguistic competence exists at all, i.e., some relatively autonomous mental capacity for language, linguistic intuitions seem to be the least obvious data on which to base the study of its structure. They are derived and rather artificial psycholinguistic phenomena which develop late in language acquisition ... and are very dependent on explicit teaching and instruction. They cannot be compared with primary language use such as speaking and listening. The domain of Chomskian linguistics is linguistic intuitions. The relation between these intuitions and man's capacity for language, however, is highly obscure.

(Levelt et al. 1977)

In this section I describe briefly the motivations for and approach to an in-depth investigation of the process of forming grammaticality judgments, which will be expanded upon in later chapters. I argue that an understanding of this process would provide the basis for an objective method of establishing which judgment data bear most directly on the grammar, and of extracting grammatical information from judgments that are confounded by other factors. The idea of factoring grammaticality out of acceptability judgments has been proposed before (e.g., Birdsong (1989); Carroll, Bever & Pollack (1981); Botha (1973)). In the words of Gleitman & Gleitman (1970), "if we could strip away various contaminating factors in behavior, we might see the grammar bare" (p. 10). That contaminants are present and in need of stripping will be demonstrated below. The traditional view of how judgments relate to language use is too naive. For instance, Cohen, while he shows considerable concern for the issues, in the end remains overly simplistic:

A native speaker's intuition that the string *S* is grammatical is just his immediate and untutored (though in principle observable) inclination to take

S as being well-formed, and in this sense he can have such an intuition if and only if he would be (equally observably) inclined to utter *S* whenever his circumstances, motivation, beliefs, etc., are precisely appropriate for a communication with the sense of *S* and also he is applying ideal standards of care and attention in the linguistic formulation of his utterance. It follows that the difference between an utterance of *S* and an intuition of *S*'s grammaticalness, as data for grammar, is just that while the former constitutes an actual occurrence of *S* in human speech, the latter establishes a potential occurrence – i.e., a potential production by some speaker. Hence intuitions of grammaticalness can always provide a vital kind of data that actual utterances may often fail to present; and because of this it is exclusive reliance on the observation of actual utterances, not reliance on intuitions of grammaticalness, that fails to mirror essential features of scientific method. (Cohen 1981: 240–241)

If one is concerned with the scientific method, it seems sensible to begin the way other scientists do, by scrutinizing the data source. Bever (1972) makes an appropriate analogy to natural science in this regard:

Such investigations are analogous to that of a biologist who checks the limits on a microscope before examining single cells with it (for example, if he does not know the refractory limitations of his microscope he may spuriously attribute color bands to the cells). However, to explore the limits of the available tools of observation is not to suggest that cells do not exist. Similarly, I have tried to examine the limits on the most extensive observational tool linguists utilize to gather data about linguistic structure: grammaticality intuitions. This investigation does not suggest that linguistic structure does not exist; indeed the investigation of interactions between manifest intuitions and inner linguistic structure cannot proceed without the *a priori* assumption that the inner structure is itself as "real" as the expressed intuitions. (p. 412)

It should not be controversial to suggest that linguists ought to study their methodology for these standard scientific reasons: to get more reliable facts by developing methods for gathering, processing, and reporting data so that the results of different investigators are comparable and their methods of analysis consistent; and to get more valid data by assessing what errors are present in the data reports and trying to eliminate their sources (Labov 1978). In Chapter 2, I present several examples showing that these measures are now necessary. The days are over when linguistics had more than enough to worry about with un-controversial, commonplace judgment data, and the sophisticated and complex judgments now in use by theoreticians assume much about human abilities that remains unproved, even unscrutinized. We simply do not know whether the ques-tions we are asking people are meaningful and can be answered in any principled way. I argue below that there is much to be gained by applying the experimen-tal methodology of social science to the gathering of grammaticality judgments, and that in the absence of such practices our data might well be suspect. Elim-inating or controlling for confounding factors requires us to have some idea of what those factors might be, and such an understanding can only be gained by systematic study of the judgment process. Finally, I argue that by studying inter-speaker variation rather than ignoring it (by treating only the majority dialect or one's own idiolect), one uncovers interesting facts.

This general approach is not a new proposal; Levelt et al. and Bever have artic-ulated the general direction of this approach with great foresight:

> Where do grammaticality intuitions come from? It makes no sense to as-sume a priori that the domain of linguistic intuition is a relatively closed one, as many linguists appear to do. Such intuitions are highly dependent on our knowledge of the world and on the structure of our inferential ca-pacities. (Levelt et al. 1977: 89)

> *What is the Science of Linguistics a Science of?* Linguistic intuitions do not necessarily directly reflect the structure of a language, yet such intuitions are the basic data the linguist uses to verify his grammar. This fact could raise serious doubts as to whether linguistic science is about anything at all, since the nature of the source of its data is so obscure. However, this obscurity is characteristic of every exploration of human behavior. Rather than rejecting linguistic study, we should pursue the course typical of most psychological sciences; give up the belief in an "absolute" intuition about sentences and study the laws of the intuitional process itself. (Bever 1970a: 346; emphasis in original)

Elliot, Legum & Thompson (1969) make the case for studying variation: "There are facts both about linguistic theory and about the grammars of particular lan-guages whose existence will be obscured unless variation is taken into account" (p. 52); "At least some variation is not completely mysterious and seems amenable to statement in terms within the realm of linguistic theory. At the same time, lin-guists have a responsibility to determine what kinds of variation exist rather than ignoring variation by basing syntactic descriptions on trivially small numbers of informants" (p. 58). Carden (e.g., 1973) makes the same case. These authors go on to show that variability on theoretically important issues such as the *do so* construction and reflexive anaphors falls into implicational hierarchies of acceptability.

Thus, the approach that I pursue in this work is to examine the process of judging grammaticality, including the role of grammar in this process and its relation to other relevant mental components. In addition to studying an intriguing form of behavior, one that has been almost entirely overlooked in favor of production and comprehension, I attempt to integrate the existing research findings in this area by sorting out the facts from the specific theories proposed in each study; assessing their consistency; clarifying how they fit into an overall theory of cognition; establishing which methodologies are most reliable, valid, and informative; and proposing new experiments to fill gaps in our knowledge. While the psychology of grammaticality judgments might hold as many complexities and and mysteries as language itself, that is no reason for despair or dismissal – it is all the more reason for us to begin the task of unraveling them.

1.3 Motivation: Whither Linguistics?

A glance at the length of the reference section of this book shows that more than a few language researchers have concerned themselves with the problems that I am addressing here. Many of the experimental findings were published a number of years ago, but experimental research seems to be on the increase again, along with continued calls for greater use of formal experimentation for collecting judgment data (e.g., Hirst (1981: 100–101)). Does all this work have any real effect on the way theoretical linguistics is carried out on a day-to-day basis? While instances in which theoretical linguistics takes experimental research into account are still few and far between, I believe that issues in grammaticality judgment collection and interpretation *are* receiving greater attention. From among the studies that make appropriate use of judgment data within the framework of theoretical argumentation I will cite three examples of what I consider to be cutting-edge work in the hope of facilitating and encouraging more research along these lines.

The first such work is by Grimshaw & Rosen (1990) (building on work by Chien & Wexler (1990)), who argue that, contrary to first appearances, children's linguistic behavior does tell us something about their grammars – namely, that they include Principle B of Binding Theory. Their reasoning is that

Performance in an experiment, including performance on the standard linguistic task of making grammaticality judgments, cannot be equated with grammatical knowledge. To determine properties of the underlying knowledge system requires inferential reasoning, sometimes of a highly abstract sort. (p. 188)

The inevitable screening effects of processing demands and other performance factors do not prevent us from establishing the character of linguistic knowledge; they just make it more challenging. ... An analysis *of* these performance factors makes it possible to see, if only dimly, through the performance filter. (p. 217)

Grimshaw & Rosen conclude that, while children do not show perfect mastery of Binding Theory, they perform above chance, and treat violations of Binding Theory differently from nonviolations. They argue that inherent properties of the relevant constructions, as well as of the experiments by which they are evaluated, conspire to worsen children's performance, especially as reflected in their apparent lesser mastery of Principle B versus Principle A. The paper is unusual in that it represents work by theoreticians in which a major goal is the explanation of the connection between behavior on judgment tasks and linguistic knowledge. While a naive view of the facts contradicts their claim, they argue that once psychological factors such as response bias and experimental demand characteristics are taken into account, the results support their theory. One may still dispute their conclusions, but their effort points in the right direction.

The second example of work that uses judgment data appropriately is a paper by Carden & Dieterich (1981), the goal of which is to establish structural conditions on pronoun coreference. Carden & Dieterich deal with cases where a pronoun precedes the noun phrase with which it is coreferent, e.g., examples (1) and (2), where cosubscripting indicates coreference:

(1)   I knew him$_i$ when Harvey$_i$ was a little boy.

(2)   We'll just have to fire him$_i$, whether McIntosh$_i$ likes it or not.

A handful of instances of these constructions have been found in texts, but proportionately very few compared to cases of uncontroversial backwards coreference like that in (3):

(3)   The boy who loves her$_i$ claims that Mary$_i$ is a genius.

Langacker (1969), who claims that sentences like (1) and (2) are bad, pairs such a sentence with a clearly good example in his paper, whereas Reinhart (1976), who claims that sentences like (1) and (2) should be good, contrasts such a sentence with a clearly bad one. This issue, according to Carden & Dieterich, also illustrates the problem with corpus data: "How do we interpret this data? Do we cheer because there *were* six examples, and conclude that Reinhart was right? Or do we boo because there were *only* six examples, as against hundreds of the uncontroversially good type? ... We may have a good but (accidentally) rare construction; or we may have a bad construction occurring a few times because of errors" (Carden & Dieterich 1981: 591). The authors investigate the status of sentences like (1) and (2) using an experiment that shows that these questionable forms are accepted no more often than an uncontroversially bad form. (In each case, only 1 of their 30 subjects accepted them.) The materials were constructed so that a preceding context sentence allowed a plausible reading where the crucial coreference relationship did *not* hold, as well as a reading where it *did* hold, so that subjects would not be forced by considerations of plausibility into accepting an ungrammatical structure. They also tested the uncontroversially bad sentences preceded by the same context sentence, so that the results would be fully comparable. The one significant shortcoming of their methodology is that they employed only two examples of each type of crucial sentence, so their results might have been affected by quirks of those specific sentences.

A third exemplary study also involves backwards coreference. It was conducted by Gerken & Bever (1986), who were apparently not aware of Carden and Dieterich's work in this area. On the basis of inter-speaker differences in the interpretation of the same sorts of sentences, Gerken & Bever propose that linguistic universals, and Binding Theory in particular, are not necessarily applied to complete sentence structures as given by linguistic competence but, rather, are applied to the speaker's *perceived* structure as generated during sentence processing. They point out that for many sentences it is not necessary to compute a complete syntactic structure in order to extract the meaning, and suggest that this computation might therefore be delayed until after the initial parse, or might never be carried out at all. Gerken & Bever are specifically concerned with Binding Theory's prediction that there should be a strong contrast between VP-attached and S-attached subordinate clauses with regard to potential backwards coreference, such that (4), in which the complement clause is under the VP, should be much worse than (5), in which the adverbial clause is attached to the S node, at least under certain versions of the theory.

(4) The dog told him$_i$ that the horse$_i$ would fall.

(5)   The dog hit him$_i$ while the horse$_i$ ate lunch.

However, Gerken & Bever's acceptability experiment failed to find any such overall difference. They argue that there are no general surface cues for the difference between S-node versus VP-node attachment, so it is possible that the distinction is not made in on-line parsing structures. In fact, there is a tendency for English speakers to segment sentences after a noun-verb-noun sequence, and those subjects who performed strong perceptual closure at this juncture (as revealed by another experiment) did not make the attachment distinction for pronouns, whereas those who made less use of the closure strategy did make the predicted contrast between (4) and (5). Subjects who exhibited strong closure did not have a VP node accessible for attachment when they got to the subordinate clause, because the VP had been closed off, and they therefore treated all such clauses as S-attached, allowing coreference in both sentence types. Thus, these individual differences do *not* require us to posit individual differences in the formulation of Binding Theory. Besides the possibility that complete trees are never computed, an alternative interpretation suggested by Gerken & Bever is that we do compute full constituent structures but cannot access them for certain tasks, being left instead with the perceptual structure alone. This raises the intriguing but rather unlikely possibility that linguists have developed introspective techniques to get at these fuller structures, while untrained speakers have not. The lesson to be drawn from these three studies is that theoretical linguistics can benefit from a concern for the judgment process.

1.4 A Working Hypothesis

In this section I set out my own basic working hypothesis regarding the interaction of metalinguistic[6] performance factors and the grammar in determining grammaticality judgments. My hypothesis is a reaction to countless studies that have demonstrated that grammaticality judgments are susceptible to order and context effects, handedness differences, etc., and have then concluded, on the basis of this manipulability (or on the basis of the gradience of judgments, or on other properties), that the grammar itself must have these properties, or that these properties must be part of the language-specific component of the brain. Such conclusions are not justified. In my view, we should start from the position that the entire behavior of making grammaticality judgments is the result

---

[6] See Chapter 3 for attempts at a definition of the term *metalinguistic*.

of interactions between primary language faculties of the mind and general cognitive properties, and crucially does *not* involve special components dedicated to linguistic intuition. Thus, my hypothesis is that for any effect on a language (judgment) task, there could be an analogous effect on a similar nonlinguistic cognitive (judgment) task. I have parenthesized the word *judgment* to indicate that I suspect that the truth of this hypothesis extends beyond judgments to other metalinguistic tasks, although they will not be my concern here. In other words, my claim is that *none* of the variables that confound metalinguistic data are peculiar to judgments about language. Rather, they can be shown to operate in some other domain in a similar way. (This is quite similar to Valian's (1982) claim that the data of more traditional psychological experiments have all the same problems that judgment data have.) It is not always easy to find convincing instances of such effects in other domains, however. The most likely candidates would be judgments in another sensory modality, such as taste, smell, or vision, which at least at a low level are unlikely to involve the language facilities of the mind. I will suggest just two arbitrary examples of cognitive domains that might be affected by the same variables that affect linguistic tasks.

First, in the visual domain, shape recognition and judgments of size, numerosity, etc., are potential candidates for parallels with linguistic tasks. Bergum & Bergum (1979a,b) have found that in judging visually ambiguous figures (e.g., Necker cubes, Rubin vase figures, and Jastrow rabbit-duck figures) certain individuals experience reversals much more frequently than others. One might predict that these people also detect linguistic ambiguity more easily than others.[7] Second, in the perfume industry, experts are employed to smell products that are to be marketed and to test for certain properties that nonexperts in this field have never heard of. These experts might differ from naive perfume smellers in the same ways that linguists differ from naive sentence judges. Wherever possible in the following chapters, I draw parallels of this sort between experimental results in psycholinguistics and known effects in other fields, or I propose a search for such effects. Such findings could greatly assist us in factoring out these effects from our grammatical judgment data, bringing us closer to an accurate picture of linguistic knowledge.

My hypothesis represents common-sense expectations about the relation between language and other behaviors, and empirical support for it would thus not be particularly surprising (Bever 1970a). However, even if the hypothesis is sup-

---

[7] The two types of individuals were architecture majors and business majors, respectively. The authors do not draw a conclusion as to whether the difference in reversal perception might be due to an innate tendency toward perceptual instability, or might be a learned ability.

ported, it still does not explain *how* cognitive principles and linguistic knowledge come to interact in the mind to produce linguistic judgments. There are (at least) two possible extreme interpretations. It could be that properties such as context dependence and susceptibility to training effects belong to separate modules of the mind that are implicated in judgment behavior but not in other forms of behavior (e.g., a decision-reporting component). At another extreme, it could be that these properties are inherent in the cognitive substrate on which language and all other higher cognitive functions are built. Both possibilities have important implications that go far beyond the present work. My intuition is that each is probably true of some properties, but it will not be possible to settle the issue here. In principle the two explanations are empirically distinguishable, since the modular theory predicts that there could be behaviors that circumvent the modules in question and do not show the relevant effects, whereas the substrate theory predicts that they are everywhere and inescapable. (These arguments are of course drastically oversimplified.) If we should find that for a given effect there seems to be no parallel elsewhere in human cognition, then and only then would we have the beginning of an argument for the special nature of linguistic judgment among human knowledge systems.

1.5 Scope and Organization

I do not attempt in this book to treat the subject of grammaticality judgments in its entirety. Rather, I restrict my investigation on two somewhat arbitrary, but fairly sensible, dimensions. First, in asking what grammaticality judgments are judgments *of,* I look only at the acceptability (and grammaticality) of word strings; i.e., I consider only syntactic, as opposed to phonological, wellformedness, although in a broad sense acceptability/grammaticality often entails conformity to the phonology as well as to the syntax, and even to other linguistic components. Second, while several sorts of experiment are potentially relevant to the subject of grammaticality judgments, I systematically exclude a number of subject populations. There will be little mention of the judgments of second language learners and other nonnative speakers, except when they bear on our understanding of native intuitions. Only a passing glance will be cast on the *development* of metalinguistic awareness (as it bears on adult awareness), which has become virtually a field unto itself. And no data from aphasic speakers or others with language impairments are considered. Putting it positively, I focus mostly on the syntactic grammaticality judgments of "typical" adult native speakers. Furthermore, I try to emphasize work on intuitions about general structures rather than work that bears only on the use of particular lexical items or constructions, since the former are generally taken to be more fundamental indicators of core linguistic knowledge.

Other sources cover parts of this territory, and the reader may wish to consult them. Newmeyer (1983) devotes a chapter of his book to the data base of linguistic theory, but his goal is to defend, rather than to (constructively) criticize, the generative modus operandi, and I disagree with many of his conclusions, although I cite many of the same sources. Chaudron (1983) deals only with experimental psycholinguistic work, but provides a useful summary chart of many of the studies I discuss,[8] and examines many procedural details that I omit;[9] however, at least half of his paper is devoted to studies of second-language learners. Labov (1975) takes a position quite sympathetic with my own, but is concerned mostly with sociolinguistic variation. While much of the experimental work he discusses is not directly relevant to the issues discussed in this book, his methodological proposals have heavily influenced my own. Finally, Birdsong's (1989) review of the literature, which occupies two of his chapters, overlaps considerably with mine, but lacks the sort of principled overall organization that I attempt to provide. His aim, like Chaudron's, is to apply discoveries about grammaticality judgments to issues in second-language learning and teaching research. Nonetheless, many of his methodological proposals have been incorporated here. Thus, none of the major previous studies of grammaticality judgments have attempted, within the basic framework of generative grammar, to explain why grammaticality judgments behave the way they do and to propose changes in the way that linguists treat judgment data. That is what I attempt to do in this book.

The book is organized as follows. In Chapter 2, I summarize the history of the concepts of grammaticality and acceptability and their associated notations, focusing on the ways in which grammaticality judgments are used by syntactic theorists today and arguing that such uses demand a careful examination of judgments, not as pure sources of data but as instances of metalinguistic performance. I also consider where their use fits in the broader scheme of introspection

---

[8] To compare the results of previous studies on the basis of Chaudron's chart would be misleading, however; the experiments differed in ways too subtle and too complex for his categorizations to capture.

[9] It will become apparent that my reports of experimental work are often concerned with two particular features of elicitation experiments, the instructions that are given to subjects, and the evaluation scheme (rating scale, categories, ranking procedure, etc.) that is used. The importance of these two factors is discussed in detail in Sections 5.2.1 and 3.3.4, respectively. Variation in these two features is perhaps the biggest reason why virtually no two studies of grammaticality judgments are directly comparable.

and intuition in social science. Chapter 3 is a discussion of several important issues that arise when a performance view of grammaticality judgments is taken: tasks one can use to elicit them, scales one can use to report them, how people might go about giving them, and how and what they might tell us about linguistic competence. Chapters 4 and 5 cover the major body of psycholinguistic research that has been devoted to discovering ways in which the judgment process can vary systematically with differences between subjects (Chapter 4) and experimental manipulations (Chapter 5). Chapter 4 considers individual differences in two major categories: endogenous, or organismic; and exogenous, or experiential. Chapter 5 examines task factors in two major categories: stimulus materials, or what is to be judged; and procedural methods, or how it is to be judged. In reviewing the literature in these two chapters, I attempt wherever possible to point out parallels with other cognitive behaviors. Chapter 6 represents the integration of the substantive and methodological findings and discussions of Chapters 3–5. I present a preliminary model of the judgment process that reflects what is known about linguistic intuitions, and I propose methods for collecting grammaticality judgments that avoid the pitfalls of previous work and take into account the factors that have been shown to influence judgments. Readers who seek immediate practical advice on the collection of judgment data may wish to consult Section 6.3 directly; it does not assume familiarity with preceding material. Chapter 7 considers ways in which mainstream linguistic theory might be affected by the growing body of research on grammaticality judgments and suggests directions that could be pursued to advantage in future studies.

2 Definitions and Historical Background

> *I dislike reliance on intuition as much as anyone. ... We should substitute rigorous criteria just as soon as possible, instead of clinging to intuition.*
>
> (Chomsky 1962)

2.1 Introduction

The history of the concepts of grammaticality and acceptability and the notations used to denote them is a long and controversial one. In this chapter I review the important theoretical developments that have defined the use of these concepts in generative grammar, because an investigation into the nature of grammaticality judgments demands a description of precisely what is meant by the term *grammaticality* and an idea of what could constitute a judgment of it. I then turn to the actual practice of linguists working within the generative paradigm today, to see how they apply these notions. The chapter is divided as follows. Section 2 is devoted to a brief history of the issues surrounding the notion of grammaticality, the associated terminology, and diverse views on its role in linguistic theory. (See Harris (1993: ch. 7) for more on this topic.) In Section 3, I survey the varied ways in which grammaticality judgments are used in the linguistic literature, considering the types of data collected and the manner in which these are employed to argue theoretical points. Section 4 raises the more fundamental question of whether judgments ought to be used at all, in the light of another bit of social science history – namely, the downfall of introspectionism in psychology. Section 5 summarizes what I perceive as the major problems with linguists' use of judgments, identifying those that we can tackle with the results of the empirical investigations discussed in subsequent chapters.

2.2 A Short History of Grammaticality

> *The obvious danger exists, however, that Chomsky's "ideal speaker-hearer" may be itself an artifact, a mere woolen outergarment worn in the attempt to achieve respectability by slipping the wolf of an arbitrary and artifactual grammar into an unsuspecting flock of linguistically naive psychologists.*
>
> (Derwing 1979)

Since my goal is to scrutinize the use of grammaticality judgments in generative grammar, I adopt the assumptions of that framework without further comment, although much of this investigation has theory-independent implications. Thus, for the relevant definitions I turn to Chomsky, and in particular to the familiar competence/performance distinction. Chomsky's basic point is that we must distinguish what speakers of a language know (subconsciously) about the structure of the language from their actual use of the language. The goal of linguistic theory, under this view, is to describe the knowledge, independent of (and logically prior to) any attempt to describe the role that this knowledge plays in the production, understanding, or judgment of language.[1] Whether a sentence is *grammatical* is a question about competence. A grammatical sentence is generated by the speaker's grammar; it is part of the language as delineated by his or her competence. I will assume for the purpose of discussion that whether a sentence is grammatical is determinate in all cases; i.e., that whatever form the competence takes in the mind, it implicitly ascribes (perhaps some degree of) grammaticality or ungrammaticality to each string of words.[2] (See below for a refinement of this assumption.) Whether a sentence is *acceptable* is a question about performance. An acceptable sentence is consciously accepted by a speaker as part of his or her language upon hearing it. This apparently simple distinction is often muddied by

---

[1] There has been considerable criticism of this view. See Greenbaum (1976b) for a list of dissenting opinions, and Derwing (1973) for the claim that competence versus performance is not an instance of the kind of idealization usually made in the natural sciences.

[2] It is conceivable, however, that competence in this sense of statically represented knowledge does not exist. It could be that a given string is generated or its status computed only when necessary, and that the demands of the particular situation determine how the computation is carried out, e.g., by some sort of comparison to prototypical sentence structures stored in memory. Since such a scenario would demand a major rethinking of the goals of the field of linguistics, I will not deal with it further.

the fact that the word *performance* has been used in different ways at different times, by Chomsky and others. It is sometimes used to refer to specific instances of behavior, or patterns of behavior in general, as opposed to static knowledge that guides behavior. In other contexts it is used to refer to anything outside of the grammar. including static knowledge of things like discourse structure or mechanisms for using language. In this book, I use the term *performance* to refer to behavior, as opposed to knowledge, including both people's behavior on specific occasions and their general patterns of behavior. (The importance of the latter distinction will be discussed below.)

Concerning the relationship between performance and competence and the approach to linguistic research, Chomsky states that

> linguistic theory is concerned primarily with an ideal speaker-listener, in a completely homogeneous speech-community, who knows its language perfectly and is unaffected by such grammatically irrelevant conditions as memory limitations, distractions, shifts of attention and interest, and errors (random or characteristic) in applying his knowledge of the language in actual performance. ...

> We thus make a fundamental distinction between *competence* (the speaker-hearer's knowledge of his language) and *performance* (the actual use of language in concrete situations). Only under the idealization set forth in the preceding paragraph is performance a direct reflection of competence. In actual fact it obviously could not directly reflect competence. (Chomsky 1965: 3–4)

Noam Chomsky (personal communication) views the competence/performance distinction as a simple truism: what we know and what we do are different things. The trick is how to learn about the former on the basis of evidence from the latter. In the mid-1960s, Chomsky was already mentioning some of the ways in which performance data, including judgment data, might be assessed: "It is not that these introspective judgments are sacrosanct and beyond any conceivable doubt. On the contrary, their correctness can be challenged and supported in many ways, some quite indirect. Consistency among speakers of similar backgrounds, as well as for a particular speaker on different occasions, is relevant information" (Chomsky (1964: 56); I return to these suggestions in Chapters 4 and 5). Nothing in the above passages implies that variation among speakers is either uninteresting for linguistic theory or necessarily an indication that incorrect judgments are involved. In practice, however, there might be a temptation to take one of these easy outs in order to avoid confronting variation; I return to this matter in Section 2.3.2. Given that linguistic competence is only one contributing factor in any observable behavior of a speaker, it is reasonable to ask how we can hope to gather behavioral evidence about grammaticality.[3] In *The Logical Structure of Linguistic Theory* (Chomsky (1955), hereafter *LSLT*)[4] and *Syntactic Structures* (Chomsky (1957), hereafter *SS*) we find the following remarks[5] (I have emphasized some hedges that indicate that no particular operational test can be expected to yield the right result in all cases):

> We know that a speaker of the language can select, among sequences that he has never heard, *certain* grammatical sentences, and that he will do this in much the same way as other speakers. We might test this by a direct determination of some sort of "bizarreness reaction," or in various indirect ways. (*LSLT*: 95)[6]

> Yet (1) [*Colorless green ideas sleep furiously*], though nonsensical, is grammatical, while (2) [*Furiously sleep ideas green colorless*] is not. Presented with these sentences, a speaker of English will read (1) with a normal sentence intonation, but he will read (2) with a falling intonation on each word: in fact, with just the intonation pattern given to any sequence of unrelated words. He treats each word in (2) as a separate phrase. Similarly, he will be able to recall (1) much more easily than (2), to learn it much more quickly, etc. (*SS*: 16)

> Such sentences with conjunction crossing constituent boundaries are also, in general, marked by special phonemic features such as extra long pauses, ... contrastive stress and intonation, failure to reduce vowels and drop final consonants in rapid speech, etc. Such features *normally* mark the reading of non-grammatical strings. (*SS*: 35–36, fn. 2)[7]

At the same time, however, it was apparent that behavioral evidence was not *always* the last word. Theoretical considerations could also dictate that some sentences *must* be grammatical, regardless of how speakers might react to them.

---

[3] See Oller, Sales & Harrington (1970) for commentary on the empirical status of generative grammars and the nature of the competence/performance distinction.

[4] All pages numbers refer to the 1975 edition.

[5] I cite many of Chomsky's passages verbatim, because the wording is often subtly nuanced and easily misparaphrased. The reader is then free to disagree with my interpretation. See Matthews (1993: ch. 4) for a detailed review of Chomsky's early writings on these and related topics.

[6] The emphasis in all quoted passages in this chapter is my own, unless otherwise indicated.

[7] Regarding this passage, Chomsky (1961) states that he was careful not to suggest *general* criteria for grammaticality.

With regard to sentences containing embedded *if-then* and *either-or* pairs, Chomsky states, "Note that many of the sentences ... will be quite strange and unusual. ... But they are all sentences, formed by processes of sentence construction so simple and elementary that even the most rudimentary English grammar would contain them" (*SS*: 23). The reasoning seems to be this: given that certain sentences are uncontroversially part of the language, our intuitions about what grammars can look like tell us that certain other sentences must also be part of it, although our judgments of these latter sentences are not so clear-cut. Such reasoning is not, in and of itself, sufficient to conclude that a sentence is grammatical.[8] It must be shown that the factors that make it less than acceptable are extragrammatical, i.e., that they exist independent of language structure.

Originally, Chomsky suggested that the evidence used to construct theories be limited to clear cases, that is, ones where our intuitions leave no doubt as to whether the sentence is acceptable or unacceptable, as the following passages state explicitly:[9]

> Our purpose is to construct an integrated and systematic theory, which, when applied rigorously to linguistic material, gives the correct analysis *for the cases where intuition* (or experiment, under more desirable circumstances) *makes a clear decision.* (*LSLT*: 415)

> We may assume for this discussion that certain sequences of phonemes are definitely sentences, and that certain other sequences are definitely non-sentences. In many intermediate cases we shall be prepared to let the grammar itself decide, when the grammar is set up in the simplest way so that it includes the clear sentence and excludes the clear non-sentences. (*SS*: 14)

What is left unsaid here is *why* it is sometimes legitimate to let the grammar decide, and how we are to know when such a move is allowed. The justification seems to be a parsimony argument: Why say that a marginal sentence is ungrammatical if that would complicate the theory? If we had access to no information about the sentence in question beyond a judgment that it is marginal, this would be a reasonable principle to follow, but I argue in subsequent chapters that we can do better by looking for additional evidence that could bear on the status of the

---

[8] Noam Chomsky (personal communication) believes that "everyone in the entire history of the subject would agree" with my claim, and that the quoted passage from *SS* implies nothing to the contrary. If that is true then the point of the passage is unclear to me; perhaps Chomsky was presupposing other kinds of evidence as well.

[9] Carden (1973) argues that in the 1960s, data on which there were disagreements were indeed considered outside the domain of the theory.

sentence. We can thus hope to avoid missing true complications in the grammar. In answer to the second question raised above, we can then also avoid the need to know when it is safe to let the grammar decide, since it is actually never safe but always potentially erroneous. Fortunately, in practice it seems to be done fairly infrequently anyway: see Labov (1975) for specific instances in which Chomsky admits that data are unclear but proceeds to construct his theory solely on the basis of his own intuitions. (This in turn is problematic for other reasons.)

Let me make a brief aside about terminology in reference to Chomsky's writings. Note that Chomsky generally does *not* use the terms *intuition* and *judgment* interchangeably. It is my understanding that judgment is a product of performance and intuition is part of competence. When Chomsky says that "the speaker has an 'intuitive sense of grammaticalness' " (*LSLT*: 95),[10] this does not translate into the ability to *judge* grammaticalness. But the very close semantics are probably responsible for the misapprehension alluded to in Chapter 1, whereby the two are equated and thus judgments are seen as directly reflecting competence, since competence consists of intuitions. This was not Chomsky's intent (see Chomsky (1965: 21)), although passages like the following could easily serve to mislead the unwary reader: "The theory is refuted if the *judgments* are not in accord with the predictions of the grammar" (Chomsky 1975: 36). In the accompanying footnote, however, we find a qualification: "Note that there is a further idealization here, in that we abstract away from other factors that may interact with knowledge of language to determine judgments." As for acceptability, which speakers *can* judge, the Introduction to Chomsky (1975) describes the concept as follows: "Sentences are acceptable (or perhaps acceptable under particular circumstances) if they are suitable, appropriate, adequate to the purpose at hand, etc. The competence grammar contributes to determining acceptability, but the latter concept involves many other factors" (Chomsky 1975: 8).[11] It seems that with linguistic training one can learn to abstract away from some of these factors: linguists certainly assume that they can judge a sentence's wellformed-

---

[10] In Chomsky's early writings, one often finds the term *grammaticalness* used instead of *grammaticality*. Most people treat these as synonymous, but this was apparently not Chomsky's original intent: "About the term 'grammaticalness,' ... I purposely chose a neologism in the hope that it would be understood that the term was to be regarded as a technical term, with exactly the meaning that was given to it, and not assimilated to some term of ordinary discourse with a sense and connotations not to the point in this context" (Noam Chomsky, quoted in Paikeday (1985: 14)).

[11] I have included passages from the 1973 Introduction of Chomsky (1975) as representative of his early work, since it provides background to *LSLT*. Of course, the intervening years might have brought a change in perspective.

ness independently of its appropriateness to any actual discourse situation, for example.

In *Aspects of the Theory of Syntax* (Chomsky (1965), hereafter *Aspects*), the relationship between acceptability and grammaticality was more explicitly discussed in the following well-known passage:

> For the purposes of this discussion, let us use the term "acceptable" to refer to utterances that are perfectly natural and immediately comprehensible without paper-and-pencil analysis, and in no way bizarre or outlandish. Obviously, acceptability will be a matter of degree, along various dimensions. One could go on to propose various operational tests to specify the notion more precisely (for example, rapidity, correctness, and uniformity of recall and recognition, normalcy of intonation). ... The more acceptable sentences are those that are more likely to be produced, more easily understood, less clumsy, and in some sense more natural. The unacceptable sentences one would tend to avoid and replace by more acceptable variants, wherever possible, in actual discourse.
>
> The notion "acceptable" is not to be confused with "grammatical." Acceptability is a concept that belongs to the study of performance, whereas grammaticalness belongs to the study of competence. ... Like acceptability, grammaticalness is, no doubt, a matter of degree ... but the scales of grammaticalness and acceptability do not coincide. Grammaticalness is only one of many factors that interact to determine acceptability. Correspondingly, although one might propose various operational tests for acceptability, *it is unlikely that a necessary and sufficient operational criterion might be invented for the much more abstract and far more important notion of grammaticalness.* (*Aspects*: 10–11)

As Jim McCawley (personal communication) points out, the above definition of *acceptable* is dispositional, in that it refers to a tendency across multiple actual encounters with a sentence, rather than to a speaker's reaction on any one occasion. Therefore, whether a sentence is *acceptable* in general cannot in principle be determined on the basis of a single situation wherein it is *accepted*. However, a *judgment* about acceptability is presumably an attempt on the part of speakers to assess what their reactions to a sentence *would be* across a range of situations. Thus, to elaborate on the definition of acceptability I gave above, whether a sentence is acceptable is a question about performance in three senses: any particular instance of a speaker accepting or rejecting a sentence is an act of performance, i.e., behavior. Any sort of generalization across many such instances

2 Definitions and Historical Background

is a generalization about performance. A judgment of one's disposition towards accepting or rejecting a sentence is itself a type of performance.

The absence of an operational criterion for grammaticality has evoked negative reactions from many quarters. As Reich (1969) puts it, "when confronted by adverse data, Chomsky retreated from his empirical position of 1957, to a theory that he himself admits cannot be tested empirically"; Marks (1967) comments on what he perceives as the incoherence of this position; Householder (1973: 365, fn. 1) calls it "the paradox of linguistics: the only possible way of determining whether or not a grammar is correct is by consulting the speaker's intuitions, but they are inaccessible"; Gleitman & Gleitman (1970: 25) have the following reaction: "[Acceptability] tests cannot invalidate, they can hardly bear on, a theory which when pushed will withdraw into successively deeper reaches of the mind". Chomsky (personal communication) believes that such comments belie a confusion between evidence and criterion: while speakers' behavior on some task – for instance, the intonation they use in reading a string of words – might constitute a piece of *evidence* concerning its grammaticality, one cannot *define* the notion *grammatical* in terms of one or several of such tests; it is defined in terms of some notion of the contents of the mind. (To borrow a favorite analogy of Chomsky's, while a litmus test might provide some evidence about whether a substance is an acid or a base, chemistry does not define the concept *acid* in terms of this test.) It seems to me that, in principle, there might someday be an operational criterion for grammaticality, but it would have to be based on direct study of the brain, not on human behavior, if it turns out to be possible to discern properties of the mind (e.g., the precise features of the grammar) from physical properties of the brain.

It does not make any sense to speak of grammaticality judgments given Chomsky's definitions, because people are incapable of judging grammaticality – It is not accessible to their intuitions (Newmeyer (1983: 51); Gombert (1992)). Linguists might construct arguments about the grammaticality of a sentence, but all that a linguistically naive subject can do is judge its acceptability. Nevertheless, in the remainder of this book I will follow the existing literature in treating *grammaticality judgment* and *acceptability judgment* as synonyms,[12] with the understanding that the former is unquestionably a misnomer, and only the latter is a sensible notion. I do so because this usage occurs in many of the passages I quote, and because *acceptability judgment* can have misleading connotations of

---

[12] It is possible that researchers who have defined grammaticality and/or acceptability in other ways might make a principled distinction between two types of judgment (this appears to be the case for Langendoen (1973)), but since I follow Chomsky's definitions I collapse the terms.

its own in certain contexts. For instance, the term can indicate that one is discussing contextual appropriateness rather than structural wellformedness. I will continue to follow Chomsky's definitions in other contexts when the distinction is important, for example, in *acceptable sentence* versus *grammatical sentence*.

Given that grammaticality is what Chomsky seeks to investigate, it would not be surprising if he saw no useful purpose in the systematization of linguistic data collection. In the end, no single empirical fact can be crucial to the issues at hand. At the time of *Aspects* this seems to have been his view, but he allowed for the possibility that circumstances might change, that there might be room at some future time for a methodology more systematic than reliance on everyday common sense:

> There are, in other words, very few reliable experimental or data-processing procedures for obtaining significant information concerning the linguistic intuition of the native speaker. It is important to bear in mind that when an operational procedure is proposed, it must be tested for adequacy ... by measuring it against the standard provided by the tacit knowledge that it attempts to specify and describe. ... If operational procedures were available that met this test, we might be justified in relying on their results in unclear and difficult cases. This remains a hope for the future rather than a present reality, however. ... There is no reason to expect that reliable operational criteria for the deeper and more important theoretical notions of linguistics (such as "grammaticalness" and "paraphrase") will ever be forthcoming. ... The critical problem for grammatical theory today is not a paucity of evidence but rather the inadequacy of present theories of language to account for masses of evidence that are hardly open to serious question. ... It seems to me that sharpening of the data by more objective tests is a matter of small importance for the problems at hand. ... *Perhaps the day will come when the kinds of data that we now can obtain in abundance will be insufficient to resolve deeper questions concerning the structure of language.* (Aspects: 19–21)

I argue that this day has come, some 30 years later. I devote Section 2.3 to demonstrating that the questions linguists are now addressing rely crucially on facts that are indeed "open to serious question."

Note also that Chomsky again assumes that there is a core of "unquestionable data concerning the linguistic intuition of the native speaker" (*Aspects*: 20), which would presumably include judgments of some sort, and that these "obvious" facts would keep linguists busy for a long time, thus postponing the need for reliable tests applicable to "less obvious" cases.[13] That is, for some sentences, acceptability judgments provide transparent evidence about grammaticality, while still not constituting judgments *of* grammaticality in the literal sense. But how is it determined whether a given datum constitutes such a clear case? For whom must it be clear (Ringen 1979)? The problem, of course, is that each investigator is free to pick and choose these "unquestionable" cases to suit the theory. (McCawley (1976) argues that, by Chomsky's own definition of grammaticality, *all* sentences must be considered unclear cases, because we never have direct information about grammaticality.) That there is no standard way to make this decision is argued in detail by Botha (1973): "The level of rationality at which grammatical inquiry and general-linguistic inquiry are conducted would be raised if it were clear ... under what circumstances an intuitive evidential statement may be properly regarded as being evident" (p. 188); "Transformational grammar lacks a set of conditions ... governing the evidentness or obviousness of intuitive evidential statements" (p. 193). Furthermore, even at an intuitive level, clear-case judgments are not necessarily windows into competence: "In terms of the notion 'clear case' spurious linguistic intuitions could, despite their spuriousness, qualify for membership of the evidential corpus; in terms of the notion 'unclear case' linguistic intuitions which were both genuine and correct could, despite their genuineness and correctness, be denied membership of this corpus" (p. 206). Botha (1981) defines a spurious judgment, in contrast to a genuine one, as one that does not reflect competence, because it has been influenced by extralinguistic factors. In this book, I propose more reliable means to make these discriminations.

As our concept of the theory is refined, the status of any given sentence can change from ungrammatical to grammatical, or vice versa. (See McCawley (1979) for a variety of definitions of grammaticality that have been used by different theoretical factions at different times.) For instance, in *LSLT* Chomsky examines the naturalness of particle movement as a function of the complexity of the intervening NP and concludes, "This is systematic behavior, and we might expect that a grammar should be able to state it" (p. 477). But in *Aspects* he says of the same sentences (and, more celebratedly, of multiply center-embedded ones), "It would be quite impossible to characterize the unacceptable sentences in grammatical terms. For example, we cannot formulate particular rules of the grammar in such a way as to exclude them" (pp. 11–12). The latter claim seems to be an exaggeration, at least with regard to center embedding. In fact, Katz &

---

[13] An argument against this position is that the large masses of unquestionable data, if indeed they exist, might still be of insufficient quality for linguistic theory, if they do not bear on the crucial issues that it must address (Botha 1973; Labov 1972a). Section 2.3 shows this to be true.

Bever (1976) elaborate Chomsky's position by saying that a recursion counter would do the job, but this is the only part of the grammar of English where it would be used, which should make us suspect that this is not the right analysis of the phenomenon. Noam Chomsky (personal communication) finds the idea of a recursion counter "ridiculous, since it is obvious that whatever is involved in constraining recursion is quite different in character from the devices made available in UG ... and may not even involve language." If the implicit empirical argument here were spelled out and supported, it would constitute a reasonable basis for not attributing limits on recursion to the grammar.

In general, there seem to be three lines of defense by which a theoretical claim is protected from potentially falsifying data, before any change in the theory can be incited. This book is intended to help objectify two of these three procedures. For instance, when faced with a sentence that apparently contradicts a claim, e.g., an acceptable sentence that a grammatical rule excludes, the first line of defense would be to argue that the data are invalid, that the sentence is not really acceptable as claimed. While it is trivial to make this statement for one's own intuitions, such arguments ought to be supported by empirical investigations of others as well. To the extent that we can standardize this process, we can reduce data disputes. The second defense is to claim that the data are not relevant to the theoretical issue at hand, that the sentence is good because it is allowed by some other part of the grammar and is not under the jurisdiction of the disputed construct. This approach generally relies on logical reasoning and might be subject to differing opinion but not to factual dispute; therefore, I do not discuss it further. The third defense, typically indicative of the least understanding on the part of the theory's proponent, is to say that the sentence *is* prohibited by the grammar, but non-grammatical factors are causing judgments not to reflect this fact. Until we have an explicit understanding of such factors, such a claim is unfalsifiable. (For a much more detailed examination of the roles of argumentation and evidence in generative theory, see Botha 1973.) This state of affairs is presumably what prompts Postal (1988) to quip:

> Great strides are being made in linguistic rhetoric, whose progress puts the stasis in mere description and theorizing to shame. In the great rhetoric laboratories of the north-eastern United States, defensive shields are being perfected that can render any theory virtually impervious to factual corrosion. (p. 129)

As I see it, this is precisely why we *should* strive for a better understanding of acceptability judgments. It would allow us a *principled* way to establish to what extent any such piece of evidence should be considered to bear on the grammar. We will still not be able to draw direct conclusions from such data, but it will at least be a matter of objective fact what the relevant data are. We clearly do sometimes use speaker judgments as evidence about grammaticality, so we should rigorously define when and why they can and cannot be used as such, and then try to expand the range of cases where they can be used. As Birdsong (1989) states, until we do so, if we do not agree on what our data represent, we cannot hope to agree on an analysis. If we can understand what factors intervene between the grammar and performance, we can circumscribe the cases where these factors might cause (un)acceptability not to reflect (un)grammaticality, and exclude these cases as evidence. Chomsky seems to agree with this approach:

> In actual practice, linguistics as a discipline is characterized by attention to certain kinds of evidence that are, for the moment, readily accessible and informative: largely, the judgments of native speakers. Each such judgment is, in fact, the result of an experiment, one that is poorly designed but rich in the evidence it provides. In practice, we tend to operate on the assumption, or pretense, that these informant judgments give us "direct evidence" as to the structure of the language, but, of course, this is only a tentative and inexact working hypothesis, and *any skilled practitioner has at his or her disposal an armory of techniques to help compensate for the errors introduced.* In general, informant judgments do not reflect the structure of the language directly; judgments of acceptability, for example, may fail to provide direct evidence as to grammatical status because of the intrusion of numerous other factors. (Chomsky 1986: 36)

If we could go a (large) step further and deduce a general reverse mapping from acceptability to grammaticality, we could in principle determine the grammatical status of any sentence operationally, and thus fully specify the range of facts over which grammars must have scope. "We require a science of linguistic introspection to provide a theoretical and empirical basis for including some acceptability judgments as syntactically relevant and excluding others" (Bever 1974: 195).

Under Bever's proposed approach, only those unacceptable sentences whose badness cannot be explained by any plausible extragrammatical aspect of speech behavior are ungrammatical. (Bever's example of such a case is *I hope it for to be stopping raining when I am having leaving*; see also Bever 1971.)[14] The argument is that "if a constraint may be adequately treated by independently motivated

---

[14] Bever goes on to make some preliminary suggestions about sentential properties that will likely affect acceptability but are outside the realm of the grammar. These include sentence

systems outside the grammar, its inclusion in the grammar is unwarranted and obscures the descriptive and explanatory power of the grammar" (Bever, Carroll & Hurtig 1976: 150). Of course, the paradigmatic example in this category would be the short-term memory limitations that are said to result in the unacceptability of multiply center-embedded sentences. More generally, the parser may be misled (garden-pathed) into an incorrect parse that makes a well-formed sentence seem bad, as in the following example from Ellis (1991), where the parser presumably first tries to attach *which book* as the object of *believes*.

(1)   Which book did you say John believes offended many people?

We must add to this proposal the converse case, in which acceptable sentences that have been ameliorated by extragrammatical factors are not the responsibility of the grammar. Again, multiple center embedding provides a plausible example. Sentences like (2a) below are clearly ungrammatical, lacking the necessary number of verb phrases, but because participants apparently cannot keep track of the number of subject noun phrases that have accumulated, they often judge such sentences to be acceptable, in contrast to the grammatical (2b), which is judged unacceptable (Frazier 1985).

(2)   a.   The patient the nurse the clinic had hired met Jack.

      b.   The patient the nurse the clinic had hired admitted met Jack.

Another class of examples in this category involves the use of resumptive pronouns, as in (3a), which is clearly better than the version without a pronoun in (3b), even though nonlinguists may generally reject both utterance types:

(3)   a.   the guy who they don't know whether he wants to come or not

      b.   *the guy who they don't know whether wants to come or not

Kroch (1981) argues that possible grammar-based accounts of the distribution of such resumptive pronouns are unappealing, and takes this as a reason to consider a processing account in terms of on-line production, which he argues is more straightforward and hence is to be preferred. On this account, resumptive pronouns are the result of the generator's inability to look far enough ahead to determine that the trace of an already uttered *wh*-expression is within an island. Thus, the production mechanism is forced to produce ungrammatical sentences in some cases, and this fact somehow renders them more acceptable than other

---

length, absurdity, difficulty of comprehension and difficulty of pronunciation – these will be the subject of Section 5.3 (see also Katz & Bever 1976).

ungrammatical sentences, for reasons that are not entirely obvious. (Examples like this motivate a link between the generator and the judgment routine in the model to be presented in Section 6.2.) While this argument for attributing judgments to performance rather than to competence is theory-internal, it makes empirical predictions, for instance that carefully planned speech or writing will not contain sentences like (3a) at all; the astute reader will find a counterexample to this claim in Footnote 17.

(See Langendoen & Bever 1973 and Bever 1974 for more instances of supposedly ungrammatical acceptable sentences.)

A third possibility we must consider when deciding the grammaticality status of a sentence is that it might have no status at all. This possibility is raised by Morgan (1972), who presents unquantified data on interspeaker judgment differences to show that certain pathological cases of subject-verb agreementagreement, subject-verb in English display a large degree of variation and uncertainty:

(4) a. ??Are/??Is John or his parents here?

  b.   I, who the FBI thinks *am/*is an anarchist, will doubtless be here.

Morgan speculates that this variation might exist because speakers' grammars simply do not contain a rule elaborate enough to apply in such cases, so when forced to make judgments they may apply ad hoc strategies. It is hard to see what the general criteria for reaching this conclusion of grammatical indeterminacy might be. Morgan's argument is based on the inability to find plausible grammatical principles that cover all the judgments that are firm, plus the fact that many speakers find *neither* variant of the problematic sentences grammatical. Presumably, indeterminacy is distinguished in principle from mere interspeaker grammar differences if individual speakers seem not to have systematic judgment patterns, but what constitutes a systematic pattern is not always obvious a priori.

Naturally, there might not be total agreement on the status of a particular effect.[15] For instance, Reich (1969) and Spencer (1973) question why limitations on center embeddings should not be taken to reflect the grammar. (See Katz & Bever (1976) for discussion of how such decisions can be argued for.) More broadly, the role of meaning vis-à-vis the grammar has been a point of great debate over the history of generative linguistics. The distinction between syntactic and semantic intuitions is liable to be based on one's own theory (Cohen 1981). McCawley, in his introduction to Postal (1976), expresses the view that such arguments are

---

[15] Newmeyer (1983) believes that discrepancies on this point account for many cases of what appear to be data disagreements among theorists.

pointless. Once you know why a sentence is bad, it does not matter whether that cause is considered inside or outside the grammar.

> If a distinction between "ungrammatical" and "unacceptable" is to be made, the ungrammatical items are those unacceptable items whose unacceptability is for a reason that the linguist takes to be in his province. That means that in order to tell whether an unacceptable item is ungrammatical, one must identify why it is unacceptable. But if one can identify why it is unacceptable, nothing is gained by in addition classing it as grammatical or ungrammatical. A grammar that specifies what is grammatical and what is ungrammatical but does not enable one to pinpoint what is wrong with all unacceptable sentences (or better, unacceptable uses of sentences) is of questionable value; and if a grammar performs the latter task, there is no obvious reason why one should care whether it performs the former. (p. 202)

I do not accept this argument. First, if one can identify why a sentence is unacceptable, then by definition one has also determined its grammatical status. It is grammatical if the cause of its unacceptability is behavioral (i.e., outside the grammar), and ungrammatical otherwise. No further arbitrary decision is required. Second, if one accepts that the nature of explanation differs for different kinds of unacceptability (e.g., that some kinds are due to UG and some are due to working memory constraints), then it is important to establish which kind of explanation a particular datum calls for. A grammar of the type that McCawley finds to be of questionable value is useful if it provides a theory of a well-defined module of the mind. It will be less useful if it simultaneously tries to provide a theory of some unrelated module.

In fact, as McCawley has also pointed out, linguists are not really interested in judgments about strings of words. Rather, they seek to know whether a given string is a grammatical expression of a particular meaning. In this sense, semantics is crucially involved.

> The alleged ability of speakers of a language to distinguish between "grammatical" and "ungrammatical" strings of words is about as rare and as perverse as the ability to construct puns, an ability to which I believe it is closely related. Anyone who has taught an introductory syntax course has had the experience of presenting an "ungrammatical" example only to be told by some smart-aleck about an unsuspected interpretation on which the sentence is quite normal. ... Such interventions are usually greeted with the sort of groans that are the accepted form of expressing appreciation of puns,

2 Definitions and Historical Background

and they provide the same sort of comic relief that puns do in the midst of what is at times a boring enterprise. However, the extent to which comical virtuosity is required for a person to notice the existence of such an interpretation, as contrasted with the ease with which one recognizes its acceptability once it has been pointed out, shows that the strings of words on which grammaticality judgments are allegedly made exist only as typographical or acoustic objects, not as perceptual or cognitive objects, just as Necker cubes exist only as graphical objects and not as perceptual objects, as contrasted with their two interpretations, which do exist as perceptual objects. These points are in fact implicitly recognized by virtually all members of the generative grammar community, as is evidenced by the fact that the "grammaticality judgments" on which they base arguments systematically ignore interpretations other than those relevant to the points at issue, and the "sentences" are often exhibited with supplementary information as to the intended interpretation, for example, subscripts to indicate purported coreference of items, much in the same way that one might present the Necker cube with shading or context that picked out one of the interpretations. Generative grammarians speak as if they were doing linguistics in terms of something like sense data, when they in fact are doing it in terms of something more like the perceptual data of gestalt psychologists. (McCawley 1982: 78–79)

It is interesting to examine what other theoretical linguists today believe about the types of evidence that are available to them. The following unusually explicit passage (whence the epigraph of Chapter 1 is drawn) confirms that judgment data are still considered the primary source of linguistic evidence, and thus underscores the importance of studying their properties. It also reaffirms that we continue to lack a principled criterion for choosing data.

No kind of data is excluded in principle, only as a matter of practice – judicious practice, we think, but not irrefutable. ... Grammarians use data like "such and such a string of words is a sentence in such and such a language" or "such and such a string of words means such and such," where such facts are determined by native speakers of the languages in question. Data of this kind vary enormously in quality – ranging from the clear fact that *He are sick* is not grammatical in English to the rather subtle judgments involved in determining whether *John* and *his* can refer to the same person in *His mother likes John.* Despite this variation in quality and despite the fact that linguists have not formulated a "methodology of sentence judgments," such data remain the principal source of information about grammar, again, not as a matter of principle, but because they have so far provided successful insights.

Thus, the study of grammar is not the study of sentence judgments; rather, sentence judgments are our best current avenue to the study of grammar. In other words, the grammar is a real thing, not an artifact erected on top of an arbitrarily demarcated set of facts or types of facts. Therefore, it is often difficult to determine whether a given fact bears on grammar or not; this is not an arbitrary decision, but ultimately an empirical question about how the world divides up." (van Riemsdijk & Williams 1986: 2)

It is at least possible a priori that the reason judgments seem to work well for linguists is that they can be manipulated and distorted to suit the purpose of an analysis. In this connection, (Birdsong 1989: 82) suggests that "linguistics is a potentially fraudulent enterprise when elicitation data can be manipulated to instantiate pet theoretical analyses. It would be hard to imagine a more powerful argument for understanding the psychology of metalinguistic performance." Indeed. Most linguists profess ignorance of the reasons why judgment data are useful. For example, Baker notes:

> We focus on those linguistic behaviors which *for some reason* are most likely to reveal the mental structures in their true light. The situation can be likened to the physicist who tries to determine the force of gravity. ... Unfortunately there is every indication that much of the linguistic behavior we have record of is like the autumn leaf – complicated by many other external factors. ... I do not claim to have the wisdom to reliably discern which linguistic behaviors are like autumn leaves and which are like steel ball bearings. (Baker 1988: 29)

Despite his lack of "wisdom," Baker implicitly chooses to continue the tradition of making primary use of judgment data.

Before closing this section, I wish to dispel one possible misinterpretation that has been an all too common result of linguists' admission that judgments are their primary data. That is the view that grammaticality judgments are the objects of study in linguistics, that its purpose is to describe them, and that they therefore constitute the only kind of data the field requires (see Sampson (1975) for views along these lines). That this is not the case has been stated repeatedly and unequivocally by Chomsky:

To say that linguistics is the study of introspective judgments would be like saying that physics is the study of meter readings, photographs, and so on, but nobody says that. ...

It just seems absurd to restrict linguistics to the study of introspective judgments, as is very commonly done. ... Many textbooks that concentrate on linguistic argumentation for example are more or less guided by that view. (Chomsky 1982: 33–34)

2.3 The Use of Judgment Data in Linguistic Theory

2.3.1 Introduction

> *I cannot make native speakers behave the way Mr. Chomsky says they do, and if they insist on breaking his rules, it might be hard to pin down the grammatical and the ungrammatical.*
>
> (Sledd 1962)

The purpose of this section is twofold. First, I wish to demonstrate the claim, made in Section 2.2, that current issues in linguistic theory require nonobvious data for their resolution. Second, and relatedly, I wish to illustrate that the use of judgments in theoretical work has moved far beyond making distinctions of good versus bad, or even graded goodness and badness decisions. The situation is characterized most poignantly by Levelt:

> In the early years of the transformational grammar [the low reliability of absolute grammaticality judgments] was not an important issue, since the 'clear cases, i.e., the highly uncontroversial cases of grammaticality and ungrammaticality, were sufficient for constructing and testing linguistic theory. It was expected that, in its turn, the theory constructed in such a way would decide on the 'unclear cases." This hope has vanished. (Levelt et al. 1977: 88)

> It has slowly but surely become clear that it is not possible, on the basis of incontrovertible, directly evident data, to construct a theory so extensive that all less obvious cases can be decided upon by the grammar itself.' It is becoming more and more apparent that decisions on very important areas of theory are dependent on very unreliable observations. ... There is a

tendency toward preoccupation with extremely subtle distinctions, not the importance, but rather the direct observability of which can seriously be called into question. (Levelt 1974: Vol. 2, p. 6)

The same complaint has been made throughout much of the history of generative grammar, e.g., by Bever (1970a: 348), Labov (1972a: 191), Langendoen (1972), Coppieters (1987), and Birdsong (1989: 81). It has come to be generally acknowledged that not all speakers of "the same language" might have the same competence, but that does not justify basing the theory only on sentences for which there is universal agreement, and extrapolating by some means to dictate the status of the remainder. In cases where people disagree, that fact cannot be ignored; the theory must be able to describe *every* speaker's competence, and thus must allow for variation wherever it occurs. This is why establishing the extent of interspeaker agreement is important. Theories are now being based on sentences whose status turns out not to be unanimous, as I discuss in Section 2.3.2. See Section 6.3.3 for further discussion of the implications of individual differences in grammaticality judgments and in linguistic competence.

Unfortunately, the vast majority of work in linguistics today, unlike that reviewed in Section 1.3, has paid little heed to the issues involved in using judgment data. What follows is surely not a random sample of the theoretical syntax literature, but it includes some very influential and widely cited papers. My particular interest will be not just the types of judgment data that are employed, and hence the judgment abilities attributed to native speakers, but also the importance of these judgments to the theoretical arguments, i.e., to what extent the arguments would be weakened if the fine-grained judgments were unavailable. In many cases I will not mention the details of the theoretical issues, since they are irrelevant to my purpose.

2.3.2 The Dangers of Unsystematic Data Collection

All too often the data in linguistic books and articles are dubious, which in turn casts doubts on the analyses. Since analyses usually build on the results of previous analyses, the effect of one set of dubious data left unquestioned can have far-reaching repercussions that are not easily perceived.

(Greenbaum 1977c)

Let us begin with an important case where interspeaker variation in judgments has been ignored, to the detriment of the theory, before examining the ways in which judgments are used by theoreticians. The belief seems to be widely held among theoreticians that the majority of the data on which their theories are based is indisputable. But one cannot assume that what is a clear-cut judgment for oneself is obvious to all, or even to a large majority of, speakers. A case in point is the widely cited article by Lasnik & Saito (1984). One of the major proposals in this work is a substantial revision of the mechanisms of Proper Government to allow sentences like (5):

(5)   Why do you think that he left? [= Lasnik & Saito's (99)]

The authors assume that such sentences are ambiguous, i.e., that *why* can be taken as questioning the reason for the thinking or the reason for the leaving. In general, they assume that adjunct *wh*-words do not show *that*-trace effects, so that all sentences of this form should also be ambiguous when *why* is replaced by *where, when,* or *how*. On the basis of these assumptions, they propose various complications to the operation of the Empty Category Principle (ECP) and a process of *that*-deletion at Logical Form so that the sentences will not violate the ECP, as they did in earlier theories. But are the crucial readings grammatical?

In a subsequent paper, Aoun et al. (1987) propose an alternative theory in the same domain, this time with the goal of accounting for the *ungrammaticality* of some of the very same sentences that Lasnik & Saito went out of their way to include in the grammar, namely those containing *why* and *how* as the *wh*-words. Anticipating reaction to the apparent data disagreement, they make the following comments:

> Some speakers claim to get a lower-clause interpretation for *why* in (51a) [*Why did she say that there are men outside*] even if a complementizer is present. However, we have found that when asked to repeat the sentence, those speakers omit *that*, as if it were not perceived.
>
> English speakers who accept (51a) may be able to use *why* referentially, in the sense of 'for what reason'. But the *acceptability* of (51a) for such speakers does not seem to us to indicate *grammaticality*, unless they also accept (26)–(28) [e.g., *Who remembers what we bought why?*] and the like; rather, an analogical process is involved. (pp. 563–564; emphasis in original)

Aoun et al. seem to be proposing two different explanations. On the one hand, they suggest that the judgment data are inaccurate, that people really cannot get the relevant reading of this kind of sentence. On the other hand, they propose that this reading *is* acceptable for some speakers, and then attempt to argue on theory-internal grounds that it still must not be generated by their grammars, since we would then expect certain other sentence to be acceptable as well.

This area provides a striking demonstration of why linguists must improve their data-gathering techniques. In the first case, Lasnik & Saito show no evidence of being aware that the only sentences that prompt their major revision of the theory are not universally accepted. If their proposal had been uncritically adopted, it would have constituted a major step in the wrong direction, in the absence of any explanation for why many speakers should find the sentences bad. In the second case, Aoun et al. conclude on the basis of a less than rigorous survey that only a small number of speakers claim the sentences to be acceptable, and that some or all of these judgments are incorrect, i.e., that subjects did not consider the crucial presence of *that*. My own preliminary survey suggests that this is not the case either. About two-thirds of the people I surveyed accepted the sentences after the presence of *that* was explicitly pointed out to them, again calling the analysis into question. Given the extent to which judgments are divided, I suspect that syntacticians would not want to base any conclusions about Universal Grammar (UG) on these sentences. But until the detailed judgment facts are known, there is no way to assess the situation accurately.[16]

A similar case is made by Sobin (1987) with regard to *wh*-extraction across *that* versus *whether*. He points out that most theories assume that these two kinds of extraction, exemplified in sentences (6) and (7) below, are equally bad – categorically ungrammatical.

(6) *Who did you say that kissed Harriet? [= Sobin's (1)]

(7) *Who did you ask whether loves Mary? [= Sobin's (4)]

But the results of Sobin's questionnaire survey (corroborated by various anecdotal observations by others) present a distinctly different picture. He asked 42 nonlinguists to classify sentences into one of three groups, representing active acceptance, passive acceptance, and rejection.[17] He found the average rejection

---

[16] Newmeyer (1983) attempts to play down the significance of a similar situation from the early 1970s, describing it as a case of "letting the theory decide" on a marginal case, as Chomsky proposed in *SS*. In the situation under discussion, however, both camps went out of their way to account for the judgments they perceived, which were not predicted by existing versions of the theory.

[17] His descriptions to subjects were worded as follows: "(a) it sounds like a sentence that you ... (the informant) ... might say in the right context or situation; (b) it sounds like a possible English sentence, one that even if you don't say it that way, you would not be particularly surprised to hear someone else say it to you that way or to see it written; (c) it sounds odd, so that you doubt that people say it that way." One might raise some questions about these instructions; for instance, they require subjects to have some sense of what a "possible English sentence" is, and to be aware of how other people might speak.

rate for sentences like (6) to be 17.5%, whereas for sentences like (7) it was 97.6%. The active acceptance rate for (6) was 45.2%. These differences certainly imply that we cannot rely on identical grammatical constraints to rule out both sentence types. While the *whether* sentences are almost unanimously rejected, the *that* sentences are quite widely accepted. Once again, several theories had been constructed on the assumption that (6) is bad for everyone, and furthermore these analyses predicted that it should be just as bad as (7), since it violates precisely the same constraint.[18] As before, these are core data for the formulation of the ECP and associated constraints. Sobin proposes that structures like (7) be ruled out universally, whereas a parametrized rule could determine whether (6) would be allowed. Whatever the eventual analysis, it is clear that ignoring variation led the theory astray in this case too.

Bley-Vroman, Felix & Ioup (1988) also gathered data on Comp-trace effects. While their primary purpose was to look at the influence of UG on second-language acquisition, they needed native English speakers as controls. Their 34 subjects made three-way judgments (accept/reject/not sure) on 32 sentences for which the authors already had a set of normative judgments in mind. On the average, subjects agreed with these norms 92% of the time (where "not sure" was never counted as agreement).[19] On 6 of the 32 sentences, however, their mean accuracy fell below 90% (the authors' arbitrarily chosen cutoff for good agreement), and two of these involved Comp-trace violations. Only 48% of subjects rejected *What did John say that would fall on the floor, if we're not careful?* and only 74% rejected *What does Mary want to know whether John has already sold?* This study also found that supposedly good sentences are not always judged very good. Only 68% of the subjects accepted *Which information would it be possible for Mary to persuade Susan to tell the reporters?*

---

[18] Such an analysis might be salvageable if something like the process of *that*-deletion proposed by Aoun et al. is going on in sentences like (6) to yield a grammatical sentence. Note that there is no closely related grammatical version of (7) (Elan Dresher, personal communication).

[19] Unfortunately, the article does not report the number of "not sure" responses, making it difficult to know how clear-cut the disagreements are.

2.3.3 A Case Study in the Use of Subtle Judgments

> *The kinds of arguments that seem
> to bear very crucially on the nature
> and operation of syntactic systems
> involve [today's grammarian] in
> grammaticality decisions that are
> extremely difficult to make.*
>
> (Fillmore 1972)

Let us now consider various ways in which judgments are used in theoretical argumentation, beginning with Belletti & Rizzi's (1988) influential work on psych-verbs in Italian. They wish to argue that (some) Experiencer subjects are underlying internal arguments, so they rely heavily on the ability to diagnose derived subjects. One criterion they use is the inability of derived subjects to bind anaphors, which generally holds for the Experiencers in question. However, they admit that with nonclitic anaphors the resulting sentences are not entirely bad; they rate them as "*?" or "(?)," where by the latter they seem to mean "very close to fully acceptable." They clearly consider the lack of total badness an important problem, since they propose an analysis to explain it. Parallel constructions in English, they point out, "are judged deviant to some extent," which they apparently consider to be support for the Italian data by implicitly assuming the same explanation in both cases. Another correlate of derived subjecthood is the impossibility of arbitrary *pro*, but again there are generic contexts where the contrast with underlying subjects is "weaker, but still detectable" as compared to specific event contexts, the predicted bad sentences being marked "?" or "??." (No definition is given for "??" in relation to "*?," but in general, people seem to assume that any rating containing a star is worse than one containing only question marks.) Here again, an explanation is proposed by Belletti & Rizzi. In both of these cases, in the absence of an explanation the marginality facts would undermine main arguments for their analysis. On the very next page, however, a "??" sentence is treated as bad with no further comment, and the same is true for a sentence marked "(*)" later on.[20] Why is it that some instances of marginality demand

---

[20] Belletti & Rizzi do not exhaust the possible annotations. In addition to the five already mentioned, they employ the standard "*" and show grammatical sentences as unmarked, for a total of seven distinctions. But there are others in the literature. For instance, there are occasional uses of "**" that mean "much worse than a sentence that is already pretty bad." As Hagège (1981) puts it, "The stars have also been eked out with further signs" (p. 137). Jim McCawley (personal communication) points out that the real problem with all these annotations is that linguists often do not use them consistently. For example, linguists are not clear on whether

comment whereas others do not? Most likely because the authors have no explanations for some marginal cases, but know that readers will not be upset if certain marginal data are left unaccounted for. Thus, we have another case of selective treatment of judgment data.

Later in Belletti & Rizzi's paper we find an instance where (citing Burzio (1981)) they equate two uses of the question mark, claiming that the marginal status of one sentence is unchanged by the application of a passivization rule, i.e., that the original sentence and its passive counterpart are equally marginal:

(8)   a.   ? John gave pictures of each other to the kids.
           [= Belletti & Rizzi's (69)]

      b.   ? Pictures of each other were given to the kids.

Their argument is that binding requirements may be satisfied at D-structure, before passive movement, so no change in grammaticality is predicted. However, in the corresponding Italian cases the apparent surface binding violations (parallel to (8b)) are "slightly more awkward, ... but the contrast is much weaker than cases involving violations of the Binding Theory" (p. 316). In the abstract, their argument takes the following form:

> The difference in grammaticality between sentences A and B is significantly less than that between sentences C and D.

> D constitutes a binding violation, but A and C are fine.

> Therefore, B does not constitute a binding violation because it is not bad enough.

The assumption is that all (Principle A) binding violations cause exactly the same change in grammaticality rating, independent of any properties of the sentences themselves. This is an assumption we ought to test.

It is interesting to look at the prose descriptions that Belletti & Rizzi use to accompany the various annotations of sentences. Their sentence (75), marked "?," is "more or less acceptable" but such sentences with one question mark "still produce a weak violation of the chain condition." That is, the sentence is bad enough that it must violate something, and just bad enough to be a violation of this condition, but must not be violating anything else or it would have to

---

"*" represents the worst point on a two-point versus a five-point scale or some intermediate point.

be worse. Examples labelled "??" are variously described as "quite strange" and "weakly deviant"; does this mean that the notation underdifferentiates, or is the descriptive prose merely being stylistically varied?

Despite their distinction of no fewer than seven degrees of grammaticality, Belletti & Rizzi remark about some other sentences that "these judgments are extremely subtle, and the usual OK vs. * notation is perhaps not appropriate for characterizing such contrasts. In fact, examples like (79a)–(80b) are already quite marked; still, there seems to be a detectable systematic difference in the indicated direction" (p. 322). Now, for some reason, any detectable pattern warrants an explanation. Furthermore, a sentence that is "quite marked" receives no stars or question marks at all. After proposing an account of the difference between the starred and unstarred items, the authors then claim independent support for it by suggesting that another subtle contrast seems "exactly on a par with" this one. That is, we must allow for judging strict equality, as well as inequality, in contrasting pairs of judgments.

In this paper we also find the paradigmatic case of comparison of degrees of badness, ECP versus Subjacency violations: "The relatively mild ill-formedness of (94b) [which they mark "??"] suggests that the empty category left after extraction is properly governed within NP, otherwise these examples would violate the ECP, and a stronger unacceptability should result" (p. 328, fn. 22). Thus, people supposedly have an absolute sense of how bad ECP violations are and the sentence in question is not bad enough to be an ECP violation. Furthermore, since Subjacency violations are usually not as bad as ECP violations, this is probably a Subjacency violation. But there is no general theory of which principles *should* cause worse violations. The theory makes no prediction about the relative badness of, say, θ-Criterion versus Case Filter violations, let alone about how bad each one is in some absolute sense. The notion of relative and absolute badness of particular violations is ad hoc, and is used in just those cases where it is convenient.

2.3.4 The Interpretation of the Annotations and Degrees of Badness

> *Twinkle twinkle sentence starred,*
> *The asterisk means that you are marred.*
> *Because of you the linguists try*
> *Inventing rules which you defy.*
>
> *Twinkle twinkle sentence starred.*
> *From linguistics you should be barred.*
> *The truth is rarely all or none,*
> *Not even with an N of one.*
> (Peter Reich, 1980)

Householder (1973) accepts both the credit and the blame for originating, around 1958, the use of asterisks to mark ungrammatical sentences. He complains that what was once a simple and unequivocal notation has come to be used in highly ambiguous ways, many of which are detailed below.[21] At the time of his writing, the asterisk seemed to have at least three possible interpretations:

1. "I would never say X";

2. "I have never seen or heard a sentence of the type of X and hereby wager you can't find an example"; and

3. "This is quite comprehensible, and I have heard people say it, but they were all K's [foreigners, Southerners, etc.]; in *my* dialect we would say Y instead." (Householder 1973: 370–372)

As we shall see, this is only the tip of the iceberg.

Another kind of ambiguity with judgment notation involves two distinct uses of marginality markings, chiefly the question mark, in the literature. One use denotes variable interspeaker ratings, i.e., a sentence that is good for some people, bad for others. The second meaning is that (most) individuals rate the sentence as marginal. One could imagine the combination of these situations as well. The same is true of disjunctive notations like "/" or "{}": Are both alternatives acceptable to all speakers, or are there two groups, each of which accepts only one? This situation is at best a notational inaccuracy that could be easily corrected by

---

[21] According to Householder, the originally marked forms that were "quite obviously ungrammatical by anyone's standards."

adopting new symbols.[22] Unfortunately, there are cases where the surrounding prose description does not make clear which meaning is intended. An example of the second kind of ambiguity appears in verb agreement with nominative objects in Icelandic. Thráinsson (1979) gives the following datum and description:

(9) Mér líkar/líka   þessir bílar.
     Me(D) likes(3rd sg.)/like(3rd pl.) these cars(N pl.)

     [= Thráinsson's (3), p. 466]

"There are some idiolectal differences as to the preference of verb forms, but the fact that some speakers prefer the 3rd sg. form here indicates that the nominative NP is not perceived as the subject" (p. 466). One interpretation of these comments might be that there is between-speaker variation across degrees of preference for each form.[23]

Andrews (1990) examined this and a number of other subtle agreement phenomena in Icelandic.. He is an unusual theoretician in that his work actually reports the results of grammaticality questionnaires that he administered. In one, Andrews elicited ratings on a 6-point scale, characterized as follows (this is one of the rare instances in which an explicit meaning is given for the symbols):[24]

✓ Completely acceptable and natural

? Acceptable, but perhaps somewhat unnatural

?? Doubtful, but perhaps acceptable

?* Worse, but not totally unacceptable

---

[22] One does occasionally find "%" used to mark acceptance by some speakers but not others. Neubauer (1976) states that he and Larry Horn introduced this symbol to indicate important dialect variation. It should be noted that *dialect* here is not necessarily meant in the sense of regionally or socially based group speech, but simply in the sense of a number of speakers who share the same judgments.

[23] Newmeyer (1983) suggests that there is an even more basic inconsistency in the use of stars, question marks, and other symbols – namely, their indication of ungrammaticality versus unacceptability. My impression is that the authors of works reviewed here, like most current authors, intend the latter interpretation. McCawley (1985) explicitly states that he uses asterisks to mark "whatever kind of oddity of a sentence ... I am at the moment concerned with; thus I use it to report data, not conclusions as to 'grammaticality'" (p. 673). As noted in Section 2.2, McCawley rejects the notion of grammaticality, as opposed to acceptability, anyway, feeling that there is nothing to be gained by classifying sources of unacceptability as being inside or outside the grammar.

[24] Labov (1972b) gives the following definitions: ? = questionably ungrammatical, * = ungrammatical, ** = outstandingly ungrammatical. See Householder (1973) for another version.

* Thoroughly unacceptable

** Horrible (p. 203)

Andrews reports results for 20 sentences, with between 12 and 17 subjects responding. Of these sentences, only three were rated uniformly "✓"; none were rated uniformly "*" or uniformly "***", and only two were rated as either "*" or "**" by everyone. But despite having access to such detailed information, Andrews fails to clarify the status of Thráinsson's variability, stating that "either of the above [agreement variants] seems to be acceptable (on the basis of questionnaires returned by seven informants)" (p. 212), which is still ambiguous. The implications of interspeaker differences versus intraspeaker marginality should be clear. The former, if not reflective of extragrammatical factors, demand different grammars for the two groups, whereas the latter demands a single grammar with a less severe constraint.

Another use of "?" is illustrated by Pollock (1989) in his widely cited paper on the structure of IP (Inflection Phrase), with regard to French sentences like the following:

(10) ?Je pensais ne pouvoir pas dormir dans cette chambre.
      [= Pollock's (20b)]

According to Pollock, "the question mark is meant here as an indication that [sentences such as the one in (10)] have a very literary ring to them, not that they are unacceptable" (p. 375). Such data are in serious danger of being misinterpreted out of context, especially since on the very next page "?" is used to indicate marginal acceptability. On this next page we also find "(?)" indicating that some speakers find another sentence better than the question-marked one, although Pollock admits to having found other speakers who hold the opposite opinion. One could see this either as again confounding marginality with interspeaker variability, or as an indication that ratings may reflect arbitrarily chosen subgroups of speakers. The contrast between "?" and "(?)" does not affect his arguments, but the difference between these marginal sentences and certain starred ones is crucial to several arguments in Pollock's paper. Later on, "(?)" is used not to mean "slightly better than ?" in a relative sense, but "perfect, with at worst a slightly literary ring," which might or might not correspond in an absolute sense to the prior usage. Indeed, literariness and marginality might be separate dimensions of ratings altogether, which cannot be meaningfully compared on the same ordinal scale, much as height and weight as integers cannot.

Finally, let us consider a paper by Browning (1987) in which more than half of the example sentences are marked with some number of question marks or stars.[25] Since the paper is concerned with (among other things) the definition of Subjacency, one of the few Government-Binding (GB) principles that has graded behavior in its very definition, it is not surprising to find extensive reliance on relative judgments. One of Browning's proposals is to account for the marginality of parasitic gaps as in (11) and (12) by the same mechanism that accounts for paradigm Subjacency violations such as those in the sentences in (13):

(11)   ?Which paper did you read before filing? [= Browning's (1)]

(12)   ?an artist that close friends of admire [= Browning's (2)]

(13)   a. Which car is it time for John to wash? [= Browning's (40)]
       b. Who did John buy a suit to impress?
       c. What did John wonder how to fix?
       d. Who did they leave before meeting?

> Consider first the degree of ungrammaticality which results from one barrier intervening between two points in a chain. Several examples are given above in [(13)]. I have been assuming the standard judgment for parasitic gaps such as [(11)] and [(12)], namely, a mild marginality. If this marginality is due to the intervening barrier, then the severity of the violation is clearly in the ball park represented by [(13)]. (pp. 68–69)

Two things are noteworthy in Browning's account. First, as we have seen before, there is a standard rating for constructions of a particular type, independent of the sentences themselves. This is surely a huge idealization – there are experiments showing that identical structural violations are given different grammaticality ratings depending on their particular lexical content (see Sections 5.3.5 and 5.3.6). To the extent that *linguists* give uniform ratings for all such sentences, it is much more likely to be because they recognize them (perhaps subconsciously) as instances of parasitic gaps than because of any pretheoretic goodness rating.[26] That is, they are judging conformity to sentence patterns or templates and then

---

[25] Hagège (1981) finds this trend unappealing: "In extreme cases, the pollution of starred, forbidden forms brings us to what has been called 'a linguistics of the impossible'" (p. 158, fn. 16).

[26] This hypothesis is supported by the fact that people's absolute judgments are highly unstable, as I discuss in later chapters. Identical ratings of the kind linguists claim to have could not arise on the basis of acceptability judgments alone.

reporting the standard rating for that pattern.[27] Second, Browning's analysis is another example of equating the badness of sentences and taking this as support for a common violation. But is it not possible that two different principles could yield the same degree of ungrammaticality when violated? Just because two sentences are equally bad does not mean they violate exactly the same constraint(s), especially since most of GB's constraints have yet to be rated according to seriousness. Browning goes on to draw support for her arguments from alleged differences in goodness between sentences with no question marks or stars whatsoever.

2.4 Introspection, Intuition, and Judgment

> *Being a native speaker doesn't confer papal infallibility on one's intuitive judgments.*
>
> (Raven McDavid, quoted in Paikeday 1985)

Over the history of generative grammar, much has been made of its heavy reliance on introspective judgments and their nonequivalence to production and comprehension. Interestingly, this same feature has been used both to criticize and to defend the generative practice. In fact, Ringen (1977) notes Chomsky's implicit suggestion that introspective psychology or psychophysics could serve as a model for the use of linguistic intuitions. But, as Ringen argues, the first of those analogies would be counterproductive to the field, and the second would be inappropriate (but see Cowart (1997: 6–7) for a different view). Let us consider how these paradigms operate, and why linguistics should not be striving to emulate them.

In the introspectionist paradigm, established by Wilhelm Wundt in 1879 in the first experimental psychology laboratory, trained subjects were asked to describe their impressions of a wide variety of physical objects and experiences (Wundt (1896); Boring (1953)). The idea was to describe internal experience in terms of elementary sensation. That is, rather than saying that one sees a book, one should relate the colors, shapes, etc., that are perceived. There were several problems with this approach. One was that the elements of most experiences simply cannot be discerned by reflecting on them, just as one cannot discern the elements

---

[27] I assume that sentence processing itself does *not* work primarily by templates.

of water by looking at it (Dellarosa 1988). Another was the fact that Wundt's subjects were far from naive with regard to the experimental procedure. They had to undergo at least 10,000 supervised practice trials before they could be used in an experiment, during which time they were taught special terminology in which to describe their sensations. One cannot help but suspect that Wundt's own ideas on what experience was like affected subjects during this training period, although at the time it was thought that subjects were merely unlearning bad perception habits. Each of these problems is applicable to the linguist's situation today to some degree (Levelt 1974: vol. 3), but perhaps the most significant drawback, which led to the demise of introspectionist psychology, is strikingly evident among modern-day linguists. Dellarosa (1988) describes it as follows:

> Despite the careful training that observers received, agreement among introspective reports was the exception rather than the rule. It was not unusual to obtain markedly different reports from two observers who were exposed to the same stimulus. Such disagreements could not be settled in any scientific fashion owing to the inherently private nature of internal events. In more technical terms, introspection failed as a bona fide scientific method because it violated a fundamental rule concerning scientific investigation: that of independent access to both causes and effects. Although the cause (i.e., stimulus) was open to public observation, the effect (i.e., internal sensation) was not. Without such independent observation of the internal sensation, it was impossible to tell which of two conflicting introspective reports was the correct one. The conflicting reports could have arisen because (a) Subject A was truly experiencing a different sensation than Subject B, or (b) Subject A was experiencing the same sensation as Subject B but was misreporting it, or (c) Subject A was simply lying. ... There was no scientific way to determine which of these three conditions was true. (p. 5)

See Householder (1965) for the view that there is no way to evaluate conflicting claims about linguistic intuitions either, and Levelt (1972) for some more general background on the historical relationship between psychology and linguistics. I should stress that I do not believe that appealing to linguistic intuitions about sentences *is* a form of introspection, for reasons that are detailed immediately below. However, the methodologies seem to have some disturbing commonalities.

Now, it is true that there has been somewhat of a resurgence in the use of introspectionist-style protocols in psychology recently, specifically in the use of "talk aloud" and "think aloud" methods. In their comprehensive review of this approach, however, Ericsson & Simon (1984) point out a fundamental difference in how such reports are used today. In a nutshell, they are not taken as facts about the inner workings of subjects' minds, but are studied from the point of view of understanding how it was that subjects were able to say what they did about a mental process, independent of its veracity. This distinction is too easily overlooked, but it is crucial, and many linguists have not taken heed of it yet. Except in those cases where they fail to suit the linguist's purpose, subjects' intuitions *are* taken to reflect their true linguistic knowledge. We do not ask, "What must be in subjects' minds in order for them to react this way to a sentence?" but, rather, "What must be in subjects' minds in order for this sentence to have the status they claim it has?" This is what Bever & Carroll (1981) mean when they say that "intuitions are not empirical primitives but complex behavioral performances in their own right" (p. 232). Thus, current psychological practice does not redeem linguistic practice.

Ringen (1977) summarizes the problem with a Wundtian approach thus: if subjects are reporting on truly private mental states (to which only they have access), then their reports are *in principle* uncheckable; therefore, if intuitions are to be any good as data, they must differ in some way from this sort of introspection. Fortunately, I believe they do. Linguists are not asking subjects to describe an internal mental process when they encounter a sentence – not even thinking aloud is involved, only reporting a reaction (Cohen 1981). Introspection is reflection, analysis, or careful thought applied to accessible contents of the mind, which do not include grammatical knowledge. Thus, linguists are not introspectionists.

Ringen goes on to consider Chomsky's second analogy, to psychophysics. Like linguistic intuition gathering, psychophysics experiments involve first-person utterances given in response to stimuli (e.g., responses to questions like "Which weight feels heavier, the one in your right or your left hand?"). But in psychophysics we can ask not only if the subjects' reports correctly describe their judgments (as opposed to being instances of lying, misspeaking, or carelessness), but also how *accurate* the judgments are (e.g., which of the two weights really *is* heavier). Psychophysics concerns the relationship between objective features of stimuli and subjective judgments of them, but grammaticality judgments have no objective standard to be measured against.[28] One is the final authority on what

---

[28] Wayne Cowart (personal communication) suggests that the analogy *is* useful because the external standards against which judgments can be measured are the linguistic norms of the community where speakers learned their native languages. Beyond the obvious practical problems in applying this idea, there is still the conceptual problem of distinguishing inaccurate judgments from real differences in the grammars of people native to the same speech community.

one's psychophysical judgments *are*, but not on whether they are correct. Thus, psychophysics also fails as an analogy to grammaticality judgment.

There is one type of report that does seem to parallel linguistic intuitions, as Ringen points out: reports about mental states, e.g., whether one is in pain. These certainly *can* be shown to be false – we can show that a person is lying about being in pain, but once we show that the report is sincere, no other evidence can disprove the assertion (it makes no sense to talk about the correctness of a sensation), and if two people's reports conflict in response to the same stimulus, that does not undermine the veracity of either report. And so it seems to be with linguistic intuitions. Pateman (1987) makes the case most eloquently:

> [Core grammatical rules] can be studied by means of *intuition*, which is a quite distinct method or process from introspection. In my view, the exercise of intuition – for example, offering intuitions as to the grammaticality or ungrammaticality of token sentences-provides us with indexical, that is, causally related, symptomatic evidence for the character of underlying mental representations. An intuition of grammaticality is not a social judgment, but the output of a computational process which the speaker as subject registers and reports, just as in the case where the viewer as subject registers and reports visual phenomena which may well be resistant to judgment proper (so, for example the Müller-Lyer illusion persists even when we know it is an illusion). Of course, this is not always true, and it is clear and admitted that intuitions of grammaticality are liable to all kinds of interference 'on the way up' to the level at which they are given as responses to questions. In particular, they are liable to interference from social judgments of linguistic acceptability. Ontologically, the difference may be expressed this way: mentally represented grammars *compute* grammaticality categorizations, but they do not care about them any more than the perceptual system cares about perceptual illusion. In contrast, speakers as subjects can and do care about grammaticality (and the veridicality of perception), and can and do convert the categorization they register into social judgments. This can sometimes lead them into error. (p. 100)

I use the term 'intuition' to designate that which gives us causally related indexical or symptomatic evidence for the character of underlying psycholinguistic (or, more generally, psychological) processes. Intuitions are not exercises of judgment which claim certainty or any kind of objectivity for the content of the judgment and hence which claim the assent of all those implicated by the judgment. Rather, intuitions are reports of appearances, hence subjective expressions which make no judgment about how others will or should respond. In intuition we tell how something strikes us, how it appears to us and thereby provide causal evidence about our minds. In Wittgenstein's terms, intuitions provide *symptoms* rather than *criteria* of what underlies them. ... Intuition is used to establish claims of form (1), not form (2), which involves the exercise of judgment (introspection in my terms).

(1)   Sentence *P* seems grammatical to subject *S*.

(2)   Sentence *P* is grammatical in language *L*, according to subject *S*. (p. 135)

See Carr (1990: 117) for a somewhat different conception of intuition versus introspection, as well as Katz (1981) and Lyons (1986) on the same topics.

Thus, much of the common terminology surrounding the use of grammaticality judgments is somewhat misleading. They are certainly not introspective. They are not judgments or intuitions in the everyday sense, in that they cannot be verified or resolved by observation or calculation. They also do not have an evaluative component as do social judgments. Perhaps more accurate terms for grammaticality judgments would be *grammaticality sensations* and *linguistic reactions*. Nonetheless, for the sake of familiarity I shall continue using traditional terminology, on the understanding that it must not be taken literally. As Pateman (1987) points out, treating grammaticality judgments like sensations does not preclude our looking for ways in which they might be inaccurate, just as our primary senses can be. Even staunch supporters of the generative enterprise such as Newmeyer (1983) admit that the theory might well be skewed by artifacts of the introspection/intuition/sensation process, but they usually resign themselves to this as being part of the early stages of the field of linguistic investigation. I suggest that a more useful approach would be to try to learn more about the creature rather than simply to accept its influence over us. If indeed metalinguistic judgment behavior can tell us anything at all about normal language use, how can we extract that information? That is the question I begin to address in the next chapter.

2.5 Conclusion

In general, it is clear that subtle judgment data have become important to theoretical argumentation. If they were not crucial, surely they would be ignored – clear-cut data make a much more impressive case. I have identified three kinds of problems in the use of these data, one of which will be the main focus for the remainder of this book. The first is that judgment data are not systematically reported or notationally identified. The second is that they are sometimes used or discarded as it suits the linguist's fancy. The third is that their use attributes various sophisticated abilities to native speakers without any evidence that speakers are actually capable of reliably making the discriminations in question, and without any attempt to systematically control the process of obtaining these judgments. The first two problems are more properly examined under the rubric of philosophy of science, and I will have little more to say about them. The third falls in the domain of psychology, which has the means to determine what people can actually do and provide a method for collecting the data when they do it. Subsequent chapters address these two goals and relate the results to the needs of the generative enterprise.

3 Judging Grammaticality: The Nature of Metalinguistic Performance

> *Metalinguistic data are like 25-cent hot dogs: they contain meat, but a lot of other ingredients, too. Some of these ingredients resist ready identification.*
>
> (Birdsong 1989)

3.1 Introduction

The purpose of this chapter is to explore some of the basic qualities of grammaticality judgments and some current thinking on their theoretical status, as a prelude to examining detailed studies of their behavior under various experimental manipulations in the two subsequent chapters. I cite some experimental work, but also a fair amount of theoretical discussion.

The structure of the chapter is as follows. In Section 3.2, I ask how it is that we can get people to assess grammaticality, what tasks have been invented for this purpose, and what their relative merits are. I then consider in Section 3.3 what has been a most important and controversial feature of the judgments that result from these tasks – namely, that people seem to judge grammaticality in a graded rather than a dichotomous fashion. This is perhaps the most widely studied topic in the literature on grammaticality judgments; a major issue is how to get at these scalar judgments *reliably*. In Section 3.4, I speculate on how the intuitions behind our judgments might arise, how a sentence is processed for judgment, the extent to which the hypothesized process could reflect the grammar, and how we might make it do so more transparently. Section 3.5 tackles more directly a view that has become almost unanimous among psycholinguists, that no privileged status can be accorded to judgment data over any other sort of performance data, and that we therefore cannot draw direct conclusions about grammar from them. Numerous researchers have made this argument in various ways, and I review the major contributions. Finally, I relate the high-level properties of grammaticality judgments discussed in this chapter to the low-level properties to be examined in the next two chapters.

3.2 Tasks that Access Grammaticality

In this section I look at some of the methods researchers have used to induce subjects to express their feelings on the grammaticality of sentences, as a prelude to the detailed discussion of experimental work that begins in Section 3.3.2. This list is not exhaustive (see Labov (1972b: 106), and Bialystok & Ryan (1985) for other types of intuitional judgments), and I concentrate on those methods that require the least inference on the part of the experimenter. For instance, I am not concerned here with inferring grammaticality on the basis of spontaneous conversations or texts, because such inference is problematic and because subjects are not engaged in explicit judgment, which is the focus of this examination.[1] Still, a number of tasks have been used productively to investigate subjects' intuitions indirectly, or to gain additional information. Many of these are represented in the studies I review in subsequent chapters. I start by extending the term *judgment* beyond the paradigm case of asking the subject, "Do you think this is a good sentence?"

The first extension we can make is to supplement judgments in various ways. For instance, we can ask subjects to explain their judgments. In the case of sentences judged bad, this can involve asking subjects why they feel the sentence is bad, or where in the sentence the problem is. Such questioning helps to ensure that the reasons for which subjects reject sentences are relevant to the theoretical issue at hand. While there is potentially a lot of information to be gained by this method, there are problems as well. For instance, it is not clear that subjects will be able to answer such questions in all cases. As Birdsong (1989: 110) puts it, the response "ungrammatical" can result from a "rather vague, gestalt-like impression"; it just sounds bad. At other times, a subject can detect something specific that is deviant about a sentence. It would be worthwhile to examine under what conditions these two feelings tend to arise, assuming subjects can reliably report the difference; the question appears not to have been studied. Some researchers deny

---

[1] As an example of such an activity, one could imagine using almost any measure that is correlated with grammaticality. For instance, Miller & Isard (1963) show that amid loud background noise, grammatical sentences can be shadowed much more accurately than ungrammatical ones, but one would not want to take such differential perceptibility as sufficient evidence for grammaticality.

that posing such questions to subjects is *ever* a useful procedure. Botha (1981), for example, believes that people do not know the reasons for their intuitive judgments and cannot justify them, so it is senseless to ask for such justification. (See Section 2.4 on introspection for more discussion of this issue.) This suggestion poses another methodological problem as well, namely, how to balance this task for the sentences that are considered good, to avoid a biased procedure. It seems to make no sense to ask, "Why is this sentence good?"[2] Some experimenters who have worried about this problem seem to have used a paraphrase task instead, which is useful in the sense that it helps to ensure that a subject actually thinks about the sentence in question and takes the intended reading. (In fact, Connors & Ouellette (1993) had their subjects paraphrase the stimuli *before* judging them.) Another type of extension of the judgment task, particularly useful in marginal cases, is to ask under what conditions, if any, the sentence could be grammatical. The subject could refer to a number of different conditions: the context of the utterance (e.g., "Only in a cartoon world where toasters can think"); prosodic features (e.g., "It's OK with heavy stress on *dog*"); restrictions on referents (e.g., "It's good as long as *they* refers to something animate"); or novel lexical items ("Then *of* would have to be a noun"). A parallel task for the ungrammatical cases might be correction, i.e., asking the subject how to fix an ungrammatical sentence (e.g., what words to add or remove). Generally, we are interested in the *minimal* necessary changes. If the initial judgment is scalar rather than binary, it might make sense to ask both kinds of questions about the same sentence, i.e., "When would it be good as it stands?" and "How could you make it completely good?"

We can also go beyond explicitly asking for grammaticality assessments and look to other metalinguistic tasks in collecting this information.[3]

---

[2] A linguist might respond to such a question by demonstrating that the sentence judged to be grammatical can be generated from the available mechanisms in the grammar, or that it satisfies all the relevant well-formedness constraints, but naive subjects cannot be expected to attempt this.

[3] Even Birdsong (1989), whose entire book is devoted to metalinguistic performance, believes this term requires a "rather vague interpretation." Its most important feature seems to be the objectification of language, or attention to linguistic form rather than content. Birdsong also suggests that metalinguistic performance describes "language-related activities typically not associated with the casual conversation and listening of non-linguists" (p. 62). Cazden (1976) describes it thus: "It is an important aspect of our unique capacities as human beings that we can not only act, but reflect back on our own actions; not only learn and use language, but treat it as an object of analysis and evaluation in its own right. Metalinguistic awareness, the ability to make language forms opaque and attend to them in and for themselves, is a special kind of language performance, one which makes special cognitive demands, and seems to be less easily and less universally acquired than the language performances of speaking and listening" (p. 603). See Gombert (1992) for a survey of uses of the term.

One simple variation is to request rank orderings of sentences by grammaticality, a procedure that I examine further in Section 3.3.4. One might also ask for a comparison of the *type* of violation in bad sentences, e.g., asking whether two sentences are bad in the same way. Another interesting method makes use of ambiguity. If we have a sentence that is uncontroversially good under one reading, but questionable under another (e.g., the *that*-trace sentences discussed in Section 2.3.2), we can ask subjects whether it is ambiguous, and then verify their answers by eliciting paraphrases of the readings they find. In fact, the latter task without the former can provide some of this information without putting subjects in a judging mode at all, which (it will be argued in Section 3.4) might be important. Getting at the grammaticality of an alternative reading of a sentence via judgments is particularly tricky, as Householder (1973) points out. The kind of judgment needed – whether the sentence is grammatical under reading X, when it is clearly good under reading Y – might require a different kind of judgment than one of simple grammaticality, in that the task involves evaluating a structure-meaning pair.

The most widely cited nonjudgment tasks, which were very popular in the 1960s and early 1970s, are the so-called compliance tests. Quirk & Svartvik (1966) are often cited as the originators of these tests. The task is to transform a stimulus sentence in some way, for example, to convert it from a statement to a question, to make it negative, or to switch its pronouns. The experimenter is actually not interested in these operations at all, but in whether the subject changes the remaining portion of the sentence while converting it. For instance, in investigating the grammaticality of a bare adjective complement of *regarded*, the task might be to convert the sentence *He is regarded insane* into a question. The dependent measure is the number of relevant noncompliances (RNCs), instances when subjects change the relevant part of the sentence, in this case the complement (e.g., by the insertion of the word *as*). This constitutes noncompliance with the instructions, since subjects are told to make only the change that the experimenter requests. An RNC suggests that the subject considers the original form to be ungrammatical, although we must be careful about potential interfering effects such as forgetting the exact syntax of the original. Key to such an interpretation is the requirement that the transformed sentence would be just as deviant as the original – the operation must neither remove nor add deviance. Of course, whether a sentence meets this criterion is up to the judgment of the experimenters. (See Itkonen (1979) for the criticism that what constitutes an RNC in these experiments also depends on the experimenters' own intuitions.)

Quirk & Svartvik's (1966) original series of experiments compared tests measuring RNCs (operation tests)compliance tests with two other types of task. Selection tests are like operation tests except that a set of possible responses is given to the subjects, who must simply select the response they prefer. Judgment tests involve rating sentences on a 3-level scale: "wholly natural and normal," "wholly unnatural and abnormal," or "marginal or dubious." The researchers argue for the use of a three-tiered scale as a compromise between the arbitrary responses that they believed would result from the use of a two-tiered scale, which they consider "absurdly gross," and the 7-point scale that is more typical in psychology, which they consider "unduly arbitrary." In eliciting judgments, they preferred to ask about natural and normal language, combining grammaticality with meaningfulness and other factors, rather than trying to focus on structure alone. They wanted to compare judgments with the other tasks because they believe that direct questioning is the *least* reliable way of getting at structural intuitions. They wanted to shift subjects' attention away from the issue of interest, and the notion of grammatical deviance in general, by the use of operation tests. The use of judgment and operation tests involving the same sentences allowed Quirk & Svartvik to pinpoint the reasons for an ungrammatical judgment without asking subjects about them directly. Interestingly, though, a graph of the number of subjects accepting various sentences does not at all resemble a graph of the number of compliances on the same sentences. Although the overall correlation of these measures is $r = 0.73$, this figure drops to 0.5 when 13 clearly grammatical control sentences are excluded. One major reason for this discrepancy is that there might be no obvious way to repair certain kinds of ungrammaticality, so that no RNC response was possible although a given sentence was clearly bad in some way, e.g., the semantically anomalous *Timber was creeping up the hill.* Based on the two graphs, Quirk & Svartvik conclude that there is no clear-cut threshold of grammaticality. Stolz (1969) correctly points out that the generalizability of their results is limited by the fact that they did not look at specific classes of rule violations, but often tended to focus on particular lexical items.

In a subsequent book, Greenbaum & Quirk (1970) describe in great detail several orally-administered batteries of operation tests, as well as relative and absolute judgment tasks. The obvious question again is whether compliance tests and judgment tests gave the same results for particular sentences. Unfortunately, their presentation does not allow a concise overall summary of the results, so we are limited to somewhat vague generalities. Greenbaum & Quirk found a large degree of agreement between the two measures, and they attempt to provide very detailed explanations of the minor systematic discrepancies. For instance, sentences that violate lexical co-occurrence restrictions are judged bad but are not changed, whereas sentences with certain word order errors are changed but not judged bad. Tottie (1977) rightly cautions, in response to performance tests like these (although her comments could apply equally well to judgment tests), that we should ask ourselves

> whether we are actually justified, from a psychological as well as from a linguistic point of view, in asking subjects to substitute one word for another or to produce negative or interrogative counterparts of affirmative sentences. Obviously, the sentences produced in that way cannot *a priori* be assumed to be equivalent to spontaneously produced linguistic structures of the same type. ... However, we need to know a good deal more about the psychology of speech production before we can arrive at anything more than a very tentative evaluation of such tests. (p. 209)

A more recent technique for assessing grammaticality, which is just beginning to show its full potential, is the measurement of event-related brain potentials (ERPs;; see Garnsey (1993) for an excellent introduction to the use of this technique in language research). These are patterns in the electrical activity of the brain, measured by scalp recordings during the presentation of stimuli, in this case, sequential visual presentation of words. Electroencephalogram readings are broken down into component waveforms and categorized by the direction of change of the potential, positive (P) or negative (N), and the typical latency in milliseconds (e.g., 300, 400, etc.) from the stimulus onset. Three ERP components have been identified with well- or ill-formedness of sentences: N400, P300, and P600. Kutas & Hillyard (1983) teased out the triggers of N400 using three types of stimulus sentence: syntactically well-formed and coherent; well-formed but containing one semantically anomalous content word; and ill-formed but semantically coherent, containing mismatches of tense or plural morphemes. In all cases, the primary task for the subjects was reading for content, although they were warned that errors might appear. The experimenters found that semantic anomalies elicited N400s, but grammatical errors did not, although they point out that the latter were considerably more subtle than the former. In a later study, Van Petten & Kutas (1991) compared syntactically well-formed anomalous sentences with random word strings and found that the ERPs elicited by the final word of each string type differed significantly. They interpreted the reaction to the well-formed strings as belonging to the P300 class of ERPs, which occurs in a wide variety of tasks, but here seemed to be associated with syntactic closure, the realization that a sentence is complete. P600 appears to indicate temporary parsing failures, whether or not they are subsequently resolved. In particular, it occurs in certain garden-path sentences at the point where the initial parsing choice fails, e.g., at *to* in (1a), but not at the same word in the superficially similar non-garden-path sentence (1b). (Osterhout & Holcomb 1992). A P600 has also been found to occur upon presentation of the word *was* in (2a), but not in (2b) (Osterhout, Holcomb & Swinney 1994).

(1) a. The broker persuaded to sell the stock …
     b. The broker hoped to sell the stock …

(2) a. The lawyer charged the defendant was lying.
     b. The lawyer charged that the defendant was lying.

Ideally, one would also hope to find a reliable ERP correlate of actual, not just temporary, grammatical violations, so that overt judgments could be independently verified, but in practice this will not be so straightforward. Not only are ERP experiments costly and difficult to conduct, requiring very carefully controlled and unnatural reading conditions, but the interpretation of the results is not straightforward. Still, we might hope that someday ERP research will at least help us to disentangle various sources of judgments of ungrammaticality (See Section 7.2 for a description of a promising study.)

There are obviously many important questions about the relationships among metalinguistic task performance of the kind we have been considering, regular linguistic performance, and competence, several of which are considered in Sections 3.4 and 3.5 below. (Many of the authors I cite in those sections construe the area of metalinguistic performance even more broadly than I have in this section, and include tasks that do not bear on grammaticality, but I believe that their discussion applies equally well to our domain.) It is not even clear whether we should speak of metalinguistic indicators as a whole, because there is considerable debate as to whether metalinguistic skill is a unitary phenomenon. From a developmental perspective, Hakes (1980) argues that it is, whereas from a cross-cultural perspective, Scribner & Cole (1981) argue that it is not, because people who do well on one task often do poorly on another (see Section 3.5, and also Section 4.4.2, for the latter). Birdsong (1989) views metalinguistic performance as a *collection* of *skills*, arguing that it shows three typical features of skilled behavior: there are differences in the number and kind of skills that individuals exhibit; there are differences in the degree to which individuals exhibit a given skill; and the skills tend to improve with practice or training. The reader is referred to Birdsong (1989: 51–54) for detailed evidence on each of these points, which are somewhat controversial (not all of Birdsong's evidence comes from judgments).

Within the scope of the present book, Scribner & Cole's work bears on the first two features of skilled behavior, and linguist/nonlinguist differences (see Section 4.4.1) bear on the third. If Birdsong's view is more or less correct, then these skills can be expected to make their own contributions to acceptability results, apart from the contributions of linguistic competence. Intertwined with these issues is the deeper question of whether we are really interested in what forms people actually use, as opposed to what they claim they use, or what they passively accept. We know that use of a construction does not imply acceptance and vice versa (Greenbaum 1976a), and sociolinguists have long known that speakers might deny using forms that they actually use frequently in everyday speech. As Labov (1975) demonstrates, this phenomenon is not even limited to socially significant linguistic variables. He describes numerous subjects who used positive *anymore* in recorded conversations, yet when asked directly, they claimed never to have heard it, felt that it is not English, misinterpreted its meaning, and showed other signs of bewilderment. Labov points out that "this puts us in the somewhat embarrassing position of knowing more about a speaker's grammar than he does himself" (p. 35). (Hindle & Sag (1975) give similar anecdotal reports.) Various metalinguistic tasks will reflect the three sets of sentences – those actually used, those claimed to be used, and those accepted – to different degrees.[4] Which set is most relevant might depend on whether one believes that linguistic competence is separate from production and comprehension mechanisms, a question I take up again in Chapter 6.

3.3 The Nature of Graded Judgments

3.3.1 Is Grammaticality Dichotomous?

The following passage, from R. Lakoff (1977), probably reflects the beliefs of most newcomers to linguistics regarding the possible grammatical status of sentences: "It was tempting to believe that linguistic markers, like other animals, came in pairs, and it was therefore natural to assume that grammaticality was an either-or question. ... This seemed to us the way things ought to be in a well-ordered universe, and we were still capable of believing, with our endearing childlike faith, that the linguistic universe was well-ordered" (p. 73). Despite Lakoff's apparent disillusionment, many linguists have wanted to maintain the principle that gram-

---

[4] For instance, Hindle & Sag (1975) present anecdotal evidence suggesting that the task of judging shows a bias towards incorrect rejections as opposed to incorrect acceptances, i.e., towards lower-than-deserved ratings, as measured by speakers' actual usage.

maticality is a dichotomous notion: "In general, then, if we find continuous-scale contrasts in the vicinity of what we are sure is language, we exclude them from language" (Hockett 1955: 17); "What with vigorous leadership and willing followership, the doctrine of discontinuity has found its fullest acceptance among American scholars" (Bolinger 1961: 2). On the other hand, it is clear that judgments of grammaticality come in more degrees, and in many cases these represent genuine multivalued phenomena (see below). Even in as early a work as *LSLT*, Chomsky asserts that "there is little doubt that speakers can fairly consistently order new utterances, never previously heard, with respect to their degree of 'belongingness' to the language" (p. 132). How are we to reconcile scalar judgments with an underlying dichotomy? Is it that the grammar assigns degrees of status to strings after all, and judgments simply reflect these? Or is it the judgment process itself that maps two-valued grammaticality to scalar acceptability by factoring in behavioral variables? Both views have been argued for in the literature, along with a third, intermediate position. Let us consider them in turn, before surveying the experimental literature to see to what extent each gains empirical support.

The best-known proponents of the view that grammaticality occurs on a continuum are Haj Ross, George Lakoff, and their followers in the late 1960s and early 1970s. Ross (e.g., 1972) used the term *squish* to refer to a continuum of grammaticality in connection with a particular construction (see Hindle & Sag (1975) for more on squishes). Lakoff (1973) summarizes the conclusions of this line of research as follows:

(i) Rules of grammar do not simply apply or fail to apply; rather they apply to a degree.

(ii) Grammatical elements are not simply members or nonmembers of grammatical categories; rather they are members to a degree.

(iii) Grammatical constructions are not simply islands or non-islands; rather they may be islands to a degree.

(iv) Grammatical constructions are not simply environments or non-environments for rules; rather they may be environments to a degree.

(v) Grammatical phenomena form hierarchies which are largely constant from speaker to speaker, and in many cases, from language to language.

(vi) Different speakers (and different languages) will have different acceptability thresholds along these hierarchies. (p. 271)

Lakoff continues, "We are saying that fuzzy grammar has a mental reality. The judgments that people make, which are matters of degree, are functions, perhaps algebraic functions, of unconscious mental judgments, which are also matters of degree" (p. 286). (See Levelt et al. (1977) for a somewhat different application of fuzzy grammar.) While I cannot review in detail the evidence that led to these conclusions, the key point is that the features of sentences that lead to graded judgments when varied do *not* have perceptually related causes, such as the taxing of short-term memory capacity, but rather are based on linguistic concepts such as clause, nominal, adverb, etc.

Let us take as an example some slightly later work by Watt (1975), who investigated whether grammaticality occurs in degrees. His domain of investigation was strained anaphora, as illustrated by the following set of related sentences:

(3) a. All those who follow Nixon say they approve of his annexing Mackenzie Territory as the fifty-fifth State.

  b. All followers of Nixon say they approve of his annexing Baffin Island as the fifty-sixth State.

  c. All Nixon-followers say they approve of his annexing The Bahamas as the fifty-seventh State.

  d. All Nixonites say they approve of his annexing British Honduras as the fifty-seventh State.

From a very detailed study of contrasts in sentences involving strained anaphora, Watt concludes that there are gradations among grammatical sentences that are *not* due to known performance factors, such as memory limits. Rather, these gradations can be accounted for in terms of factors that are already part of the grammar itself, such as linear order, contrastive stress, and specificity of reference. Watt argues that to try to account for such gradations by extragrammatical means would require needless duplication of the grammar in another part of the mind. This is the complement of Bever's argument, presented in Section 2.2. Bever attempts to avoid duplicating *within* the grammar features that are already required *outside* of it.

Despite their seemingly complementary lines of argumentation, it is clear that Bever and Watt disagree strongly in the conclusions that they draw. Bever (1975a) is unequivocal in his position:

> To give up the notion that a grammar defines a set of well-formed utterances is to give up a great deal. This is not to say that it is impossible in

principle that grammars are squishy. Rather the possibility of studying precise properties of grammar and exact rules becomes much more difficult, as Ross himself points out. Thus, if we can maintain the concept of discrete grammaticality, we will be in a better position to pursue an understanding of grammatical universals. (p. 601)

Bever argues that, if at all possible, judgment continua should be derived from independently-motivated theories of speech perception and production, while the grammar should be left discretely intact. He and Carroll lay out two alternative positions, then proceed to knock them down:

First, we may with Ross assume that non-discrete data directly imply non-discrete theories of grammar. This is not satisfactory: Non-discrete grammar offers no account of why the continua are the way they are. The correspondences between such grammatical analyses and the predictions of our behavioral account would have to be viewed as mere coincidence. Moreover, no distinction at all could be drawn between the squishy intuitions we have been concerned with here and the ineluctable intuitions upon which linguistic theory relies. A second option is to treat *all* acceptability phenomena as behavioral and non-structural (Clark & Haviland 1974). This alternative also is inadequate: It cannot explain the categorical (un)acceptability of examples at either end of a continuum.

The third alternative is that examples with intermediate acceptability rest on an internal confusion by the informant between the application of a linguistic process to a category (e.g., "S") and to the typical behavioral reflex of that category (e.g., "perceptual clause"). This explanation explains a variety of acceptability facts as well as predicting hitherto unnoticed ones. However, it is important to specify what the general conditions are that will lead to an acceptability squish. ...

An underlying theme of our proposal is that *all* grammatical properties are categorical and that all apparent departures from this have a general explanation in an interactionist framework – a totally discrete system of grammar interacting with behavioral processes. (Bever & Carroll 1981: 232–233)

(An argument for the third alternative is presented in the study by Gerken & Bever discussed in Section 1.3.) Thus, the claim that the grammar is discrete does not preclude the existence of graded phenomena like those studied by Watt, it merely asserts that part of their explanation must be extragrammatical; see Katz & Bever (1976) for a more detailed general argument.

Bever & Carroll's dismissals of positions other than their own are not entirely convincing. First, I do not see how one could ask for more of an account of "why the continua are the way they are" than Ross et al. provide, unless one already presupposes that the continua do not come from the grammar – language just *is* the way it is. Second, Clark & Haviland do not wish to exclude structural accounts of acceptability phenomena; rather, they argue that structural sources cannot be disentangled from the effects of processing. They claim that grammatical knowledge is not separable from comprehension and production processes, and that traditional grammatical constraints can be alternatively formulated as constraints on the comprehension process, but the latter can still contribute to structurally based judgments. There is no reason why they cannot get categorical judgments from their model. Furthermore, it is an open empirical question whether there really are large classes of sentences at either end of the scale within which people do not find any acceptability differences.

The discrete, dichotomous view of grammar has been defended from a somewhat different angle by Carr (1990):

> It is as well to respond briefly to a frequently voiced but unworrying objection concerning grammaticality judgements as evidence. It is at times pointed out that there are cases of 'asterisk fade', where intuitive responses supply us with a gradient scale of well-formed to ill-formed expressions. The objection is that the evidence here contains grey areas and that the ill-formed vs. well-formed distinction upon which [autonomous linguistics] rests is thus undermined.
>
> A moment's reflection shows that, far from undermining the distinction, asterisk fade *presupposes* it: one cannot coherently speak of a cline from well-formed to ill-formed without a clear conception of what these are. Furthermore, once we have erected a set of theoretical proposals to deal with the ill-formed and well-formed cases, the theory itself will allow us to decide on the status of asterisk-faded expressions, as Chomsky has long since observed. (p. 57; emphasis in original)

I argue against Carr's second point in Sections 2.2 and 2.3; his first argument also does not stand up to scrutiny. One can certainly speak coherently of a continuum, e.g., from rich to poor, without there being any non-arbitrary dividing line between the two. To my mind, the most compelling reason to believe in grammars embodying small numbers of discrete choices comes from learnability. Given the standard poverty-of the-stimulus argument, arriving at settings of continuous valued parameters would seem to be impossibly hard for children.

Although Chomsky already assumed in *LSLT* that there were degrees of ungrammaticality, he went further in *Aspects*: 148–153), proposing that the grammar predicts at least three levels or kinds of deviance, corresponding to the violation of selectional restrictions, subcategorization, and lexical category requirements. It is important to recognize that Chomsky's theory assumes the existence of absolute grammaticality. Sentences that violate no constraints of the grammar are assumed to be uniformly grammatical. If a sentence is less than absolutely grammatical, it must violate some constraint(s) of the grammar, and these constraints come in varying degrees of importance. Thus there are no degrees of grammaticality, but there are degrees of ungrammaticality. (See Levelt (1974: vol. 3) and below for some alternative proposals.) In terms of string sets, then, we have a primary dichotomy of good versus bad, with no distinctions among the good sentences but graded distinctions among the bad. It is reasonable to ask whether there is any psychological evidence that this theoretical distinction reflects cognitive reality. Even though acceptability is affected by factors other than grammaticality, one might expect the good/bad dichotomy to show through them, if the other factors are relatively independent of grammaticality and ungrammaticality. I am not aware of any clear evidence of this sort. Ross (1979), reported in Section 4.2, did make a distinction between good, marginal, and bad sentences (on the basis of questionnaire data) and found that judgments on the first class showed the least interspeaker and intraspeaker variation, but his study was so methodologically naive that this result cannot be taken as anything more than suggestive until further experimentation is done. Quirk & Svartvik (1966) make a similar distinction. Watt (1975) claims that his findings argue against Chomsky's proposal because his sentences are all generated by the grammar of English, and yet they show differences of goodness. Furthermore, there is no evidence that these differences are of some other kind than the differences we find among ungrammatical sentences. Chomsky's proposal also suffers from a major theoretical problem – namely, there is no algorithm for determining which grammatical sentence to compare an ungrammatical sentence to, in order to compute its degree of ungrammaticality (Fillmore 1972). (See Watt (1975) for a review of Chomsky's later proposals, which I do not discuss here.)

More likely than Chomsky's proposal is a scenario in which grammaticality rating works in much the same way as conceptual classification ratings of the sort elicited by Rosch (1975) under the rubric of prototype theory. Just as we can ask, "How good an example of a bird is a robin/ostrich/butterfly/chair?" we can ask, "How good an example of a grammatical sentence is *X*?" for any string *X*. The responses will likely spread along a continuum with no indication of a clear-cut break of the sort discussed above, provided they are not biased by a lopsided rating scale. Kess & Hoppe (1983: 47) concur: "Apparently shared linguistic abilities operate on the same type of a graded continuum scale that cognitive abilities of a more general sort do." (See Section 6.2 for an attempt to formalize judgment gradience along these lines.) We must be cautious in extrapolating from such a result (if it is found) to the nature of grammar, however. Prototypicality effects do not necessarily imply the absence of an underlying discrete system. As G. Lakoff (1987) reminds us, Rosch herself never suggested that graded classification effects reflect degrees of category membership or representation in terms of prototypical features or exemplars. In fact, empirical demonstrations to the contrary have been made.

Armstrong, Gleitman & Gleitman (1983) applied Rosch's original experimental paradigms to uncontroversially discrete concepts such as *even number* and *female*. Subjects were instructed to rate the extent to which exemplars represented the meaning of the category, and were timed on their responses to true/false categorial questions. They found that the discrete concepts presented the same pattern of results as Rosch's original taxonomic materials. Specifically, the goodness of various exemplars was rated quite uniformly across subjects, and reaction times for deciding membership in a category were longer for the worse exemplars, again with as much cross-subject consistency as for the taxonomic concepts that Rosch studied. Despite being able to grade exemplars consistently on a continuum, the subjects demonstrably knew that membership in categories such as *even number* was an either/or proposition. Which behavior reflects subjects' true cognitive representations of these concepts? Armstrong, Gleitman & Gleitman do not see these results as contradictory, because their experiment involved two different tasks, judging exemplariness and deciding membership. They discuss various possible theoretical explanations of their results, assuming that the real concepts are discrete and suggesting possible origins of the gradations, e.g., that they might stem from a quick, heuristic identification procedure. Lakoff argues against this last idea, and proposes that prototype effects reflect a mismatch between potentially discrete conceptual knowledge and the real world. For example, in the real world not all unmarried men are eligible to be married, and hence cannot be rated as bachelors to the full extent. However, there are still concepts for which there appears to be no discrete decision criterion, e.g., whether someone is rich, and these also exhibit prototypicality effects. Thus, it appears that graded structure in prototype tasks tells us nothing about the nature of the underlying mental representations. Is the same true of graded structure in grammaticality judgments and its bearing on mental grammars?

Barsalou (1987) suggests that graded structure might be a universal property of categories, and that the properties of an exemplar that determine its goodness as an instance of some category can vary depending on the situation. These properties might include, but are not limited to, similarity to the central tendency; similarity to the ideals of the category frequency of occurrence; and context. Barsalou summarizes his conclusion as follows:

> The graded structures within categories do not remain stable across situations. Instead a category's graded structure can shift substantially with changes in context. This suggests that graded structures do not reflect invariant properties of categories but instead are highly dependent on constraints inherent in specific situations. (p. 107)

As I argue, particularly in Chapter 5, Barsalou's view jibes well with the findings on grammaticality. Judgments are not invariant, and any of a large number of factors can come into play in making a judgment. Barsalou also looked at intra- and intersubject reliability across a wide variety of conceptual types. When people order exemplars by typicality, the average between-subject correlation is about .45. For the same subject judging the same stimuli on two occasions one month apart, it is roughly .75. In both cases it is the moderate exemplars (neither very good instances nor very good noninstances) that are the most unstable. These results also jibe with Ross's findings. Barsalou goes on to argue that there simply are no invariant representations of categories in the human cognitive system. Invariant representations are merely analytic fictions created by psychologists; perhaps linguists should be added to the list of culprits. Nonetheless, he suggests that the task of judging typicality might not make use of the same representations as judging set membership; the former might use probable properties, while the latter might use discriminative ones.

It might be that the nature of the particular tasks used by prototype theorists (and linguists) inherently induces graded behavior, independent of the nature of the underlying knowledge. If this is so, the status of that underlying knowledge as discrete or continuous must be demonstrated by other means. But how could we ever know whether a grammar, if it exists independent of performance mechanisms, classifies sentences dichotomously? If performance mechanisms induce graded structure by themselves, and if (as I argue) they can never be circumvented because competence is not directly accessible, then it might not be possible to investigate empirically how a grammar itself classifies sentences.[5] There

---

[5] Wayne Cowart (personal communication) suggests that part of the problem here could lie at

are many possible combinations of mental structures that could yield graded acceptability judgments. For instance, Fillmore, Kempler & Wang (1979b) argue that judgment ratings might reflect the interaction of discretely varying elementary components that only have the appearance of continua.[6] Carroll (1979) follows Bever in suggesting that graded acceptability can result from a discrete grammar plus performance rules of some sort. In either case, neither grades of grammaticality nor grades of ungrammaticality would be part of the grammar. It could be that while fully grammatical sentences can be judged as such without much reference to their meaningfulness, interpretability becomes an important factor in judging some ungrammatical sentences. That is, the closer we can come to figuring out what an ungrammatical sentence is supposed to mean, the more likely we are to judge it to be acceptable. (See Fowler (1970) for essentially this argument; he insists that "an ungrammatical sentence is an ungrammatical sentence is an ungrammatical sentence," regardless of how it might be interpretable on the basis of extragrammatical information. Others, such as Katz (1964), have claimed that there is an identifiable class of semigrammatical sentences, by which is meant ungrammatical utterances that are comprehensible.) Questions about the nature of the concept *grammatical sentence* might eventually be answerable, but for now I leave them open and move on to a related question that likely *is* answerable – can we obtain useful judgments of degree of acceptability from subjects?

3.3.2 Experiments on Chomsky's Three Levels of Deviance

An enormous amount of research on degrees of (un)grammaticality was generated by Chomsky's identification of three levels or kinds of deviance. (See Schnitser (1973) for comparison of Chomsky's ideas with other contemporary ideas about degrees of badness.) The discussion in *Aspects* spurred a flurry of experiments designed to test Chomsky's idea by obtaining judgment ratings. In retrospect, these experiments seem somewhat misguided. Chomsky himself never claimed that degrees of *grammaticality* would correspond to degrees of *acceptability*; in fact, he explicitly states that the two do *not* coincide (see Section 2.2).[7]

---

the level of implementation: although our brains may be trying to realize a discrete system, their hardware is analog, which makes the implementation imperfect.

[6] Technically there cannot be a true continuum of grammaticality values of sentences, because continua involve an uncountably infinite number of values, and most linguists believe that there are only a countably infinite number of sentences. When linguists speak of grammaticality being a continuum, they typically mean that it is a discrete scale with more than two possible values.

[7] It is ironic, then, that current work in syntactic theory regularly makes heavy use of relative degrees of badness.

Predictably, the ensuing results have often been contradictory.[8] Nevertheless, we can learn quite a bit about the nature of scalar judgment from these experiments. I present here a selective review; see Moore (1972) and works cited therein for further references.

Downey & Hakes (1968) studied the effects of Chomsky's three levels of deviance on acceptability ratings, paraphrasing, and free recall. Subjects rated sentences on a scale from 0 ("completely acceptable") to 3 ("completely unacceptable"). Subjects were given two examples of how a sentence could be unacceptable, but Downey & Hakes do not provide details of these examples. The order among subjects' mean acceptability ratings was as predicted, although the difference between subcategorization and phrase structure violations was not significant. However, the recall scores showed a reversal of this pattern, with sentences containing selectional violations being harder to remember correctly than those with subcategorization errors.[9] Stolz (1969) performed a replication of this study, adding finer distinctions from Chomsky's hierarchy of selectional features, e.g., that the difference between mass nouns and count nouns is greater than that between human nouns and nonhuman nouns, although problems with materials made the possible effect of this difference inconclusive. Stolz also used a 4-point response scale, and told subjects that their responses should be based on *any* kind of deviance, including anomalous meanings as well as form. His results showed that sentence types were rated in the following order from least to most acceptable: random strings; sentences with subcategorization violations; sentences with selectional violations; analytic grammatical sentences; and contingently true grammatical sentences.[10]

Moore (1972) set out to test a hypothesis somewhat more general than Chomsky's proposal, which applies only to verbal features. He asked whether there is an acceptability hierarchy created by Chomsky's three types of violation, regardless of where in a sentence they occur. He also sought corroboration for such a hierarchy from sources other than judgments, in particular, subjects' reaction times in making those judgments. Moore's prediction was that a severely ungrammatical sentence should be processed faster than a marginally ungrammatical one, because more thorough processing would be required to detect a

---

[8] There has been much selective interpretation of acceptability as bearing on grammaticality in this area. If the results go the right way, they are taken as evidence; if not, they are dismissed as performance artifacts.

[9] Results from the paraphrase task were not quantitatively analyzable; the authors merely discuss what strategies they believe the subjects used.

[10] An analytic sentence is true simply by virtue of the meanings of its words, whereas a contingently true sentence makes a true claim about something in the world.

subtler error. His first experiment used a paradigm that was adopted in many subsequent studies. Subjects were shown a written sentence with a blank line where a missing word would go (e.g., *Sincerity may* _____ *the boy*). They were then shown a word that could fill the blank on a separate screen and were asked to decide as quickly as possible whether the sentence would be "appropriately completed" by that word.[11] The incomplete sentences were designed so that there was no way of assessing their grammaticality until the missing word was seen. The sentences in (4), (5), and (6) below illustrate stimulus sentences with blank lines in verb, subject, and object position, respectively (shown by the underline under the subsequently presented target word). In each set, the first sentence contains a lexical category violation. Example (4b) violates strict subcategorization, while (5b) and (6b) violate selectional restrictions between the verb and the noun phrase. Example (4c) violates a selectional restriction of the verb, while (5c) and (6c) violate selectional restrictions between the noun and its modifying adjective.[12]

(4)   a. Smart voters <u>uncle</u> honest politicians.

    b. Noisy dogs <u>growl</u> night animals.

    c. Catchy slogans <u>believe</u> unwary citizens.

(5)   a. Modern <u>wanders</u> improve factory efficiency.

    b. Sensible <u>ideas</u> distrust public officials.

    c. Nosey <u>ditches</u> annoy suburb dwellers.

(6)   a. Large factories utilize efficient <u>hesitates</u>.

    b. Big corporations appoint many <u>machines</u>.

---

[11] Moore apparently wanted to ensure that subjects took selectional restrictions into account in making their decisions. He says, "The [experimenter] explained to [the subject] that terms such as 'appropriate' and 'acceptable' were deliberately being used, instead of 'grammatical,' because of the fact that the inappropriate sentences were inappropriate for varying reasons, some more syntactic than semantic. Inasmuch as 'ungrammatical' is frequency employed as being synonymous with 'syntactically deviant,' such instructions attempted to preclude any such dichotomy being set up by [the subject]." Since his subjects were not linguistics students, however, being presented with this terminology may only have confused them.

[12] Moore did not consider strict subcategorization to be a property of nouns, and therefore could not make all violations in the (b)-level sentences of the same type. He seems to assume that Chomsky's theory predicts that all selectional restriction violations are equally ungrammatical, so (5b) and (5c) should be equivalent, and (6b) and (6c) should be equivalent. However, since I am not particularly concerned with the theoretical implications of Moore's study, I do not address this issue here.

c. Factory foremen appreciate eager <u>tools</u>. (Moore 1972: 553)

The main effect of level of violation seemed to support Chomsky's theory: re-action times increased from (a) to (b) to (c) sentences. Interestingly, the mean reaction time for filler sentences that were grammatical was between those for (a) and (b) sentences. However, there were several mitigating interactions. In particular, there was no difference between reaction times for sentences like (4b) and (4c), while sentences like (5c) and (6c) did show longer decision time than their (b) counterparts (but Chomsky's theory might not have predicted the latter difference). Moore takes this as evidence that the process of checking grammaticality occurs in two passes. First, the major relations between subject, verb, and object are checked, and then relationships within the NP constituents are examined. Under this view, both verbal subcategorization and selectional restrictions are examined in the first pass and have no differential status, as reflected in the reaction time data. Several results support the importance of the verb in determining requirements for the rest of the sentence. For instance, although (4c) and (5b) constitute exactly the same type of violation, (4c) took significantly longer to reject. A large problem with this paradigm, of course, is that the sentences differ in many ways not relevant to the violations under study.

A second experiment examined whether grammaticality ratings of the same sets of sentences on a 20-point scale would conform to Chomsky's hierarchy. A new group of subjects was told that a sentence was "acceptable" if it "could occur in normal, everyday usage."[13] Subjects were asked to rate acceptable sentences with a score of 1, whereas scores of 2 to 20 represented increasing unacceptability.[14] Once again, the main effect of level of violation was as predicted. Mean ratings for (a), (b), and (c) sentences were 13.5, 11.0, and 9.2, respectively, but the latter two ratings did not differ significantly for sentences with blank lines in verb position, contradicting several previous studies. [15] Moore & Biederman (1979) attempted to distinguish various possible serial and parallel models that could account for subject-verb-object relations being checked faster than noun-adjective ones, using the same blank-line paradigm that was used in Moore's first experiment, but with sentences that contained *two* kinds of violation, e.g.,

---

[13] Moore does not explain why the definition of acceptability was changed from that of the first experiment.

[14] One positive feature of Moore's instructions was that they explicitly encouraged subjects to look over a few of the (practice) sentences to get an idea of the range within which they were working. Subjects were told to make use of the full range of the rating scale.

[15] Moore suggests that other studies failed to control for the location of the violation, and hence would not have seen the crucial interaction.

Old houses quarrel valuable relics, where both subject-verb selection and verbal subcategorization are violated. If both kinds of violation are searched for in parallel, one would expect an average judgment speed gain on such sentences as compared to the judgment time required to search for either of the two violations by itself (assuming the search for ungrammaticality is self-terminating), but no such significant gain was found. On the other hand, no significant increase in judgment time was found, suggesting that the search does terminate when one violation is encountered. Moore & Biederman take this as support for a serial model, where subject-verb-object relations are checked before internal NP relations. A follow-up rating task with no time constraint showed that double violations did decrease the grammaticality of sentences as compared to single violations, so that this rating process, unlike the speeded determination of grammaticality, does not terminate on encountering the first violation.[16]

The most recent study dealing with Chomsky's three levels of deviance was performed by Nagata (1990b). His subjects used a 7-point scale to rate three types of violation: lexical category violations; selectional restriction violations between verbs and their objects; and selectional restriction violations between nouns and their modifying adjectives. Nagata found significant differences of rating in the predicted order; his results thus support Chomsky's distinctions.

3.3.3 Other Experiments

Chomsky's three levels of violation are not the only theoretical constructs that have spawned experimental work on levels of grammaticality. Around the time of Chomsky's proposal, some researchers were taking different approaches to the study of degrees of grammaticality. Coleman (1965) looked at four kinds of stimuli, ranging from random strings to strings where each word correctly matched a valid phrase structure rule in lexical category. His intermediate levels were less sensible; they involved choosing words from the correct *phrasal* category, e.g., approximating a noun phrase by choosing any two words that could appear in a noun phrase. Example (7) shows sample sentences from each of Coleman's four levels.

(7) a. Think apron the wits for about.

b. One the could to a her.

c. The grass seldom were struck Lindy.

---

[16] This experiment used a 100-point rating scale, but the authors do not say why they felt that such a wide range of possible ratings was necessary.

d. The dust could always be Disneyland.

Coleman found that subjects' rank-orderings were significantly monotonically correlated with degree of grammaticality defined in this way. Moreover, other measures besides judgment correlated with this scale. For example, the more grammatical strings were easier to memorize and to perform a cloze test (Taylor 1953) on correctly. Like many cases to be reviewed in this subsection, these results seem neither particularly surprising nor particularly informative.

Around the same time, Marks (1968) looked at those most mystical of linguistic beasts, multiply self-embedded sentences. He instructed subjects to judge their grammatical structure, not their length, complexity, difficulty of comprehension, or frequency of usage. For sentences with up to five self-embeddings, his results showed a power-law correlation between degree of embedding and subjects' ratings. That is, unacceptability grew as a function of the number of embeddings to a constant exponent. Another study by Marks (1965; 1967) was inspired by Chomsky's informal statement that some ungrammatical sentences obviously have more structure than others. Marks's hypothesis was that, in forming judgments of ungrammatical sentences, people consider the serial position of a violation within a sentence as well as the sentence's status as described by the grammar. Since sentences are processed from left to right, earlier errors should interfere more with processing, because early words prepare the processor for later ones and set up expectations and restrictions. Marks constructed stimulus materials by taking simplex sentences and sentences with infinitival clauses and reversing the order of two adjacent words in various positions, producing a paradigm like the one in (8):

(8) a. The boy hit the ball.
     b. Boy the hit the ball.
     c. The boy hit ball the.
     d. The hit boy the ball.
     e. The boy the hit ball.

Sentences were presented in groups with random order and subjects were asked to rank them from the best English to the worst English. As predicted, noun-determiner inversion was judged less acceptable if it occurred earlier in the sentence. Moreover, sentences like (8d) were judged to be worse than those such as (8e), although Marks points out that the two types of inversion found in these sentences are not the same, and serial position might not be the important factor here. But at least in the former case, it is hard to see how any traditional grammar would distinguish the grammaticality of the sentences, since such grammars treat all noun phrases as equivalent. Serial position of anomaly thus constitutes a reasonable candidate for an extragrammatical factor that contributes to acceptability.

Scott performed a series of similar experiments (Scott 1969; Scott & Mills 1973), except that he used a single basic sentence order (subject-verb-object-qualifier) and rearranged whole constituents rather than words. His subjects rated each permutation as "acceptably grammatical" or "not grammatical."[17] The percentage of subjects who accepted various permutations ranged from 100% to 0%. Scott takes the results to show that there are at least five degrees of grammaticality among these sentences, but this number seems to be arbitrary. We should also keep in mind that, unlike Marks's subjects, Scott's were only giving good/bad judgments, so the gradations appeared only in the pooled results and do not bear on the judgments of individual subjects. Scott tries to account for the numbers of acceptances on the basis of how many constituents were moved and in how many places the canonical constituent order was split. This index does not yield a perfect correlation with judged grammaticality, so Scott & Mills looked for other factors that might have determined the outcome – in particular, meaningfulness.[18] This factor was found to have no significant effect, but a useful outcome of the experiment was that when the permutations were not presented all together with their canonical form, grammaticality was rated much lower, suggesting that people accept a sentence more often if they can see that it is a rearrangement of a grammatical sentence.

In yet another study of the effect of word order on grammaticality judgments, Danks & Glucksberg (1971) considered violations of adjective ordering constraints (e.g., *Swiss red big tables* versus *big red Swiss tables*) using a ranking test with the six possible permutations of three prenominal adjectives. The results showed that the position of the adjective that was most closely related to an intrinsic property of the noun was the primary determinant of acceptability: the closer it was to the noun, the higher the sentence was ranked.

More recently, Crain & Fodor (1985, 1987) looked at the effects of different kinds of ungrammaticality on a sentence matching task, where the subject must decide

---

[17] Subjects were offered a third choice, namely, "grammatical but with a different meaning from the unpermuted sentence"; we shall not be concerned with this possibility here.

[18] Scott & Mills cite various psychological sources for their definition of *meaningfulness* as "the association value of a single written verbal unit," for which they use frequency of occurrence as a metric. This does not correspond to what other authors have meant by the meaningfulness of a sentence.

whether two simultaneously displayed sentences are identical. The basic finding was that number agreement and quantifier placement errors (shown in (9) and (10), respectively) increase matching times, while Subjacency and (certain) Empty Category Principle violations (shown in (11) and (12)) do not.

(9) *Mary were writing a letter to her husband.

(10) *Lesley's parents are chemical engineers both.

(11) *Who do the police believe the claim that John shot?

(12) *Who did the duchess sell Turner's portrait of?

While previous work had attributed this difference to different levels of ungrammaticality, Crain & Fodor argue that it was due instead to the correctability of the error: the first two types of error are easy to correct automatically, while for the other two there is no obvious correction that can convert them directly into grammatical sentences. Their claim is that if a correction is made, it must be *undone* in order to perform the matching task, sentence matching task since the subject must decide whether the sentences are literally identical. In cases like (11) and (12) no correction is possible, hence the bad sentence can be compared directly. Forster & Stevenson (1987) question this interpretation, suggesting that the correlation with correctability is epiphenomenal and cannot be the cause of the observed time differences. Both sets of authors acknowledge that other factors are at work as well, but the possibility that the correctability of a sentence could be a factor in relative ratings of acceptability should not be dismissed; whether it bears any relation to theories of degree of grammaticality is a matter of debate.

3.3.4 Ratings, Rankings, and Consistency

It is a fundamental assumption throughout this book that empirical facts are useful (and interesting) if they are systematic, because they must tell us something about the minds of the subjects who produce them. It remains a matter of analytical interpretation to decide *what* these facts tell us. Thus, we must determine whether graded judgments are systematic, and the results mentioned throughout this section strongly suggest that they are. The next thing one might wish to determine is just how many meaningful distinctions of levels of acceptability (relative or absolute) can be made. This would provide a basis for establishing a procedure for eliciting such distinctions.[19] Chaudron (1983) cites several psycho-metric studies showing that rating scales generally increase in reliability with increasing numbers of levels up to 20.[20] Presumably this can be shown by giving subjects different sizes of scale on which to rate the same stimuli: if you have too few levels, people collapse true distinctions arbitrarily, whereas if you have too many, people create spurious distinctions arbitrarily. Thus, the "true" num-ber of distinctions will show the greatest consistency within (and perhaps also between) subjects. It follows that studies that choose inappropriate numbers of levels add spurious variation to their results, possibly concealing the effects they are supposed to uncover. As far as I am aware, a psychometric investigation along these lines has never been done with specific regard to grammaticality judgments.

Even if we can find the optimal size of rating scale, there will still be problems with this measure of grammaticality judgments. One major problem is how to quantify inter- and intrasubject consistency, which is an important part of much work in this field. If we use a 20-point scale, should we require two subjects to give exactly the same rating of a sentence in order to consider them consistent? Would plus or minus one position be sufficient? What if two subjects show ex-actly the same distances between ratings of multiple sentences, but their absolute ratings are offset by some constant? Can we merely say that one is biased toward more conservative or more liberal judgments, and consider their responses to be fully consistent? Depending on the size of the offset constant, that might not seem appropriate, but neither would a conclusion of total inconsistency. If we standardize using z-scores, can we be sure we are not throwing away real dif-ferences?[21] Similar problems arise if some subjects simply fail to use the whole range of the scale, which can easily happen unintentionally if subjects have no idea what range of sentence types they will see. (For this reason alone, practice trials with representative anchor sentences are a good idea) If we are attempt-ing to compare consistency of subjects between studies that use different rating scales, the consistency measure will have to be scaled accordingly. Such prob-

---

[19] But see Cowart (1997: 7–12, 70–72) for the claim that the choice of response scale might not make much difference to patterns of relative acceptability.

[20] Snow (1975) points out the apparently contradictory finding that psychologists who measure attitudes have shown that subjects find scales with more than seven points hard to use.

[21] In doing so, we would be implicitly adopting the theoretical position that any such differences simply are not part of what we are studying. For instance, the fact that Speaker A could be consistently more conservative in grammaticality judgments than Speaker B does not tell us anything about their grammars. I do not think we are in a position to say this with any degree of certainty. See Cowart (1997: 13–14, 114) for more on the use of standard scores.

lems have prompted many researchers to consider whether, instead of asking for absolute ratings of sentences, we should instead require subjects simply to rank order them from most to least acceptable. This approach does have certain advantages. For one thing, psychometric research indicates that people are much more reliable on comparative, as opposed to independent, ratings (Mohan 1977). Rank orders also solve the problem of different baselines on a rating scale, and there are nonparametric statistical tests for assessing the consistency or correlation between sets of rank orders. Relative judgments are not without problems, however. One problem is efficiency (Maclay & Sleator 1960): the amount of information one can extract from a given number of relative judgments is much less than the amount one can extract from absolute ratings. While exhaustive pairwise comparisons are not necessary to arrive at an ordering of a set of sentences, there is surely a limit to how many sentences subjects can handle in one group; intergroup orders must then somehow be elicited.

A further problem with the interpretation of relative judgments is that pairwise differential acceptability might not be transitive. That is, a subject who judges sentence A better than sentence B, and also judges sentence B better than sentence C when considering them two at a time, does not necessarily judge sentence A better than sentence C when they are examined side by side.[22] Hindle & Sag (1975) cite an instance of this situation with regard to the sentences in (13), which contain *anymore*, although they only present group data.

(13) a. They've scared us out of eating fish anymore.

  b. It's dangerous to eat fish anymore.

  c. All we eat anymore is fish.

Twenty-two such sentences were presented to 36 subjects, who were asked to compare them and then give each a grammaticality rating on a 5-point scale.[23] It was determined for each subject which of a given pair of sentences he or she had rated more grammatical, or whether the pair had been rated equally grammatical, and subjects' ratings were tallied on this basis. Hindle & Sag found that while more subjects preferred (13a) over (13b) than vice versa, and more preferred (13b) over (13c), more preferred (13c) over (13a).[24] They conclude that their comparison

---

[22] A hybrid solution that solves this and some other problems is to *elicit* absolute ratings but *convert* them to rankings. Under this solution, circularity can never arise.

[23] These data are not quite equivalent to ranked comparisons, since a maximum of five distinctions could be made.

[24] The differences in ratings were quite small, with many subjects rating the pairs as equally grammatical, which is not surprising given the small size of the rating scale compared to the number of sentences.

data are spurious, because they involve an apples-and-oranges comparison: the sentences are too structurally diverse and hence their acceptability might be affected by different determining factors. Danks & Glucksberg (1970) encountered similar circular triads on an individual level, and take them as a measure of a subject's inconsistency. While a detailed examination of this issue would take us too deeply into psychometric theory, my purpose is merely to point out that such methodological problems will have to be dealt with if a paradigm involving relative judgments is followed. (See Gardner (1974) for a discussion of nontransitive paradox in various domains, and the argument that these *can* be rational if the pairwise comparisons involve different criteria. This could easily happen in the case of relative grammaticality judgments; see Watt (1975) for this view. Einhorn (1982) notes similar phenomena under the name of "intransitive choices" and shows how they can easily occur in everyday situations.)

It is also an open question what to make of discrepancies between absolute ratings and rank-orderings given by the same subjects, as have been found by Snow & Meijer (1977) (see Section 4.2) and others. Even if we can establish that the discrepancies are due to context or contrast effects from neighboring sentences, this does not determine which kind of judgment is closer to the truth. Greenbaum & Quirk (1970) also examined the question of intra- and intersubject consistency, and this rating-ranking contrast in particular, using tests of evaluation versus performance. Their evaluation test involved a rating on a 3-point scale: "perfectly natural and normal," "wholly unnatural and abnormal," or "somewhere between." Their performance test involved the presentation of multiple variants of a sentence together, and required subjects to rank them as well as to rate each sentence individually (my summary is necessarily imprecise, since these researchers describe in great detail numerous experiments with minor variations). Greenbaum & Quirk typically used groups of 20–30 subjects and found that cross-group consistency was quite high, with very few significant differences on judgments (and other kinds of metalinguistic tasks). Also, their design allowed for several sentences to be judged a second time. Most sentences showed 90–95 percent consistency (measured as the number of subjects giving the same judgment both times a sentence was presented), but consistency for some sentences was as low as 54%. A very few sentences were both rated and ranked. The two measures generally correlated with each other, but sometimes sentences that were rated equally grammatical were ranked differently, even though tied rankings were allowed. This might mean that the 3-point scale was too limiting, not allowing enough room for the distinctions subjects wanted to make.

Yet another study comparing rating and ranking was conducted by Mohan

(1977). Ratings were on a scale of 1 ("completely well-formed") to 10 ("completely ill-formed") that was anchored by an example sentence for each of the extremes (probably a very good idea). There were 11 sentences to be ranked; procedure was a within-subjects variable, the two tasks being separated by a 2-week interval. Unfortunately, the instructions seem a bit too usage-oriented: "Consider each of the sentences and decide if it would be possible that you would say this in conversation." The study was actually concerned in part with establishing whether individual speakers can do ordinal scaling of sentences, or whether such scaling only emerges by pooling multiple speakers' dichotomous judgments, where speakers might have different thresholds of acceptability and no differentiations within the good and bad sentence groups. Nonparametric statistical analysis showed that the cross-speaker agreement in rankings was much higher than would be expected under the latter interpretation. Mohan also found some evidence for a yea-saying factor, a tendency to favor acquiescence, i.e., accepting some sentences regardless of their grammatical status, by correlating the number accepted by each individual on two unrelated sets of sentences; there was a small but significant positive correlation. As for rating versus ranking, correlating the number of acceptances under the two procedures again gave a highly significant result,[25] although the correlation itself was modest (.57).

3.4 The Judgment Process

In this section I will consider what people might actually be doing when judging the grammaticality of a sentence. Just about the only thing we know for sure is that we do not know what they are doing. What follows is some considered speculation. Many researchers want to relate this question to another unanswered question, namely, what happens in the ordinary processing of a sentence that one performs during the course of a conversation or while reading? There are two extreme positions one can take on the relation between these two processes: they might be identical, or they might be totally different. In the first case, some might argue (this is perhaps the null hypothesis) that the only difference between processing for judgment and processing for conversation is that in the former case the reply consists of a "yes" or "no" (or a numeric rating, or whatever), instead of a pragmatically related utterance. Obviously, the decision between the possible judgments has to come from somewhere, but on this view the processing of the sentence itself is identical. The differences come in deciding

---

[25] Sentences rated 1–5 were treated as acceptances; subjects drew a threshold line in their rank orderings, which allowed the comparison.

on a rating versus deciding what to say next, both of which are separate from the parsing, semantic analysis, etc., that go into decoding the incoming utterance. At the other extreme, one might say that judging is nothing at all like understanding and involves none of the same cognitive mechanisms. If you are told you will have to judge a sentence, you route it to the sentence-judging processor in the mind, rather than the sentence-comprehending processor. These two modules are entirely separate and might differ in arbitrary ways. (If this were put forward as a serious proposal, one would have to address the question of how and why such a separation would come to exist in the mind.) As with most interesting psychological questions, many researchers suspect that the answer lies somewhere in the middle. We hope reality is not like the second position, but fear it is not like the first either. Let us consider which positions the major researchers in this field have espoused, the extent to which these positions have empirical support, and what their implications are for investigating grammar. I present my own speculation on this issue in detail in Section 6.2.

I have already reviewed one line of thinking about the judgment process in Section 2.4, namely, that it has something in common with introspection, which might introduce some artifactual phenomena. But grammaticality judgments seem to have much more in common with other psychological judgments. Graeme Hirst (personal communication) has suggested the following analogy to food tasting. If someone asks you what you remember about last night's dinner, chances are you will not have much to say. Unless there was something strikingly good or strikingly awful about the food, you will likely have only a general impression that it was OK, if no particular attention was drawn to it at the time you ate it. On the other hand, if someone offers you some food and asks you for your impressions *before* you taste it, you will pay particular attention to the flavors, textures, aromas, etc.; perhaps you will chew more slowly; and you might be able to give much more detailed comments, concerning, e.g., particular herbs you detect, how tender the meat is, and so on. Your host could ask you more detailed questions, too, such as whether you think there is too much garlic in the tomato sauce. Intuitively, it seems at least plausible that the taste stimuli are being processed in a different way, or to a different degree, than if no attention were being drawn to them, and the same might hold for sentence tasting.[26] Hirst also suggests a third, hybrid scenario, in which the opinion is solicited im-

---

[26] This argument has been made for other metalinguistic tasks as well. For instance, Kess & Hoppe (1983) suggest that in an ambiguity detection situation, looking for ambiguity puts subjects in a different mode from that used in a paraphrase task where the stimulus just happens to be ambiguous, so different processing can be expected, with different results.

mediately *after* the tasting. If the question is unexpected, then tasting will have proceeded as usual (as in the first situation), but since no time has elapsed we might have access to information that will later be lost or forgotten, impressions that were induced by the stimulus but ignored because they were irrelevant. To the extent that processing for prewarned judgment differs from regular processing, this last scenario could provide the best of both worlds: regular processing, but access to additional information, which Hirst refers to as the traces of processing. (See also Section 4.4.1 on parallels to wine tasting, and Section 5.2.7 on speed of judgment.)

If the reader has not wandered off to the fridge by now, let us apply these ideas more directly to linguistic judgments (see also Birdsong (1989: 202–203)). In the worst case, we could imagine that expected judgment causes people to revert to conscious reasoning *about* sentences, rather than processing *of* them. Consciously known rules could be applied in this way to decide grammaticality, but the only rules about language that most nonlinguists have conscious access to are those learned in grade school, which tend to be of the prescriptive variety. Thus, subjects might reason that a sentence is ungrammatical because it ends with a preposition, since they remember a rule stating that this is a bad thing. Schmidt & McCreary (1977) showed that many people are clearly aware of prescriptive standards even if these are not reflected in their spontaneous speech. These researchers also found strong discrepancies between subjects' production on performance tests similar to Quirk & Svartvik's (1966) and their choice of which forms were correct, so it seems that, at least in some cases, subjects *can* distinguish their linguistic intuitions from their prescriptive knowledge, but it is not yet clear whether we can induce them to exclude prescriptive knowledge from their judgments. Because prescriptive grammar does not necessarily have any relation to descriptive reality, judgments involving prescriptive knowledge are of no use to us. But if we avoid the generally well-circumscribed prescriptive cases, can we not then expect to avoid conscious processing? Hirst argues in the negative. In general, people seem to be able to invent spurious rules or principles as post hoc rationalizations of behavior (Nisbett & Wilson 1977), including language behavior. In Chapter 5, I report on studies in which respondents who had to justify their grammaticality choices gave (by linguistic standards) quite outrageous answers. Alternatively, even if people sense their true intuitions about a sentence, they might not express them if they cannot fabricate a justification. Thus, conscious reasoning/parsing by subjects is most undesirable. But does conscious reasoning ever occur? As drastic and ad hoc as it seemingly must be, would it not result in judgments so far from what we know about actual usage that the discrepancies would be strikingly obvious? Hirst argues that such discrepancies might well exist. Perhaps there really *is* a huge shift, comparable to the difference between written and spoken language, which also might not be obvious until systematically studied. This is all the more likely, given that judgments typically involve such rarely occurring forms anyway: the usage data with which to compare them are extremely sparse.

There is suggestive experimental evidence for differences between judgments and usage. Nagata (1990a) wanted to examine the extent to which ungrammaticality affects our initial parsing of a sentence, as opposed to our post hoc evaluation of it. To do this, he measured reaction times of subjects who were asked to judge the grammaticality of sentences quickly on a good-bad scale, and plotted them against their grammaticality rating on a scale from 1 to 7 (where 1 = grammatical and 2–7 represent increasing degrees of ungrammaticality), which was elicited after the initial judgment and was not speeded. To control for the length of the sentences involved, each sentence was presented in two parts, with the subject pressing a button to expose the second part and start the timed trial. Stimulus sentences were paired such that the identical target strings could be used as the second parts of two different sentences. The sentences were designed so that the target string completed one sentence grammatically, but completed the other ungrammatically, thus matching the length of the timed portion exactly. Nagata's initial hypothesis was that highly ungrammatical sentences would show longer reaction times than mildly bad ones, because minor violations could go unnoticed whereas major ones would disrupt parsing. His findings showed something quite different, however. When reaction time is plotted against mean grammaticality rating, the result is an inverted U-shaped curve. Sentences of intermediate ungrammaticality took more time to judge than very good or very bad ones. We note that this differs from the data that Moore (1972) reported (see Section 3.3.2): he found reaction time inversely related to severity of violation. We must keep in mind, however, that Moore was looking only at three very specific types of violation, which might not have encompassed the full range of possible severity. Thus, his results might all come from the higher end of Nagata's spectrum, with which they are consistent. Nagata's data do confirm Moore's finding that completely grammatical sentences take somewhat longer to judge than the worst violations, presumably because the latter do not require the whole sentence to be read.

There are many possible interpretations of such a general finding, but here are some speculations. Judging perfectly good sentences and very bad sentences occurs quickly because their status as good or bad is immediately obvious. Marginal sentences, on the other hand, do not fall clearly into one class or the other; hence more time is required to make decisions about them. Severe ungrammaticality did not slow down parsing because subjects were not trying to analyze or comprehend the sentence in any normal manner. As soon as a violation was detected, the decision could be made, perhaps without even considering the remainder of the string. If this interpretation is correct, then Nagata's study really did not get at the on-line nature of grammaticality as it affects normal parsing. Since subjects knew they would be timed on judgments, they went into "quick judging mode," which might be quite different from normal parsing for comprehension. Nagata's purpose would be better served by not eliciting judgments at all, but rather by assessing processing speed while subjects are engaged in reading for comprehension, as proposed below.

One possible course of action at this stage would be to look for more evidence of drastic differences between judgments and actual use, by employing corpus-based analysis, for instance (but see Hirst (1981: 55), for problems with real-world texts, such as the fact that one can generate bad sentences in writing without realizing it). But if such differences are found, we will not be any closer to a general method for discovering the linguistic knowledge that underlies regular performance. So let us move on to how we *would* like the judgment process to work, and see whether we can make it happen. In the abstract, it would be nice if the language processor could run as usual, but a homunculus could be allowed to inspect the process and then report back on what he has seen. He could then observe not only the fact that, say, the parser had failed to parse a sentence, but exactly where in the sentence this occurred and why. Unfortunately, there is little evidence to suggest that people can introspect on the language mechanism in this way. If that is not possible, then at least the homunculus should be allowed to inspect the state of the processor when it is finished, although, being a rather robust device, it might have managed to get through the sentence somehow and left little trace of a problem. This latter method, the interpretation of the "trace of execution," is what we might hope to achieve through postpresentation testing. Speed will be of the essence, because much research in psycholinguistics has shown that our memory for the form of an utterance decays extremely quickly as compared to our memory for its content (see, e.g., Sachs (1967) and many subsequent studies). Others have reasoned along similar lines:

There is very little evidence in the literature that people *are* conscious of many of their own mental processes. Awareness seems to be restricted to the outcome or results of such processes, and if people do report on processes, this is – Nisbett & Wilson (1977) contend – usually a logical reconstruction of how such a result might have come about (often in the form of a motivation) rather than a memory trace of the process itself (Levelt, Sinclair & Jarvella 1978: 7).

Thus, extreme caution in interpretation is called for. Nisbett & Wilson warn that "people sometimes make assertions about mental events to which they may have no access and these assertions may bear little resemblance to the actual events" (p. 247). Thus, our hopes for the homunculus might be unattainable in principle. Any introspective access we might have is insufficient to produce generally correct or reliable reports on how we reach decisions. People base their reports of thought processes on their theories about what is likely to have influenced them, and thus even when they are correct, this is not due to direct introspective awareness. Nisbett & Wilson also make the interesting point that certain types of factor will rarely occur to us as possible influences in a judgment, because their effects seem implausible. Among these factors are many manipulations that have been clearly shown to affect grammaticality judgments, such as serial order effects and contrast effects. Linguists beware: we might feel certain that we are not subject to such effects, but we are.

With the above caveats, let us go on to consider how a postpresentation method could conceivably be used in linguistic judgment. The obvious problem is going to be that before too long, the subject will be on to us, i.e., will realize that we are going to ask for judgments, and so might revert to "judging mode" on any sentence after the first. (It is not difficult to imagine bogus tasks that would keep the subject in the dark until after the first sentence was presented.) This seems to require interspersing judgment trials at a low concentration among nonjudgment trials, or at the very least making the distractor task sufficiently engaging or realistic that the subjects do not have an opportunity to reflect on the purpose of the study. For instance, we might present sentences in the guise of a text that has been translated from a foreign language (say, a play or television show), and ask the subjects to point out places where the translation is bad English (or whatever language) while keeping track of the plot for a later recall test, which forces them to keep processing for content.[27] The alternative is to try to deduce judgments from some nonintrusive measure, so that the subject is never aware that grammaticality is at issue. For instance, we can simply ask subjects to read a passage for content while taking some standard measure of reading speed and location (e.g., eye tracking or self-paced reading). It is reasonable to predict that when unexpected ungrammaticality is encountered, a delay in reading will result; we might even learn something about where in the course of processing the error was detected. (Kutas & Hillyard (1983) review some other on-line measures of this type.) We could also use event-related brain potential ERP measurements in this way, or look for people to balk or do a double take (Newmeyer 1983). Of

---

[27] This idea arose from a suggestion by Bill Poser (personal communication).

course, there are other variables that affect reading speed (and ERPs) that will have to be factored out, the sensitivity of these measures to structural violations might not be terribly high, and the concentration of ungrammatical sentences should still be kept reasonably low. Any of these methods is probably best used as corroboration for data derived by other means.

I conclude this section by briefly describing the work of Bialystok & Ryan (1985) (see also Ryan & Ledger 1984 and Bialystok 1986), who have proposed a high-level model of language skill that encompasses many of the metalinguistic (and linguistic) tasks we have discussed so far and attempts to unify their cognitive requirements in terms of the demands they place on two fundamental dimensions of language proficiency. The first, which they dub *analyzed knowledge*, consists of explicit, structured knowledge about language that is accessible to conscious reasoning and can be manipulated in solving problems, e.g., explaining errors in bad sentences. While regular language production and comprehension make relatively little use of analyzed knowledge, metalinguistic tasks like judging grammaticality require considerably more of such knowledge. This type of knowledge would include the prescriptive rules alluded to above. Bialystok & Ryan's second dimension is labeled *cognitive control*. This is a skill required for focusing one's attention on particular information and attending simultaneously to multiple facets of a stimulus, e.g., its form, meaning, and context, and coordinating them within time constraints imposed by the task. Behaviors that have become automatic, such as attending to the meaning of a conversational utterance, require very little cognitive control, whereas moving one's focus away from meaning and onto form (decentering, in Piagetian terminology), as in making judgments, requires considerably more cognitive control. This might be a large part of what happens when we go into "judging mode." Thus, on both counts metalinguistic tasks are more demanding than conversation. Also, since the two dimensions are theoretically orthogonal (although in practice there is a correlation across the tasks people actually perform), we might expect that people's proficiency can vary along them independently and each could be subject to improvement through training or experience. (For instance, as will be argued in Section 4.4, schooling and literacy might contribute to such improvement;[28] experience as a newspaper editor will increase one's ability to detect errors in written text; linguistic training might also be expected to improve one's abilities, but the matter is not nearly so simple – see Section 4.4.1.) Also, particular tasks and particular stimuli within those tasks will vary in the demands they make on the

---

[28] Bialystok (1986) claims that schooling contributes most to development of the control dimension, whereas literacy increases analyzed linguistic knowledge.

two dimensions. For example, more salient errors require less cognitive control in order to be detected; more analyzed knowledge is needed in the absence of a supporting context. Bialystok & Ryan propose that grammaticality tasks can be ordered as follows, by increasing amount of analyzed knowledge required: grammaticality judgment, locating ungrammaticality, correcting ungrammaticality, explaining ungrammaticality, and stating a rule that is violated. The sort of evidence they use to demonstrate such claims is that second-language learners differ significantly on their ability to perform the various tasks even when precisely the same grammatical phenomena are involved in all of them. If it is true that (at least) these two types of skills are involved in making judgments, we must examine the nature of the interface between metalinguistic behaviors and competence grammar.

3.5 The Interpretation of Judgments with Respect to Competence

Many researchers have been convinced that there must be some differences between linguistic knowledge as revealed by judgments and that which underlies language use (e.g., Carden & Dieterich (1981)). The question for those who accept this assumption then becomes whether and to what extent judgment data can be used as evidence of competence. If they are not pure reflections of that competence (as argued eloquently by Levelt (1974: vol. 3: 5–7)), if they have no special epistemological status vis-??-vis the grammar (Levelt, Sinclair & Jarvella 1978), then how can the impurities be removed? In this section I look at the views of a number of researchers who have made the further argument, in various ways, that judgments are somehow special or abnormal, unique among language behaviors and built on a different competence base. I examine whether there is any evidence to support these claims, and whether they lead to any substantive proposals on how to make the best use of judgment data.

Bever has been the most widely cited proponent of the view that many of the properties that linguists attribute to the grammar, i.e., to a process-independent competence, really do not belong there at all. They are in actuality properties of the *particular* behavioral process through which the data were obtained, be it intuitive judgments, production, or some other kind of data:

> Even if our linguistic intuitions are consistent, there is no reason to believe that they are *direct* behavioral reflections of linguistic knowledge. The behavior of having linguistic intuitions may introduce its own properties. ...

> A linguistic grammar may have formal properties that reflect the study of selected subparts of speech behavior (for example, having intuitions about sentences), but which are not reflected in *any* other kind of speech behavior. (Bever 1970a: 343–344)

A major tenet of the current investigation is that, if such properties in fact are not part of linguistic competence, they might be part of more general nonlinguistic cognitive systems, in which case we could expect them to be apparent in other tasks besides evaluating sentences (this proposal was discussed in Section 1.4). Bever goes on to make a distinction between properties of the linguistic processing mechanism and properties of the introspective process, neither of which should be reflected in the grammar, but both of which have played a role in grammar construction in actual practice. Thus, we might be constructing *two* different "contaminated" grammars.

> The relationship between linguistic grammar based on intuition and that based on the description of other kinds of explicit language performance may not just be "abstract" … but may be *nonexistent* in some cases. First, apparently "linguistic" intuitions about the relative acceptability of sequences may themselves be functions of one of the systems of speech behavior (for instance, perception) rather than of the system of structurally relevant intuitions. Second, the behavior of producing linguistically relevant intuitions may introduce some properties which are *sui generis* and which appear in *no* other kind of language behavior. (Bever 1970a: 345)

Thus, one of our general goals in this area should be to sort out which properties are attributable to which performance procedures, so that we can treat data from each type of task most appropriately, rather than trying to identify *general* performance artifacts that might actually not apply across the board.

Let us now consider some specific properties that judgment data have been claimed to exhibit, in contrast with usage data. Several suggestions come from work by the Gleitmans and their colleagues:

> We take judgments about language to be manifestations of an executive, or metalinguistic, skill that has psychological interest in its own right. The metalinguistic capacity shows more individual and population differences than the linguistic capacity; it appears relatively late in development; and it is sensitive to linguistic levels. Specifically, the more "surface" aspects of language are more difficult to access for the sake of giving judgments

than are the "deeper" or more meaningful aspects. This distinction in performance may reflect differences in decay rates for less and more highly
processed linguistic material. (Hirsh-Pasek, Gleitman & Gleitman 1978: 99).

[Generative] grammars reflect the judgmental ("metalinguistic") aspects of
language knowledge more directly than they do knowledge of language itself. ... Whatever differences exist between these organizations may derive
from the fact that the "executive" thinking capacities have properties of
their own, which enter into the form of the grammars they construct. ...
Differences in tacit knowledge are small in comparison to differences in the
ability to make such knowledge explicit (Gleitman & Gleitman 1979: 121).[29]

Let us consider the suggested properties one at a time.[30]

First, it is claimed that metalinguistic abilities exhibit more individual differences than other linguistic abilities, and that different people's grammars are
more similar than our externalizations about them would suggest.[31] (For instance,
Gleitman & Gleitman argue that there is more variation in learning to read than
in learning to talk, because the former requires additional metalinguistic skills
that the latter does not.) I suspect that this impression arises because metalinguistic tasks are typically used to probe areas of linguistic knowledge that rarely
occur in regular speech and that therefore likely do exhibit more interspeaker
variation than the most common sentence structures, but it remains to be shown
whether differing judgments result from grammars or from differences in the
intuitional mechanism – this must be determined empirically.

Another claim of Gleitman & Gleitman is that low-level properties are harder
to make intuitions about than high-level (i.e., meaning-related) properties and
that intuitions about the latter show less variability. They paraphrase this by
saying that "fully processed" forms of language are easier to judge than only partially processed ones, such as syntactic forms without their semantics. Now, it is
certainly true that meaning is the property of language we deal with and use on
a conscious level most frequently, and so one might expect that meaning-related
tasks such as paraphrase or ambiguity judgment would come more naturally
than structural well-formedness judgments. But the actual evidence provided by

---

[29] See Van Kleeck (1982) for a critique of this paper.
[30] I defer discussion of the developmental argument until I have reviewed some of the relevant
experiments below.
[31] See Van Kleeck (1982) for a review of studies that find strong correlations between primary
linguistic abilities and metalinguistic abilities, and some methodological problems that they
share with Gleitman & Gleitman's work.

Hirsh-Pasek, Gleitman & Gleitman is not general enough to warrant their conclusion, since it all comes from the phonological domain. They show that children's word detection abilities are superior to their syllable identification, which in turn is better than their segment differentiation. Since the authors consider the word level to be "deeper" (more basic) than the syllable and segment levels, they draw the more general conclusion, but in fact meaning versus form is not the relevant contrast.

The actual generalization is that the difficulty of such detection or monitoring tasks depends on the size or level of unit one is searching for relative to the level of the units among which one is searching, with no target level being easier than another in any absolute sense (McNeill & Lindig 1973). At another point, Gleitman & Gleitman argue that giving judgments is more difficult than participating in conversation, by virtue of requiring self-consciousness, i.e., taking a prior cognitive process as the object of a higher process. Fillmore, Kempler & Wang (1979b) agree that metalinguistic performance requires more skills than regular language use. But while the "objectification of cognitive processing" view has a certain analytic appeal, and might even seem intuitively right, we have no solid evidence that anything of the kind is actually going on; our impressions might be epiphenomenal. In all these cases, then, the claims are unsupported. This is not to say that they are false, but one can envisage much more direct experimental ways of verifying or falsifying them, which would be a worthwhile undertaking.

These authors also go on to make specific suggestions as to where we should look for the source of properties that are special to metalinguistic behavior. They propose viewing it as an instance of the class of metacognitive behaviors.

> There need be no formal resemblance between metacognition and the cognitive processes it sometimes guides and organizes. Rather, one might expect to find resemblances among the higher-order processes themselves. On this view, judgments (and therefore grammars) have little direct relevance to speech and comprehension, but rather to reasoning. Whatever resemblance exists between language processing strategies and grammars may derive from the fact that the human builds his grammar out of his observation of regularities in his speech and comprehension. Whatever differences exist between these organizations may derive from the fact that the reflective capacities have properties of their own, which enter into the form of the grammars they construct (Hirsh-Pasek, Gleitman & Gleitman 1978: 128)

(Bialystok & Ryan derive the same prediction from their model.) For the hypothesis that there are resemblances among higher-order processes to be of any use, we must find some other metacognitive tasks to compare grammaticality judgments to. Unfortunately, very few have been studied. In the domain of memory, recollection (i.e., knowing that you remember something) could be considered metamemory (see Ryan & Ledger 1984 for a literature review), and as a special case, the tip-of-the-tongue phenomenon involves metamemory in the (temporary) absence of memory itself (Gleitman, Gleitman & Shipley 1972). The authors propose that intentional learning, or learning how to learn through deliberate memorization strategies or other means, constitutes another type of metacognitive activity. But no one has yet illustrated how comparisons with such processes can shed any light on the nature of linguistic intuitions. (See Van Kleeck 1982, Goldman 1982, and Gombert 1992 for more on this topic.)

The arguments that we have seen so far for the secondary nature of grammatical intuitions have been based on comparisons between fully developed linguistic versus metalinguistic abilities in adults. Another major set of arguments about the nature of linguistic intuition comes from developmental work on the acquisition of metalinguistic abilities. This is a huge area in its own right, to which I cannot hope to do justice here; see Chaudron (1983), Ryan & Ledger (1984), Birdsong (1989), and Gombert (1992) for literature reviews. Instead, I will concentrate mainly on one research project that makes a particularly provocative suggestion about how metalinguistic abilities develop – the work of Hakes (1980). His thesis, written within a Piagetian framework, starts from the observation that judgments and explanations of syntactic well-formedness emerge developmentally at about the same time as the ability to explain judgments of space and number and to develop intentional memorization strategies, which is considerably later than corresponding production and comprehension abilities (which seem to appear in the preoperational period). He suggests that these are all forms of concrete operational thought, since they all involve controlled processes, whereas sentence comprehension and casual memory are automatic processes. (See Van Kleeck 1982 and Ryan & Ledger 1984 for more on this approach.)

To test this idea, Hakes presented children aged 4 to 8 with various metalinguistic tasks (comprehension, judgments of synonymy and acceptability, phonemic segmentation), as well as other cognitive tasks (e.g., conservation tests). His finding was not only that performance on these tasks shows improvement strongly correlated with age, but also that the nature of the improvement was similar, in the direction of objectifying or "decentering" (using controlled processing to stand back from and evaluate a situation), a process that Piaget attributed to the period of middle childhood. Hakes thus argues that a *general* metalinguistic ability underlies successful performance in all these tasks. (Another task that fits this trend, according to Ryan & Ledger (1984), is reading – performance on grammaticality judgments correlates widely with reading ability.) For instance, Hakes found that synonymy judgments were based on superficial form in the youngest children, but on meaning and form together at a later stage. Acceptability for the youngest children was determined by whether they understood the sentence.[32]

At a later stage acceptability was based on the truth or desirability of the situation described in the sentence, its moral correctness, etc.[33] Still older children generally based acceptability judgments on linguistic form, although even some 8-year-olds labeled sentences unacceptable due to falseness of content. (Ryan & Ledger (1984) take their own data to show that until about the age of 8, children's reactions to ungrammatical sentences are just unsystematic.) Another general trend was that fewer bad sentences were judged good as the child grew older, which Hakes interprets as indicating that more grammatical rules were being learned.[34] (He additionally provides an interesting discussion of the methodological problems in getting linguistic judgments from young children, which must be much harder again than getting them from adults.)

The claim that controlled processing is a crucial developmental factor is supported by the fact that children seem to have the necessary skills to perform concrete operations earlier than the operations actually emerge. Children have been known to display metalinguistic behavior spontaneously in conversation, and can make use of deliberate memorization strategies when so instructed, but until a certain stage do not seem to be able to choose the appropriate routines to fit a situation. To follow up a point deferred earlier, Hirsh-Pasek, Gleitman & Gleitman use data such as that obtained by Hakes to argue that metalinguistic ability emerges late in development, and therefore must differ in important ways from language use. They also report that children have been known to judge bad sentences as grammatical, even though they have demonstrably mastered the relevant grammatical form in their own speech. But if Hakes is on the right track in pointing to objectification as the crucial skill that must be added to comprehen-

---

[32] There is obviously a great deal of variation in the ages at which particular abilities emerge. Certainly it would be incorrect to say that children under the age of 4 cannot assess grammaticality. Gleitman, Gleitman & Shipley (1972) showed that 2½-year-olds can detect and correct certain grammatical errors in simple imperatives (but see Gombert (1992) for a critique), although it was rare for them to correct just syntax, and that 6-to-8-year-olds could correctly explain a wide variety of grammatical errors.

[33] Such factors are not entirely abandoned in adulthood; see several studies reported in Chapter 4, notably Hill (1961) and Vetter, Volovecky & Howell (1979).

[34] However, the procedure that Hakes used could have been subject to a response bias, since he asked the children to explain their reasons for rejection but not for acceptance (see Section 6.3.2).

sion processing to allow judgment, then it does not necessarily follow that this objectification distorts the data that it provides, and we certainly cannot conclude on this basis that there is a *separate* knowledge base underlying intuitions.

It must be noted that there is a great deal of disagreement concerning how early children can provide useful grammaticality judgments. McDaniel & Cairns (1990) find that if one undertakes a training session first, children as young as 4 can make grammaticality judgments. They compared child judgments of sentences with their responses to the same sentences in an act-out task, and found that while there were few actual conflicts between the two measures, act-out responses failed to reveal the full range of possible readings of the sentence. For example, a child would act out a sentence in only one particular way and yet judge it grammatical for other meanings as well, for instance by allowing multiple possible referents for a pronoun. The reader may consult their work for methodological details.

Besides adult native speakers and children, data from a third group, adult second-language learners, have been used in exploring the relationship between judgments and competence. Coppieters (1987) attempted an experimental demonstration that syntactic intuitions do not improve as speaking ability in the second language increases. Specifically, he wanted to show that native and near-native speakers could have identical linguistic performance but radically different intuitions, and then take this to support the indirectness of the link between language use and linguistic intuitions as "a particularly striking illustration of the relatively independent status of two linguistic planes: language use and language form." He began his procedure by finding nonnative speakers of French who could not be clearly distinguished from native speakers in interviews that he conducted and who were considered to have native proficiency by their colleagues or friends; many of these subjects were linguists. He also interviewed a group of native speakers in the same way. He then proceeded with informal interview elicitations of judgments on a number of sentence types (requiring judgments of subtleties of French syntax such as adjective placement, choice of past tenses, etc., usually with two alternatives) that were rated as "correct or good," "uncertain or problematic," or "incorrect or bad." Subjects were also asked to explain meaning differences between pairs of minimally distinct sentences. The average ratings of the native speakers were used as a norm against which to evaluate individuals from both groups. Native speakers differed from their norm on 5–16% of the sentences, while near-natives disagreed on 23–49% of the judgments. Qualitatively, Coppieters reports that near-natives had strikingly different feelings about how sentences differed and the contexts where they could be used, and showed much variation in their explanations, whereas the native speakers where quite homogeneous in their answers. But do these results really show intuitional differences in the face of identical performance? The fact is the two groups were never compared on their *use* of the crucial constructions tested in the judgment task (e.g., by injecting the constructions surreptitiously in casual conversation), so it is equally possible (and seemingly more likely) that the same differences would be found in performance as well.[35] There might be no differential effect of judgment whatsoever in this case. (A related experiment by Snow & Meijer (1977) is reported in conjunction with a discussion of their other experiments in Section 4.4.3.) Thus, it seems that in ordinary language use the more subtle points of grammar can be avoided or go unnoticed, a state of affairs that many computer programs employing natural language exploit in order to engage in reasonable dialogues with humans using only rudimentary grammars.

Other authors have followed the same approach to argue that the degree of individual differences in metalinguistic ability implies that such ability relies on skills beyond those required for language use. In trying to pin down these skills, Masny & d'Anglejan (1985) looked at advanced students of English as a Second Language for statistical relationships between second language (L2) grammaticality judgments and corrections and selected cognitive and linguistic variables: L2 proficiency, first language (L1) reading competence, reasoning (nonverbal intelligence), field (in)dependence (a measure of cognitive style; see Section 4.3.1), and others. Using multiple regression analysis, they found that the best predictor of L2 metalinguistic ability was L2 proficiency. In apparent contradiction of Gleitman & Gleitman's claim, they found no correlation between metalinguistic ability and reasoning ability or cognitive style. Birdsong (1989) tries to make the same case on the basis of Scribner & Cole's (1981) study of Vai speakers in Liberia. Among these people, literacy and/or schooling seems to be a prerequisite for the ability to *explain* grammaticality judgments, which leads to large individual differences, but not for the ability to *make* them, which shows relatively little variation. I will discuss their findings further in Section 4.4.2. Regardless of the questionable effectiveness of this particular line of argumentation, it is hard to dispute the general conclusion that metalinguistic behavior is not a direct reflection of linguistic competence. In fact, much of the remainder of this book will lend credence to that argument. Birdsong concludes, "Inasmuch as metalinguistic performance reflects idiosyncratic skill parameters, which vary across tasks and across individuals, it cannot, in any rough-and-ready manner, reflect the grammar or linguistic competence presumably possessed by all speakers of

---

[35] Coppieters himself admits this as a likely possibility.

a language" (p. 61); "the inference of grammatical competence from linguistic and metalinguistic performance requires convergent evidence from a variety of validated sources, as well as a profound understanding of the variables that determine the form of the evidence" (p. 44).

3.6 Conclusion

I began this chapter by considering various ways to elicit subjects' impressions regarding the grammaticality of sentences, considering the pros and cons of several methods. These should be kept in mind when examining the studies that are reviewed in Chapters 4 and 5. Along the way, I considered how judgments fit into the larger class of metalinguistic behaviors, a theme to which I return in Chapter 6 in attempting to model the judgment process. I looked in detail at one heavily explored property of judgments, their scalability, and the methodological problems this property raises. I examined the much broader question of what really occurs during the judgment process and how we might manipulate that process to keep it more in line with language use. I then reviewed several kinds of evidence for just how different judgments seem to be from competence, the major determination being that the evidence is inconclusive. Following from the approach outlined thus far, the next two chapters attempt in part to show how the general features of judgments described in this chapter are the result of lower-level cognitive effects.

4 Subject-Related Factors in Grammaticality Judgments

Speakers perversely disagree among themselves about what is grammatical in their language; some of the principal sources of suffering and dispute within generative linguistics have been over ways of coming to terms with such realities.

(Fillmore 1979)

4.1 Introduction

Despite their common genetic makeup, humans exhibit individual differences in virtually every aspect of behavior. It should not be surprising to find that linguistic intuitions are no exception. The central question I address in this chapter is the extent to which differences in linguistic intuitions are systematically attributable to differences either in properties of the organism or in its life experiences. In some cases, there are some features on which people differ that contribute rather transparently to their grammaticality judgments, and to linguistic behavior generally, whereas in other cases the connection is surprising and still poorly understood. Throughout the chapter a major theme is consistency, or the extent to which the same subject gives a sentence the same rating on different occasions, or different subjects give a sentence the same rating. In the former case, inconsistencies are liable to be the result of factors having nothing to do with subjects' linguistic representations, e.g., whether they are fresh or fatigued, uncooperative, attentive or distracted, etc. (Bradac et al. 1980). In the latter case, interspeaker differences might be attributable to differences in deeper properties of the minds of the people in question, in their grammars or in some other module that affects grammaticality judgments. The implications of these various possibilities are taken up in Chapter 6.

I begin this chapter with three important studies that have looked quantitatively at individual differences in grammaticality judgments (Section 4.2). The amount of variation found there motivates a search for systematic factors that might account for some of it. In Section 4.3, I examine organismic factors in this regard. Two such factors have been studied extensively: field dependence, a concept from the personality literature (Section 4.3.1), and handedness, which seems to be an important indicator of linguistic structures in the brain (Section 4.3.2). Some other factors, such as age, sex, and general cognitive endowment, seem to be obvious candidates but have been given little or no attention in the literature, so I consider them only briefly in Section 4.3.3. Section 4.4 turns to features of the person's experience. The most controversial and most discussed of these is linguistic training. Innumerable critics of the linguistic enterprise have made their case on the basis of linguists being their own speaker-consultants. I look at several studies that have tried to establish whether linguists are suitable sources of grammaticality judgment data (Section 4.4.1). A less-studied but very intriguing source of variation in judgment abilities might be the amount of literacy training and general schooling a person has received. Investigations with remote cultures are the major source of evidence on this topic (Section 4.4.2). I conclude the section with a discussion of a grab bag of miscellaneous experiential factors, such as the amount of exposure one has had to a language (for instance, as a near-native speaker versus a native speaker) and accumulated world knowledge (Section 4.4.3). Section 4.5 concludes the chapter by summarizing the findings and using them to motivate the investigations of Chapter 5.

4.2 Individual Differences: Three Representative Studies

> *Note that, as usual, a given reader is not really expected to agree with a given writer's placement of asterisks.*
> (Neubauer 1976)

The term most often used for individual differences in language judgments is idiolectal variation, although Heringer (1970) is on the mark when he says, "This term is chosen for want of a better one and is not intended to imply that groups of people do not show the same patterns of variation in acceptability judgments, at least with individual sentence types. To call this dialect variation, however, seems not to be appropriate since there do not appear to be geographical or sociological correlates to this variation" (p. 287). Carden (1973) uses the term *randomly distributed dialects* in order to emphasize his belief that these should have the same theoretical status as geographically and socially defined dialects. The first set of experiments I review concerns the single most widely studied instance of individual differences: the interpretation of quantifier-negative combinations, as exemplified in (1a), which might be paraphrased as (1b) or (1c):

(1)   a. All the boys didn't leave.

        b. Not all the boys left.

        c. None of the boys left.

(Note that the spoken intonation pattern of (1a) likely would be very different for the two readings, although no one appears to have studied this issue systematically; see Section 5.2.6.) In an early study, Carden (1970b) claims that speakers fall into three categories with regard to their interpretation of sentences like (1a): some can only get the meaning of (1b), some can only get the meaning of (1c), and some find the sentence ambiguous.[1] He, along with many other researchers of the day (e.g., Elliot, Legum & Thompson 1969), argued that there are important theoretical insights to be gained by examining the full range of dialects, rather than accounting for one and ignoring the others. Carden was particularly interested in finding implicational relations among dialect differences. In a follow-up study that attempted to elicit judgments on these sentences, Heringer (1970) was faced with "the problem of asking naive informants to judge the acceptability of ambiguous sentences on specific readings," a problem we have also encountered with regard to adjunct *wh*-movement (see Section 2.3.2). When a sentence is uncontroversially good under one reading, one's initial impression is that it sounds fine. This undoubtedly biases ratings of other readings. Therefore, Heringer constructed a situational context in which only one of the readings was possible, either in the form of a scenario of which the target sentence formed the conclusion, or a prose description of the kind of situation where the sentence might occur. These two types of context are illustrated in (2) and (3), respectively:

(2)   All the students didn't pass the test, did they? [Professor Unrat believes he finally has succeeded in making up a midterm which every single one of his students would fail miserably. However, he doesn't know the test results yet, since his poor overworked teaching assistant Stanley has just

---

[1] While these three categories represent the major dialects, Carden admits that he found many subdialects. He also reports anecdotally that some speakers who originally could only get the (1b) reading started accepting both readings after repeated exposure to sentences that forced the (1c) reading. A similar finding is reported by Neubauer (1976) regarding individual differences in uses of the word *pretend*: subjects moved toward a more liberal dialect when pushed.

this moment finished grading them. Unrat asks Stanley this question in order to confirm his belief.]

(3)   All the treasure seekers didn't find the chest of gold. [Used in the situation where none of them found it.] (p. 294)

Heringer's instructions stated that acceptability should only be considered in the context of the material in square brackets. Unfortunately, acceptability was not defined for the subjects (a complaint made by Carden (1970a) as well) and they did not receive any training on practice sentences.

At any rate, several interesting results are found in this study. One is the ability of context to prompt subjects to see potential acceptability where there otherwise is none, a result that I discuss in Section 5.3.1. Another interesting finding is that, while there were very few speakers who accepted only the (1c) reading, there were many more who accepted neither reading. In Carden's study this pattern does not show up at all. In general, the results of the two studies differ quite substantially, leading Heringer to speculate on why this should be so. First, the mode of presentation was different in the two studies. Carden presented sentences orally in interviews, whereas Heringer used a written questionnaire. A second possibility, which I discuss more fully in Section 6.3, is that interviews of the sort Carden conducted are more susceptible to experimenter bias. A third potential problem, mentioned by Carden (1970a), is that Heringer used only one stimulus sentence for each reading in most of the constructions, so it is worth asking whether peculiarities of the sentences chosen could be responsible for some of the results. Nonetheless, Heringer's data apparently refute Newmeyer's (1983) claim that people differ only on their bias of interpretation on these quantifier-negative sentences (i.e., which reading they think of first),but that everyone *can* get both readings. Even when context forced a particular reading, many of Heringer's subjects did not accept that reading, so subjects seem to differ on something deeper than processing preferences.[2] (See Labov (1972a) for a survey of work on quantifier-negative dialects.)

---

[2] Newmeyer cites a paper by Baltin (1977) to support his claim that everyone can get both readings, but in fact Baltin found nothing of the kind. He found the three dialects that Carden had reported, using question answering rather than judgments as his primary source. (He also found a significant correlation between subjects' preferences on quantifier-negative constructions and their interpretation of prenominal modifiers as restrictive versus nonrestrictive.) However, Labov (1975) does report results along the lines described by Newmeyer, where non-linguistic tasks were used to force one reading or the other, with almost complete success across subjects.

Stokes (1974) performed a follow-up to Carden's work, starting from the criticism that the interview technique is subject to experimenter bias. Stokes used a questionnaire, and determined which readings of quantifier-negative sentences were grammatical by using judgments of synonymy rather than of grammaticality, with the hope that the former would be less likely to tap prescriptive feelings. He too found "extraordinary variation" in the results, a much wider range of response patterns than the three dialects Carden discussed. Among his 48 subjects, there were 17 different patterns of responses to the stimulus sentences.

The second study I review is by Snow & Meijer (1977), who performed three experiments to substantiate their claim about the secondary nature of syntactic intuitions and language data, which corresponds in many respects to the position presented in Section 3.5.[3] (The second and third experiments will be discussed in subsequent sections.) Their first experiment used as subjects native speakers of Dutch who were studying linguistics but had not taken any courses in syntactic theory. We might expect them to show somewhat more sophistication than truly naive subjects. Their materials all involved issues of word order, so multiple arrangements of each set of words were constructed. There were two conditions, absolute judgments and rank-ordering. In the former condition, each of 24 sentences appeared on a separate page and the instructions stated, "Will you please read the sentence, then indicate whether you think it is a good Dutch sentence (by 'good' we mean 'acceptable in spoken language' and not 'grammatically correct'). Write + if the sentence is good, − if it isn't good, and ? if it is in-between or if you don't know." In the rank-ordering condition, the sentences were divided across four pages of six sentences each, and the instructions read in part, "Will you please rank these sentences within the groups of six by rewriting them at the bottom of the page with those sentences which are good Dutch, or the best Dutch, at the top and those sentences which are the worst Dutch at the bottom. Sentences which are equally good or bad can be written on one line." Immediately we see a potential confound, since the rank-ordering subjects were not told to rank by spoken acceptability as opposed to grammatical correctness (of course, we do not know whether this terminology was understood in a uniform way by the first group either). Snow & Meijer decided to make this a within-subjects factor, administering the two kinds of tests a week apart to the same subjects, and found no effects of the order of test types, but the instructions could still confound any differences between the two types of task.

---

[3] They argue that syntactic intuitions are developmentally secondary, as evidenced by studies such as Hakes (1980); pragmatically secondary, because their function is not communicative; and methodologically secondary, as demonstrated by their experiments reported in this chapter.

The results were first analyzed for between- and within-subjects consistency in the two conditions. The between-subjects consensus on rankings was significant for all sets of sentences, as measured by Kendall's coefficient of concordance, but was not extremely high (ranging from .466 to .670 on a potential range of 0–1). The most agreed-upon sentence, which the authors claim is perfectly normal, showed disagreement by 3 of 25 subjects, and all other sentences showed at least 7 disagreements as compared to their mean rank. The absolute ratings similarly showed no total unanimity, although there was one sentence type on which 24 of the 25 subjects agreed.[4] On the other hand, five sentence types showed disagreements, i.e., at least one subject rated them bad both times while another rated them good both times, and two of these represented almost equal splits of the subjects. Within-subject consistency was 70.8% for the absolute judgments, where two identical ratings for two structurally identical variants counted as consistent, even if they were both marked "?". The majority of inconsistencies involved one "?" rating rather than strictly opposed judgments. One subject out of the 25 was consistent on all 10 sentence types, while the two least consistent subjects were consistent on only 5. Snow & Meijer correctly advise caution in interpreting this as a good level of consistency, however, because many of their subjects showed strong response biases toward a "+" response or toward a "−" response. In the extreme case, someone labeling all sentences as good would be 100% consistent. (Since we are not told the normative status of the stimulus sentences, we do not know what an unbiased distribution of responses might look like.) The authors devised a complex scoring system to assess within-subject consistency between rank-orderings and absolute ratings, which ranged on average from perfect consistency to about three out-of-sequence rankings in a set of six sentences. There was no significant correlation between this cross-conditions consistency score for a given subject and his or her consistency within absolute judgments. Even when judgments are pooled across all the subjects, the absolute ratings do not agree entirely with the rank-orderings. There was at least one reversal of position for each set of six sentences. On the basis of these results, it is hard to argue with the authors that "testing even a relatively large group of subjects, all of them relatively intelligent and language-conscious, does not assure internally consistent judgments concerning the relative acceptability of sentences" (p. 172).

The third of our example studies is perhaps the most widely cited study on individual differences in grammaticality judgments, that of Ross (1979). Ross asked

---

[4] In the absolute condition, subjects could indicate that they were unsure, which the 25th subject did here; therefore, this constitutes only a weak disagreement.

30 subjects to rate the grammaticality of 12 sentences on a scale from 1 to 4, and elicited their perceptions about these judgments.[5] Specifically, the subjects were asked to state how certain they were of each judgment (pretty sure, middling, or pretty unsure), and how they thought that judgment compared to the judgments of most speakers (liberal, conservative, or middle-of-the-road). Since I am particularly concerned with the design of instructions for such experiments, I present Ross's description of the rating scale as it appeared on his questionnaire:

1. The sentence sounds perfect. You would use it without hesitation.

2. The sentence is less than perfect – something in it just doesn't feel comfortable. Maybe lots of people could say it, but you never feel quite comfortable with it.

3. Worse than 2, but not completely impossible. Maybe somebody might use the sentence, but certainly not you. The sentence is almost beyond hope.

4. The sentence is absolutely out. Impossible to understand, nobody would say it. Un-English. (p. 161)

Note the reference to comprehensibility in item 4. In general, the instructions are quite explicit regarding differentiation of the levels, but give little indication of what counts as a criterion for grammaticality.

By his own admission, Ross intended this experiment only as a pilot study. As he acknowledges, his presentation of the results shows no knowledge of statistical whatsoever. Instead, he invents his own numerical measures to assess variability, covariation, etc., and gives numerous large tables of raw data.[6] While these shortcomings make the paper tedious to read and the results hard to interpret, at least his raw data could be used to do proper statistical analyses. I will report only the more obvious results, with the understanding that none of them should be taken as firm. First, I present the sentences employed in the questionnaire, with their mean ratings on the 1–4 scale. (Ross did not calculate mean ratings, but computed an overall score by weighting the numbers of subjects who gave each of the four responses, in effect treating the scale as centered about a zero point. Since his formula is arbitrary and unjustified, I use the standard

---

[5] There were actually 13 sentences in his questionnaire, one of which was geared to the semantics of *barely* and *scarcely* and did not yield results comparable to those for the other sentences.

[6] Another potential problem of interpretation is that 8 of his 30 subjects were nonnative speakers of English.

computation instead. Thus, in his ordered list, the third and fourth sentences are transposed.)[7]

The doctor is sure that there will be no problems.	1.07	*Core*
Under no circumstances would I accept that offer.	1.23	
We don't believe the claim that Jimson ever had any money.	1.63	
That is a frequently talked about proposal.	1.70	
The fact he wasn't in the store shouldn't be forgotten.	1.80	
The idea he wasn't in the store is preposterous.	2.03	
I urge that anything he touch be burned.	2.03	*Bog*
Nobody is here who I get along with who I want to talk to.	2.60	
All the further we got was to Sudbury.	2.77	
Nobody who I get along with is here who I want to talk to.	2.83	
Such formulas should be writable down.	3.07	*Fringe*
What will the grandfather clock stand between the bed and?	3.30	

The designations *core, bog,* and *fringe* are used by Ross to refer to the range of good, marginal, and bad sentences, respectively. These divisions are made by eyeballing, not by any formulaic procedure.[8] He found three variables that correlated with this distinction in the order core-fringe-bog (i.e., variables that changed monotonically such that good sentences were at one extreme and marginal ones at the other): increasing variability among subjects, decreasing confidence in their judgments, and increasing self-rating as conservative. The finding about variability jibes with Barsalou's results reported in Section 3.3.1 for conceptual typicality judgments. The pattern of confidence agrees with the findings of Quirk & Svartvik (1966: 52, fig. 9), based on the number of subjects choosing the "marginal or dubious" rating on their 3-point scale; they dub this phenomenon the "query bulge." At an intuitive level, these results are not surprising, but the only explanation RossRoss, John Robert adduces, namely that "the mind sags in the middle," does not add much insight.[9] While an additional goal of the questionnaire was to assess whether people know where their judgments stand in relation to those of the rest of the population, the data were not interpretable due to apparent misunderstandings of the liberality scale.[10] Interestingly, Ross

---

[7] The general problem of how to come up with a single rating for a sentence on the basis of multiple judgments on a graded scale has arisen in many other studies as well. Standard deviations should probably be reported.

[8] Ross does not commit as to exactly where the divisions should be drawn for the sentences he studied, so I have placed the boundaries arbitrarily within his suggested ranges.

[9] This quotation is attributed to George Miller.

[10] Ross suggests that a better way to get at this information is simply to ask subjects directly what ratings they think most other people would give.

found no cases of strongly polarized judgments, i.e., sentences that some people rated 1 and the rest rated 4, with no one in between. In all cases, the two most frequent ratings were adjacent on the scale, that is, there were no bimodal distributions. He suggests that this might be an artifact of the particular sentences chosen; if one deliberately chose known dialectal peculiarities, bimodality might still appear. However, as a measure of just how different people are, no 2 of the 30 subjects agreed on their ratings for more than 7 of the 12 sentences on the 4-point scale. In fact, Ross did not try all combinations of sentences, so it might even require fewer than 7 sentences to differentiate all of the subjects. (By way of comparison, Quirk & Svartvik (1966) (see Section 3.2) reported that with 76 subjects judging 50 sentences on a 3-point scale, only two sentences were unanimously rejected, and only two accepted.) These sorts of striking results lead Ross to ask, "Where's English?" (his proposed answer is discussed below). One experiential factor that contributed to variability among Ross's subjects was that some of his subjects were linguists while others were not. He found systematic differences between the two groups, which I discuss in Section 4.4.1.

Most linguists acknowledge that no two people will agree on even binary judgments of a large collection of sentences, let alone ordinal rankings.[11] What, if anything, does this tell us about people's grammars? Ross's data prompted him to take a very pessimistic view. He proposed in dismay that a language might be defined only as an *n*-dimensional space for some *n* in the thousands, where each point is a sentence and each dimension an implicationally ordered axis such that acceptance of a sentence on a given axis implies acceptance of all sentences closer to the origin along that axis. Then each person's idiolect is an *n*-dimensional vector specifying that person's acceptance threshold for each axis. Most linguists find this an appallingly messy and uninteresting view of language.[12] I discuss

---

[11] Newmeyer appears to be the exception, claiming that "there is good reason to think that idiosyncratic (i.e., nongeographical and nonsocial) dialects are nothing but artifacts of the now-abandoned view that grammaticality is dependent on context" (Newmeyer 1983: 57). However, he only cites one case as evidence for this very broad generalization, that of quantifier-negative sentences, and the facts there are still controversial, as discussed above.

[12] This view seems to have originated in Ross's earlier proposal of the concept of a squish (see Section 3.3.1). A squish is a two-dimensional matrix where the cells represent judgments. On one axis are forms graded by some property, e.g., increasing volitionality. On the other are environments where the forms might occur, graded by the extent to which they demand that property. One can make claims about how orderly the implicational pattern in the matrix should be across speakers. Unfortunately, after some research in this paradigm it started to look like both hierarchies could vary across speakers, or even that this pattern could be violated by a single speaker through the syntactic analog of statistical interactions: the effect of one dimension on grammaticality depended on the level of the other.

some alternative positions in Chapter 6. The reader is referred to Fillmore, Kempler & Wang (1979a) for a very wide-ranging discussion of individual differences in language behavior. Let us now consider the potential sources of these differences.

4.3 Organismic Factors

4.3.1 Field Dependence

Field dependence/independence is a concept that originated in the personality assessment literature in psychology. It is meant to diagnose how people perceive and think, specifically the extent to which they perform *cognitive differentiation*, the process of distinguishing stimuli along different dimensions. Nagata (1989b) investigated whether field (in)dependence would influence grammaticality judgments. A field dependent (FD) person fuses aspects of the world and experiences it globally, whereas a field independent (FI) person is analytical, differentiating information and experiences into components. These are seen as more or less permanent traits of individuals (Weiner et al. 1977). There are a number of diagnostic tests for field (in)dependence that have been shown by psychologists to be very well correlated. One of these is the tilting-room-tilting-chair test, which involves an apparatus consisting of a small box-shaped room containing a chair, mounted on mechanical devices such that each can be rotated independently in two dimensions. Subjects seated on the chair cannot see outside the room, and are required to judge whether they are seated upright or on a tilt relative to the outside world. FD individuals tend to believe that they are on a tilt if the orientation of the room makes it appear so, i.e., they have trouble distinguishing visual cues from kinesthetic/vestibular ones, whereas FI individuals have less trouble. A simpler test to perform, used by Nagata to divide up his subjects, is the embedded figures test. In this test subjects must rapidly pick out simple geometric figures embedded in larger, more complex ones. FDs have more difficulty with this than FIs. We might expect that these differences in cognitive style could show linguistic side effects. FI individuals show an impersonal orientation and have well-developed cognitive restructuring skills, while FD individuals show more interpersonal competencies. For example, they recall social words better than FIs and use them more often in free association tasks. Thus, we could anticipate that FDs would use strategies involving the enrichment of stimulus sentences with context when judging them, while FIs would be more prone to employ structural differentiation. (The nature of these strategies is described in more detail in Sections 5.2.4 and 5.2.5, in conjunction with discussion of Nagata's other experiments.) However, as reported in Section 3.5, Masny & d'Anglejan (1985) found field dependence had no discernible effect on L2 judgment ability. They also review numerous other studies attempting to relate it to language ability, the results of which were mixed. An additional facet of this distinction is that FDs are more prone to changing their opinions under external influence, since they pay greater heed to others, so we should look for differential reactions to knowledge of other people's judgments.

Nagata's experiment involved repeated presentation of sentences. After rating the grammaticality of a number of sentences (on a scale of 1 to 7), subjects were exposed to each sentence 10 times for 3 seconds per repetition, during which time they were told to think of the grammaticality of the sentence. After the tenth repetition, they rated each sentence a second time. Then they were told that their judgments differed from those of the average college student (which Nagata considered negative reinforcement), and were asked to think about the grammaticality of each sentence again and rate it a third time. Other experiments have shown that for a general population, the repetition treatment makes judgments significantly more stringent (i.e., sentences are rated less grammatical after repetition); see Section 5.2.3 for details. In Nagata's experiments, the judgments of FIs did become more stringent after repetition, but those of FDs showed no significant change. After the negative reinforcement, both groups' ratings became more lenient (the FDs' nonsignificantly more so). Nagata concludes that FDs approach the task of judging grammaticality differently from FIs, since they resist the usual repetition effect. One might have expected their judgments to become more lenient with repetition, as they considered more potential contexts for the sentences, but this trend was not found either. Apparently it is much harder to make sentences get better than to make them get worse (again, see Chapter 5 for more on this point). The idea that FDs would be more responsive to negative reinforcement was not substantiated. In summary, we can say that field dependence is a factor that can induce variability among subjects on grammaticality judgment tasks, just as it does in other domains. For instance, Lefever & Ehri (1976) found a moderately positive correlation between field independence and the ability to detect several kinds of ambiguity in sentences. They propose that the common features among the various tasks involve restructuring a stimulus pattern, overcoming the influence of context, and shifting mental set.

4.3.2 Handedness

There is already considerable evidence that handedness correlates with differences in language processing, for instance in the review by Hardyck, Naylor &

Smith (1979). Recently, some preliminary studies have been done on possible correlations between handedness and grammaticality judgment strategies. Work by Bever, Carrithers & Townsend (1987) was the first to suggest that such differences might be found. The purpose of their study was to show that the assumption that the basic mechanisms of sentence processing are the same for everyone is a severe oversimplification. Specifically, they demonstrated how right-handers from families with at least one closely related left-hander ("mixed background right-handers") show different processing patterns from right-handers with no familial history of left-handedness ("pure background right-handers"). The former group tend to process in a more structure-independent way than the latter, that is, they attend less to syntactic and semantic structures of language and more to conceptual and lexico-pragmatic features. These differences were found despite the matching of subject groups on several other variables, including age, sex, native language (English), and verbal SAT score.[13] In one study the authors used the classic tone location paradigm, wherein a subject hears a tone while listening to a sentence and must subsequently identify at which point in the sentence it occurred. They demonstrated that mixed-background subjects did not show a superiority effect for clause boundary location of the tone, that is, they did *not* locate the tone more accurately when it occurred exactly between two clauses, while pure-background subjects did. A second experiment showed that mixed-background subjects respond more quickly in a word recognition task (supposedly because they "make more use of the reference of individual words in their processing") and are insensitive to the position of the target word in the clause, unlike their structure-dependent counterparts, who showed serial order effects. Pure-background righthanders also performed more slowly on word-by-word reading tasks. These results support the authors' general conclusion that pure-background people depend more on aspects of sentence *structure*, mixed-backgrounders more on lexical and conceptual knowledge.[14] There is some neurological evidence to corroborate this proposal. Familial sinistrality seems to be correlated with a less localized, more widespread language module in the brain, which Bever, Carrithers & Townsend (1987) suggest leads to more contact between language and other kinds of knowledge. Whatever the eventual explanations of these differences, it would not be surprising to find that the different processing strategies are also reflected in different judgment strategies between

---

[13] These studies do not use left-handed subjects because they are harder to find and to match on these dimensions.

[14] It is important to note that there were no instances in which the two groups showed reverse effects; either they showed the same trend to different degrees, or else one group showed no effect.

such groups. In fact, the two types of strategies proposed by Bever et al. are not so dissimilar from those proposed by Nagata for field dependents versus independents. A replication of his procedure with mixed-background subjects could prove fruitful. See Bever et al. (1989) and Bever (1992) for more studies of language differences correlated with familial handedness.

Cowart (1989) conducted the first study to look explicitly for the effects of familial sinistrality differences in a judgment task. The experiment involved a written questionnaire using a 4-point scale, the extremes of which were designated "OK" and "odd" (since the details of the procedure are not reported, we cannot assess the extent to which subjects were instructed on how to evaluate sentences in terms of these labels). The sentences in question followed the paradigm in (4):

(4) a. What did the scientist criticize Max's proof of?
     b. What did the scientist criticize a proof of?
     c. What did the scientist criticize the proof of?
     d. Why did the scientist criticize Max's proof of the theorem?

Example (4a) has traditionally been called a violation of the Specified Subject Condition, while (4b) and (4c) are considered good in some theories and claimed to violate only the lesser constraint of Subjacency by others; (4d) is an uncontroversial control sentence. It was hypothesized that since the violations in (4a–c) are all of a purely structural nature, mixed-background subjects would be less sensitive to them and therefore rate them more grammatical than their pure-background counterparts. This prediction was borne out. For cases like (4a–c) the ratings of the latter subjects were significantly lower than those of the former, but no difference was found for grammatical control sentences like (4d).[15] If this insensitivity to structural violations is found throughout the syntax, it could constitute an explanation for a significant amount of intersubject variation in judgments. (See Section 7.2 for the possibility that Subjacency is really a parsing constraint and not a grammatical constraint.)

4.3.3 Other Organismic Factors

In this subsection I suggest some other organismic factors that might induce systematic differences in grammaticality judgments. First, let us consider two of the most obvious factors: age and sex. Ross (1979) suggests that, in general, more

---

[15] Another result was that cases like (4b) and (4c) were rated significantly worse than (4d), suggesting that they might indeed constitute Subjacency violations (but see the caveats in Section 2.3).

contact with a language leads to higher grammaticality ratings for it, an idea inspired by the fact (reported in Section 4.4.1) that linguists rated sentences higher on average than nonlinguists in his questionnaire experiment, which obviously has other possible explanations. If Ross is right, we would expect increasing age to be correlated with increasing tolerance in judgments. His own data do not bear this out, but they were not even based on accurate ages, just his guesses, so there is certainly room for more investigation here. Greenbaum's (1977) review of the literature cites age as a factor that correlates with difference in acceptability judgments, but he does not provide details. As for sex differences, Chaudron (1983) states in his wide-ranging survey of metalinguistic research that sex has rarely been experimentally analyzed and "does not appear to be a relevant factor," but if the former is true then how do we know the latter for certain? R. Lakoff (1977), while dealing with what she calls acceptability differences between men's and women's speech, makes it clear that such differences are conditioned by situational and social factors (i.e., *when* a particular kind of utterance is appropriate), and not differences in grammars. For instance, she has found no instances of syntactic rules that only one sex possesses, at least not in English. However, Bever (1992) *has* found preliminary evidence for sex differences in methods of language processing, which presumably could be reflected in judgments as well. He argues that there is a spectrum of "abduction strategies" or possible ways one can develop abstract representations (linguistic or otherwise), whose extremes are hypothesis refinement (using new data to refine an existing hypothesis) and hypothesis competition (using it to choose between alternative hypotheses). In one of Bever's experiments, the tasks involved producing, comprehending, and judging sentences in an artificial language. Under learning conditions that are supposed to support hypothesis competition, men do significantly better than women on the judgment task, while the opposite is true with hypothesis refinement. While there is as yet no conclusive basis for deciding whether these differences are biologically or socially caused, it is intriguing that similar sex differences surface in spatial learning tasks, which leads Bever to suggest that there might be a general abduction mechanism implicated in both activities. However, it does not necessarily follow that any sex differences we might find in judgments of one's native language would be attributable to the same mechanism. One can imagine that differences in conversational strategy could lead, say, to women judging fewer sentences ungrammatical than men because they are more supportive in conversation. (See Wardhaugh (1988: ch. 13) for a brief review of the literature on sex differences in language and their social correlates.) The attribution of sex differences to biological versus psychological causes is notoriously tricky, and is the subject of much ongoing research; see Halpern (1992) for an excellent review, and Philips, Steele & Tanz (1987) on the possible relevance of sex differences in the brain to language. It appears that no one has yet looked for sex differences in the processing of individual sentences, as opposed to overall skill level on verbal tasks.

The second direction we might explore while looking for organismic factors involves general cognitive differences that we suspect are implicated in the task of judging grammaticality. For instance, we will see evidence in Section 5.3.5 that part of this process involves imagining a situation to which a sentence could be applied. Therefore, the ability to imagine situations, i.e., some form of creativity, is a dimension on which people undoubtedly vary and one that could correlate with judgments. Various perceptual strategies have been implicated in language processing, and hence also (somewhat controversially) in the generation of judgments. Subjects might differ in their ability to use these strategies (Botha 1973). Similarly, a number of extragrammatical factors often implicated in acceptability (as distinct from grammaticality) might be subject to inherent differences, such as working memory capacity, ability to reason by analogy, and so on. At a more general level, intelligence and cognitive development might be pertinent, at least up to a certain ceiling. Hakes (1980) (reported in Section 3.5) attempts to show that qualitative changes in children's ability to make grammaticality judgments are correlated with Piagetian stages of development, and Masny & d'Anglejan (1985), mentioned in Section 3.5, looked for correlations between IQ and judgments of second-language learners, although they failed to find any significant patterns. Finally, Bialystok & Ryan (1985) propose a model of (meta)linguistic ability as factored into two major dimensions, analyzed knowledge and cognitive control (see Section 3.4). Each is the product of underlying cognitive abilities on which people might differ. Analyzed knowledge is related to intelligence and logical deduction abilities, while cognitive control depends on reflective and impulsive tendencies, as well as field dependence, discussed in Section 4.3.1. The authors do not provide specific evidence for these interdependencies, however. In general, demographic variables are hard to study rigorously in this context, because their effects seem to be small relative to stimulus factors and can often interact, which demands large samples of subjects in order to detect the effects reliably.

4.4 Experiential Factors

4.4.1 Linguistic Training

It is well-known among linguists that intuitions about the acceptability of utterances tend to be vague and inconsistent, depending on what you had for breakfast[16] and which judgment would best suit your own pet theory.[17]

(Dahl 1979)

Only the most sophisticated speakers can supply the exquisite judgments required for writing a grammar.
(Gleitman & Gleitman 1970)

One of the most frequent criticisms of generative grammar has been the fact that, to paraphrase Labov, the theories that linguists develop are based on data that they themselves create, a situation that constitutes an intolerable conflict of interest and seriously undermines the external validity of the findings. In this subsection I enumerate some of the specific reasons why it has been suggested that linguists' intuitions differ from those of naive native speakers and thus should not be used as linguistic data. I then turn to experimental attempts to establish whether such differences actually exist, of which there have been surprisingly few. It must be kept in mind throughout that finding differences in the way linguists and nonlinguists judge sentences does not inherently count as a strike against using data from the former group. We must examine each difference to see what the potential benefits and drawbacks are for linguistic investigation.

The following passage from Bradac et al. (1980: 968) is typical of the views expressed by many outside the generative enterprise: "as a result of their special training, linguists may tend to judge strings differently from nonlinguists. Training in linguistics may produce beliefs or attitudes which are not shared by

---

[16] Since it is not clear whether what one had for breakfast should be treated as a between- or a within-subjects factor, it will not be discussed further.

[17] Jim McCawley (personal communication) points out that the relevant factor is actually which judgment linguists *believe* would suit their theories, because their beliefs about the consequences of their own theories may turn out to be erroneous.

those who have not received such training. This suggests that the knowledge produced by linguists may become increasingly artifactual; it may fail increasingly to model natural language." While the authors' premise of differing beliefs is almost certainly true, it does not follow that linguists' judgments are artifactual in the sense that they are influenced by factors that are not relevant to the grammars of naive speakers. A priori it is equally possible that their training allows them to factor out various irrelevant factors that *do* influence naive judgments, but actually reflect cognitive factors *other than* the grammar that is the object of study (Levelt 1974). However, there are legitimate reasons to suggest that this ability of linguists might have come at the price of a loss of objectivity. Labov (1972a) argues that linguists have become removed from everyday language experience. Greenbaum (1976a; 1977c) believes that linguists are bound to be unreliable subjects, for at least three reasons. First, after long exposure to closely related sentences their judgments tend to become blurred. A famous quotation from Fraser (1971: 178), exemplifies the point: "I think this issue is fairly clear. It will be resolved by speakers whose intuitions about the sentences in question are sharper than mine, which have been blunted by frequent worrying about these cases." Even Chomsky himself has experienced this phenomenon: "I had worried so much over whether *very* could occur with *surprised*, that I no longer had a firm opinion about it" (Chomsky 1962: 172). Haj Ross coined the term *scanted out* in the early 1970s to describe this state.[18] Second, linguists are liable to be unconsciously prejudiced by their own theoretical positions, tending to judge in accordance with the predictions of their particular version of grammar.[19] Botha (1973), Derwing (1973), Sampson (1975) and Ringen (1979), among many other critics, also express this view. Additionally, Levelt (1974) suggests that hypercritical linguists might be biased *away from* the judgments predicted by the theory they are working on. Carden & Dieterich (1981) speculate on the subconscious process by which this could arise in a particular case. Greenbaum's third source

---

[18] The term apparently originates from Ross's feeling that just trying to produce any judgments on sentences containing the word *scant* was sufficient to induce a loss of intuitions in short order.

[19] Elan Dresher (personal communication) suggests that the reputed argumentativeness of linguists and the existence of multiple competing theories would guard against such bias. However, in the first place, Wayne Cowart (personal communication) points out that it is almost impossible to get an article published if all one has to offer is disagreement with some other linguist's judgments. Furthermore, even if one has a theory to go with new judgments, this will only help the field if one's theory is of interest to the linguist in question. If the source of bias is an uncontroversial assumption within GB, say, but that assumption is disputed by proponents of Lexical-Functional Grammar, the bias will be difficult to discover, because the two camps rarely interact.

of linguists' unreliability is that they look for reasons behind their acceptance or rejection of a sentence, which takes away spontaneity and makes their judgment processes different from those of naive subjects, who presumably have neither the inclination nor the knowledge necessary to perform this analysis. On the issue of whether this is actually less desirable, see the discussion in Section 5.2.7 on the relative merits of spontaneous versus reasoned judgments. Nonetheless, I agree with Greenbaum that this constitutes an additional difference between the two groups. Let us now see whether any of the above hypotheses have been borne out empirically.

I begin with a summary of differences found by Ross in the study mentioned in Section 4.2. The summary is brief because the study's methodological shortcomings make its results suspect at best. On average, his linguists were more unsure than his nonlinguists (i.e., they had less confidence in their ratings), perhaps because thinking about language makes you realize how little you know about it and shatters your confidence in your own judgments – "Doing syntax rots the brain."[20] Nonlinguists rated themselves more conservative, were tougher graders (i.e., they rated sentences less grammatical overall), and made fewer distinctions between levels of grammaticality (i.e., they tended not to use the whole scale). We will find a counterexample to the relative stringency finding in another study.

The most widely cited work on linguist/nonlinguist differences is that of Spencer (1973). The paper is perhaps more important for the many issues it raises than for Spencer's experimental results. She starts from the position that:

> it is possible that the behavior of producing linguistically relevant intuitions has developed into a specialized skill, no longer directly related to the language behavior of the speech community (Bever [1970a]). The linguist views language in a highly specialized way, and perhaps is influenced by a perceptual set. The resulting description may not be an ideal representation of linguistic structure. It may be an artifactual system which reflects the accretion of conceptual organization by linguists. (p. 87)

Spencer's experiment used two groups of subjects: the naive subjects were students of introductory psychology, while the nonnaive subjects were graduate students who had taken at least one course in generative grammar.[21] She states

---

[20] Ross attributes this adage to John Lawler without providing a reference.

[21] Apparently the nonnaive subjects did not possess a uniform amount of linguistic background, however, since some were graduate students in linguistics, while others were psychology or speech students. The latter groups might have watered down the linguistic biases of the first group.

that Chomsky's (1961) definition of grammaticality and examples were used as the basis for the instructions in her experiment, but all she actually tells us about these instructions is the following: "Each [subject] was read the same instructions – he would be asked to make a decision on each statement as to whether it was complete and well-formed or not. There were a series of guidelines and examples as to what the [experimenter] meant. ... After the instructions had been read, the [subject] was asked to tell the [experimenter] what he had understood his instructions to be, and any confusions or omissions were corrected" (p. 91). Apparently Spencer (or her editors) did not consider it important to describe the details of these instructions, but they are crucial for interpreting the results. If they did not correspond to the concept of grammaticality that linguists use, then we have a confounding variable.[22] The stimulus sentences were drawn from six linguistic articles, and had all been labeled unequivocally good or bad by the original author. Unfortunately, none of the sentences are reported in the paper. Newmeyer (1983) surmises, on the basis of the source articles, that many of them were pragmatically very odd and required an unusual context to sound acceptable. Spencer's design was intended to draw out two possible results that would undermine linguists' use of their own intuitions: intersubject variation by naive subjects on allegedly clear cases, and naive subject consensus that conflicted with a linguist's judgment. There was also a check for consistency: six randomly chosen sentences were resubmitted for judgment at the end of the experimental session, and subjects who contradicted themselves on three or more of these had all their results discarded.

The first result was that an average of 81.4% of the 150 sentences were considered clear cases, as defined by the degree of consensus among subjects. At least 65% in each group gave the same rating (either good or bad, there were no other available answers). That is, the division between accepters and rejecters had to be at least 15% from an even split. But this is not a particularly strong consensus; 35% of the subjects could still have disagreed. If a 75% criterion had been set, the percentage of clear cases would have been lower. Spencer does not provide figures from which we can calculate it exactly. She acknowledges that her choice of cut-off is arbitrary. (For comparison, Snow & Meijer (1977) report 20% of their sentences as unclear cases among naive native speakers. Their definition of unclear is that a sentence received approximately equal numbers of acceptances and rejections.) As for whether naive and nonnaive subjects differed in their responses, it is impossible to be certain on the basis of Spencer's reported figures, for two reasons. First, while she shows that the proportion of sentences

---

[22] Newmeyer (1983) makes this criticism as well.

accepted by the two groups differs by 6%, she reports no statistical test of significance for this difference. Second, this comparison would not reveal a situation where the groups differed on *which* sentences were accepted, but total *numbers* of acceptances happened to come out roughly the same. Spencer merely states that there were "no noticeable differences in the distribution of exemplars found unacceptable, unclear, and acceptable."[23]

As for comparing the subjects to the linguist authors, 73 of the 150 sentences showed disagreement, defined by the subjects' pooled rating being either unclear or opposite to that of the linguist. Table 4.1 (from Spencer (1973)) gives a breakdown of the results. Of the disagreements, 81% were unanimous across the subject groups, and in the majority of the remaining cases it was the naive subjects who disagreed with the linguists while the nonnaive subjects agreed, but again this difference is not analyzed for significance. We must keep in mind, however, that this 50% disagreement rate is made up by comparing the pooled judgments of 65 subjects with that of an individual linguist, a point that many subsequent articles have emphasized. Thus, while we can certainly conclude that the published judgments did not show a good correspondence with the population as a whole, we crucially cannot conclude that linguists *as a group* have systematically different judgments from nonlinguists. A comparison with any single randomly chosen naive subject could well have shown just as much disagreement. Nevertheless, Spencer concludes that linguists should not trust their intuitions: "It is reasonable to state that the judgments of the linguists used are representative of many linguists as a group," since there had not been any published rebuttals in the 4–5 years since the original articles appeared. But there are many possible alternative explanations for that state of affairs. As for the direction of the disagreements, the table shows that on 42 sentences nonlinguists were more accepting, while on 17 they were more stringent and on 14 they were mixed. This pattern, though not overwhelming, contradicts Ross's findings that linguists are more accepting on average.[24] Thus, the only firm recommendation we can draw from this study is that a reasonable sample size be used in determining the representativeness of judgments; we cannot conclude that this sample should not consist of linguists.

Despite the less-than-convincing nature of her findings, Spencer goes on to make the familiar point that linguists who use only their own intuitions as data are really no different from trained introspectionists, whose intuitions ended up

---

[23] For Spencer, an unclear sentence is one on which the subjects did not show consensus by the measure defined above.

[24] If we expect that linguists should be more aware of their actual speech tendencies than untrained speakers, then this result also contradicts the general recommendation of Hindle & Sag (1975) to trust "OK" judgments more than stars.

Table 4.1: Comparison of Linguists' and Nonlinguists' Acceptability Judgments (Spencer 1973)

Number of sentences	Judgment (+ = acceptable; – = unacceptable; ± = unclear case)			
	Linguist (as published)	Naive group	Nonnaive group	Total
Consensual Agreement				
51	+	+	+	
26	–	–	–	77
Consensual Disagreement				
17	+	– or ±	– or ±	
42	–	+ or ±	+ or ±	59
Judgments Mixed				
3	+	+	– or ±	3
4	+	– or ±	+	
7	–	+ or ±	–	11

being totally removed from the layman's experiences (see Section 2.4 for a discussion of of introspectionism in psychology). In addition to the possibility that linguists' theoretical perspectives influence their judgments, she suggests that working with many sentences revolving around a given issue might also contribute to context biases in their judgments. That is, satiation first leads to a loss of symbol meaning, then illusory changes occur in the form and meaning of the sentences, constrained by the context (e.g., one's theory).[25] Thus, the linguist can reperceive and reorganize a sentence after repeated consideration, taking into account the theoretical constructs that it bears on. Finally, Spencer addresses the question of whether linguist/nonlinguist differences might not in fact be a good thing:

> It might be claimed that any difference between linguists and naive speakers found in this experiment is due to the increased awareness and sophistication in language that linguists have developed through their study. Perhaps linguists are simply more sensitive to language and therefore are able to

---

[25] This notion of the effects of satiation derives from experiments such as those of Taylor & Henning (1963). They used a tape loop of a short phrase or sentence repeated for 15 minutes. When the instructions suggested that the stimulus would change, subjects perceived illusory changes. Furthermore, the number of non-English forms they perceived among these changes was heavily increased when they were told to expect non-English forms. Thus, the context constrained illusory variation.

detect finer differentiations than naive speakers in intuitions concerning natural language, rather than creating differentiations which do not exist within the natural language. If linguists are dealing with artifacts, however, nonnaive speakers, who have studied modern linguistics, should perform in a manner similar to naive speakers. Thus, to anticipate this criticism, non-naive speakers also participated in the experiment. (p. 90)

Of course there is a certain Catch-22 quality to this last point. One could always counter that, however much linguistic training these nonnaive subjects had, it did not raise them to the same level of linguistic sophistication as practicing linguists, and so the latter's judgments might still be valid. Conversely, if the nonnaive subjects behave more like linguists than like naive subjects, one could maintain that linguists' judgments were artifactual and that the nonnaive subjects had too much linguistic training, such that they were exhibiting the same biases as linguists. Thus, subjects with some knowledge of linguistics can never be used to decide this issue definitively. What is needed is truly naive subjects who nonetheless have been given a very good understanding of what is meant by grammaticality.[26] (One might, however, question whether this is possible even in principle.)

At least three other studies have compared linguist and nonlinguist judgments directly.[27] One of these was an informal experiment conducted by Greenbaum (1988: 93, fn. 4) that was similar to Spencer's and found similar results. Another, reported in a very brief article, is by Rose (1973). Rose also took his stimulus items from linguistic articles, asking subjects to classify them as acceptable or unacceptable (details of the method are not given). Half of the subjects were told to play the role of an editorial assistant working for a strict editor, while the other half had to play the role of a person attempting to help a foreign friend speak properly. Rose states that, overall, subjects agreed with the linguist authors 89% of the time. I assume this is a percentage of the total individual judgments, rather

---

[26] I am aware of only two paradigms that have systematically addressed the issue of training naive subjects. Ryan & Ledger (1984) found that explicit training on how to perform a grammaticality judgment task did not improve the performance of their kindergarten-age subjects, while McDaniel & Cairns (1990) found that training did help even their 4-year-old subjects.

[27] The only other empirical basis we have for comparing linguists and nonlinguists would have to come from separate studies that use the same procedure but with different kinds of subjects. For example, a study by Elliot, Legum & Thompson (1969) used mostly linguists, whereas Greenbaum's (1973) replication, described in Section 5.2.2, used all nonlinguists and got different results, but Greenbaum tried to eliminate other procedural problems with the design of Elliot, Legum & Thompson (1969), so the studies are no longer directly comparable. This is the only such instance I am aware of.

than a pooled scheme like Spencer used. This number is not nearly as informative as Spencer's, since it could represent a variety of scenarios, such as each sentence showing strong agreement, or most showing uniform agreement and some showing uniform disagreement. A chi-square analysis showed that linguist judgments and subject judgments were significantly related, but we have no indication as to which direction the disagreements took. There was no difference between the two roles played by subjects.

Snow & Meijer's (1977) second experiment repeated the procedures of the first, as reported in Section 4.2, but used eight linguists as subjects, allowing direct comparison with the results of their nonlinguist group. The linguists showed significantly greater within-subject consistency than the nonlinguists in the first experiment: 94.3% on the absolute judgments. In part this might be attributable to a bias towards "–" responses, which exceeded that of nonlinguists. (The authors do not report sentence-by-sentence comparisons, so we cannot say with certainty how often linguists were more stringent than nonlinguists; there is no basis for comparison with Ross or Spencer on this issue.) Linguists' consistency between absolute ratings and rank-orderings was also significantly higher, and they showed greater between-subjects agreement, with Kendall coefficients of between .581 and .844. As for whether the linguists' judgments differed from those of the nonlinguists, the mean rankings of sentences by the two groups showed a high correlation (Spearman ρ = .89), as did the absolute ratings (ρ = .84). While this is a higher rate of agreement than Spencer found, we must consider that Snow & Meijer use the mean ratings of a group of linguists, rather than a single linguist's judgments. Also, as they themselves point out, Spencer counted as disagreements any cases where nonlinguists showed disagreement among themselves; this was not taken account of in Snow & Meijer's study. Thus, the two ratings are not directly comparable. The authors draw a number of methodological conclusions, including the interesting suggestion that while comparing absolute judgments with rank-orderings provides a useful check of judgmental consistency, the fact that a sentence is judged inconsistently might say more about the sentence than about the quality of the judges, for instance that it has some shifty properties. With regard to the implications of linguists' higher consistency of judgment, they suggest two alternative interpretations. Either linguists have learned to ignore minor irrelevant differences among sentences, such as their semantic plausibility, or they have learned to apply their theory to unclear cases. The extent to which each of these turns out to be right will obviously determine whether this improved consistency is a desirable property.

Valian (1982) has explored in some detail the parallels between linguists' use of their own judgments and expert judgment in other fields. She argues that linguists giving judgments are in relevant respects just like experts judging wine, tea, or cheese, so to the extent that the latter have proven to be useful, in fact essential (e.g., in maintaining uniform taste of a product year after year), the former could also. It is instructive to enumerate these parallels. Tasters, like linguists, are fallible, but their errors are within acceptable limits, and they know their task well enough to be able to take systematic steps to reduce the likelihood of error. For example, they arrange their samples in a particular order, not tasting a heavy-bodied wine before a light-bodied one. Linguists are similarly aware that order of judgment can affect their intuitions. Tasters have a priori biases, e.g., by being Bordeaux lovers rather than burgundy lovers, which makes them differentially sensitive to certain tastes. Similarly, linguists clearly have a priori biases. Tasters also come at their task with prior information about the samples they are tasting, e.g., what region a wine is from. Linguists' theories similarly provide a classification of sentences that are judged. In both cases, this additional information can allow finer judgments to be made and can focus attention on particular aspects of a sample. Valian argues that to have a completely open mind about the material at hand is to lack any experience with it, which results in the inability to make consistent or fine discriminations. In the case of wine, things may all taste the same. Some people excel at different kinds of judgments than others do. In general, while all kinds of judgments are in some sense subjective, this does not mean they cannot be reliable and valid, especially when we acknowledge that there are strategies we can adopt for making them so.

4.4.2 Literacy and Education

Birdsong (1989: 31–44), Bialystok & Ryan (1985), and Masny & d'Anglejan (1985) provide extensive reviews of research examining the relationship between literacy, education, and metalinguistic skills, including grammaticality judgments, and comment on the debate over which one(s) might be prerequisite(s) for the other(s). Bialystok (1986) suggests that schooling contributes to her dimension of linguistic control, implicated in the ability to objectify language for judging purposes, while literacy adds to one's analyzed knowledge. (See Section 6.2.1 for more discussion of this model.) I present here a few studies from this field.

The largest and most fascinating project on this topic was conducted by Scribner & Cole (1981), who did several years of field work among the Vai people of Liberia. These people have invented their own syllabic writing system, which is taught to some children in the home. Formal schooling, for those who manage to get it, is conducted in English; some Vai also know Arabic. Scribner & Cole were interested in teasing apart the effects of schooling and literacy, and so the fact that there were Vai monoliterates who had no formal schooling was crucial.[28] It was their hypothesis that writing contributes to the objectification of language, independent of any general cognitive advantages it might entail. (In fact, they found very little evidence that literacy in either Vai or Arabic produces advantages for problem solving or other cognitive tasks.) More specifically, they believed that deliberate written composition in one's native language increases one's understanding of its formal properties, an idea that dates back to Vygotsky.

Scribner & Cole used three kinds of metalinguistic task to test this theory. The first involved orally presenting paired sentences, one good and one bad, and asking subjects to choose the good one and explain why the other one was bad. Examples (5) and (6) below give rough English equivalents of the type of structures involved:

(5)   a. He shot me at the gun.

   b. He shot the gun at me.

(6)   a. These children, what is its name?

   b. These children, what are their names?

The second task called for subjects to explicitly identify some grammatical principle of Vai. This is illustrated in (7), where the relevant distinction is alienable versus inalienable possession.

(7)   People say "my (ŋ) father," but "my (na) book"; they say "my (ŋ) sibling," but "my (na) wife." Why do people sometimes say ŋ and sometimes say *na*?

(Apparently a wife is viewed as an acquired possession rather than a relative.) Subjects' explanations on these two tasks were scored on a scale of 0–7. Zero denoted irrelevant answers, such as "The old people say it like that," "Bad Vai," and "Not a good Vai speaker." A score of 1 was given to responses that claimed the sentence was semantically inappropriate, and higher scores denoted increasing degrees of grammatical relevance. While all groups were able to identify the bad sentence in the first task, their explanation abilities on the two tasks differed according to literacy and education. On one survey, the average explanation scores

---

[28] I should point out that theirs was a huge anthropological and psychological study, of which the metalinguistic tasks reported here constituted a tiny part.

were 3.9 for illiterate speakers, 4.6 for Vai literate speakers, and 5.6 for Vai-Arabic biliterate speakers. A replication found scores of 2.3, 2.9, and 3.2, respectively. Multiple regression analysis showed that, of all the demographic data that were available about the subjects, Vai literacy was the only factor that predicted these differences.[29]

The third task involved correcting errors of various types (shown in (8)) and explaining what was wrong with an ungrammatical sentence.

(8)   a. My child is crying yesterday.

    b. This house is fine very.

    c. I don't want to bother you (plural) because you (singular) are
       working.

    d. This is the chief's child first.

    e. These men, where is he going?

    f. They have planting the oranges.

On this task explanations were scored on a scale of 0–5. The authors provide Table 4.2, summarizing the number of errors fixed correctly and the total of the explanation scores on the six sentences. Here the regression analysis showed that schooling was the biggest contributor to explanation scores, and Vai literacy was also a factor. It is important to note that literate and performed equally well on other tasks examining their ability to explain things, so the effect seen in this experiment is specific to the linguistic content of the problem. We can conclude from this work that literacy and schooling have little effect on the ability to identify ungrammaticality, and hence to make grammaticality judgments in the narrow sense, but both factors appear to affect explicit grammatical knowledge, and hence will confound many other metalinguistic tasks.[30]

---

[29] Interestingly, similar differences were found by Liles, Shulman & Bartlett (1977) when comparing the judgments of children with language disorders versus unaffected children. They found that children with language disorders not only make fewer accurate judgments on certain types of syntactic errors, but they can recognize some errors without being able to correct them, whereas unaffected children have almost no trouble correcting detected errors. In this case, however, the authors suggest that inferior production skills might be responsible, although their reasoning is quite speculative.

[30] A similar result in another domain is reported by Reed & Lave (1979), also based on work in Liberia. These authors examined the arithmetic abilities of Vai and Gola tailors to assess the contribution of formal Western education as compared to traditional apprenticeship. Their findings suggest that these abilities can be very domain-specific: the same problem framed in terms of monetary units may be more difficult than when framed in terms of numbers of buttons to be sewn on pants, for instance. They also found that the types of errors made differ

Table 4.2: Comparison of Vai Error Correction and Explanation as a Function of
Literacy (Scribner & Cole 1981)

	Maximum possible score	Nonliterate	Arabic monoliterate	Vai monoliterate	Schooled literate
Number correct	6	5.1	4.5	5.0	5.6
Explanation score	30	6.9	8.1	9.9	15.7

Other researchers of literacy effects include Scholes & Willis (1987), who studied 10 English-speaking illiterate adults and found that they seem to process sentences without making use of all the syntactic information available. For instance, they report anecdotally that a spoken sentence like *The window in the room with the chair was broken* is taken to mean that the chair got broken.[31] Birdsong (1989) cites other work by these authors suggesting that illiterate speakers are insensitive to passive morphology, and that they judge grammaticality according to pragmatic validity and moral correctness or desirability. Scholes & Willis conclude that illiterate speakers have vastly different grammars from literate speakers, but Birdsong counters that their judgments might be based on different criteria, without the underlying grammars necessarily differing. Heeschen (1978) had similar experiences with the Eipo, an illiterate, neolithic horticultural people of West New Guinea. He states that they are "uneasy and unsuccessful" in trying to objectify language, and concludes that 90% of their grammaticality judgments of possible but rarely occurring verbal affix combinations were simply wrong.[32] However, their judgments on word order were "absolutely correct." Heeschen suggests why this difference should be found: some affix combinations are rare and hence hard to see as correct out of context, whereas word order is a feature of every utterance that cannot be avoided. This hypothesis is supported by the fact that in *natural* situations (e.g., when native speakers corrected him in conversation), as opposed to structured judgment tasks, "their judgments as native speakers proved to be perfectly reliable" (p. 177). Thus, at least for this culture,

---

systematically between the two groups with different types of education, and seem to reflect the different ways in which arithmetic is taught in school versus on the job. The general result is that skill in applying knowledge to a particular domain does not always imply the ability to use that knowledge in the abstract.

[31] One might suspect the presence of some third, pathological factor affecting both ability to acquire literacy skills and ability to comprehend sentences, but Scholes & Willis's very brief description gives no indication of such a factor.

[32] Heeschen does not explain how he determined what the correct forms actually were.

it seems that illiteracy does not imply the inability to make accurate judgments, but just makes it hard to do so in an abstract context.

4.4.3 Other Experiential Factors

As in the previous section, I conclude with a collection of remarks on other types of experience that might systematically affect judgments of grammaticality. The most obvious would be the amount of experience with the language in question. There have been numerous studies of metalinguistic skill in nonnative learners of a second language, as part of the second-language teaching literature, which is beyond the scope of this investigation (see Ellis (1991) for a review). Clearly, one would expect nonnative speakers to differ from their native counterparts in judgments as well as in language use, but the results of a third experiment in Snow & Meijer's (1977) study (see also Sections 4.2 and 4.4.1) suggest that native intuitions may be acquired independently of native skill in language use.

This experiment involved the same procedure as was used in Snow & Meijer's first and second studies, this time with nonnative speakers of Dutch as subjects. Their within-subject consistency was at least as good as that of native speakers, but predictably they showed more between-subject disagreements, since their degree of familiarity with Dutch was not matched. Nonetheless, their pooled judgments agreed somewhat better with the native speaker group than those of the linguists did. And, surprisingly, the three virtually bilingual non-natives did not match the native group better than the remaining poorer Dutch speakers (as measured by correlations in rank-ordering). The authors interpret this to mean that one's skill in speaking a language can improve without one's syntactic intuitions becoming more nativelike.[33] Conversely, they suggest that classics scholars, for instance, show the opposite: they develop strong intuitions without being able to speak the language. Together with the large amount of variation in judgments among native speakers found in the first two experiments, Snow & Meijer's results lead them to conclude that speaking and understanding involve a different language faculty from judging, since skill in one is not a good predictor of skill in the other. On the other hand, Coppieters (1987) claims that his subjects appeared to have achieved native levels of production and comprehension, and yet their judgments were significantly different from those of native speakers. But, as discussed in Section 3.5, Coppieters's study had not actually shown that the two groups were identical in their *use* of the crucial forms, but

---

[33] Chaudron (1983) points out that there were only eight nonnative subjects in this experiment altogether, so due caution is advised in interpreting the results.

only on unrelated general measures of fluency, mastery of various constructions, and so forth. Thus, we have no basis for concluding that nonnative speakers display differences unique to their judgments. More likely, their grammars simply differ from those of natives on the points investigated, and this would show up in everyday use as well if these constructions occurred. It has also been proposed that experience in *another* language (e.g., bilingualism) leads to differences in metalinguistic ability (Van Kleeck 1982; Bialystok 1986; see Section 5.3.2).

One would expect certain types of nonlinguistic experience to influence judgments as well, for example, factual world knowledge, and cultural and social experiences and beliefs. Greenbaum's (1977) review cites correlations between judgments and occupation or socioeconomic class, without elaborating. Svartvik & Wright (1977) found differences on judgments by 14-to-17-year-olds concerning the use of *ought* correlated with the different academic standing of three groups of English schools they attended. I am not aware of any studies showing that these variables can affect *structural* judgments. A purported example of how world knowledge is relevant to grammaticality is provided by Belletti (1988). According to her, the following two sentences involving subject postposing contrast in grammaticality in Italian:

(9) a. È   stato rubato il   portafoglio a Maria.
        has been stolen the wallet   to Maria

    b. *È   stata rubata la   pianta a Maria.
        (has been stolen the plant   to Maria)

The crucial difference here is claimed to be that we can assume people normally own only one wallet, but the same is not true for a plant. If this is true, someone from a different culture presumably would not show this distinction. Unfortunately, according to one native speaker I consulted (Mirco Ghini, personal communication), while (9b) does require the presupposition of a unique plant that the speaker is referring to, it is structurally fine. In fact, it represents the unmarked word order for expressing this idea, and is clearly better than other starred examples given by Belletti that do seem to violate structural constraints. Evidently, a systematic investigation of this point is called for. G. Lakoff (1971) has argued that the well-formedness of a sentence can *never* be assessed without reference to a set of presuppositions about the nature of the world, and cites numerous sentences where people differ in this regard. For example, whether *My cat enjoys tormenting me* is grammatical depends on whether one believes cats to have minds. In cultures where events are believed to have this property, the equivalent of *My birth enjoys tormenting me* is perfectly normal. Similarly, Lakoff has argued that grammaticality judgments of *John called Mary a Republican and then SHE insulted HIM* depend on the speaker's beliefs, and perhaps even on John's and Mary's. Chomsky (1972) argues instead that such sentences should be considered grammatical regardless of anyone's beliefs, and that it should be left to the semantic component of the grammar to specify the presuppositions they require. (See also Bar-Hillel (1971), who argues against those who feel "obliged to force a clearly pragmatic matter into a syntactico-semantic straitjacket.")

4.5 Conclusion

The studies reviewed in this chapter show that a considerable proportion of individual differences in grammaticality judgments can be attributed to specific linguistically relevant features of the person, be they inborn or the result of experience. Nonetheless, we can be fairly certain that there remains much variation that we cannot factor out in this way. In this regard grammaticality judgments are like most other forms of behavior, including other metalinguistic tasks such as ambiguity detection (Kess & Hoppe 1983). A common genetic endowment provides for a certain degree of commonality, and certain gross parameters of variation, but beyond that differences abound. This state of affairs, however immutable, presents frustrating problems once we acknowledge that the study of grammar, while in principle a study of each individual's mental structures, must appeal to the judgments of many individuals. However, before we resign ourselves completely, we should consider that not all the variation that shows up within and across experiments is attributable to real differences between subjects. Subtle differences in procedures or in the sentences themselves can add error to the actual variation. In the next chapter I turn my attention to such confounding sources.

5 Task-Related Factors in Grammaticality Judgments

MEANDER (a linguist): I have a theory that everybody's eyes are colourless.

SIMPLON (a psychologist): But, Meander, everybody's eyes look brown, blue or green to me.

MEANDER: That's because they are actually wearing contact lenses to color their eyes.

SIMPLON: But, Meander, I know that I don't wear contact lenses, and when I look in the mirror my eyes look blue to me.

MEANDER: Ah: but then, there's a lot we don't know about mirrors.

(Bever 1974)[1]

5.1 Introduction

By now it should not be a surprise to find that grammaticality judgments may vary depending upon the procedure by which they are obtained and properties of the stimulus items that are presented. In fact, the latter assertion might seem tautologous. Obviously, if judgments are to be of any value they must vary depending on the sentences being judged. My focus here, therefore, will be on variation caused by factors that are *irrelevant* to the concept that we are trying to access through grammaticality judgments, namely grammaticality. Clearly there is room for disagreement here, since what should count towards grammaticality is a matter of theoretical assumption or fiat. Similarly, whether an experimental procedure interferes with grammaticality judgments depends on one's view of how best to obtain them. For the most part, the variables I examine in this chapter would be uncontroversially labeled as confounds by the majority of linguists.

Even where there is disagreement, for instance, as to whether context is a nuisance or an integral part of the grammaticality of a sentence, systematic study

---

[1] Tom Bever (personal communication) states that this is a dialogue version of a joke attributed to Haj Ross.

should lead to a better understanding of the phenomenon, and thus improve the linguist's chances of designing effective elicitation procedures. The recommendations I make on the basis of the research reviewed here reflect my own point of view on the nature of grammaticality.

This chapter is essentially a top-down survey of the experimental literature. Section 5.2 covers features of the elicitation process as a whole, beginning with what subjects are asked to do, that is, how the procedure of judging grammaticality is explained to them (Section 5.2.1).[2] This issue will pervade the entire chapter, since differences in instructions could be largely to blame for the staggering discrepancies among experiments, and much of the existing literature is undermined because vague instructions make many of the results virtually uninterpretable. [3] Then I examine the effects of the order in which sentences are presented for judgment (Section 5.2.2). The next three subsections largely follow the research program of one experimenter, Hiroshi Nagata, whose initial work looked at the effects of repeated exposure to the same sentences (Section 5.2.3). This also raises the issue of intrasubject consistency, which was a subsidiary concern of several other experimenters mentioned in this chapter. Later work by Nagata and others brought in mental state manipulations and their interaction with repetition (Section 5.2.4), and sought support for his hypothesized explanations by correlation with subjects who were explicitly told to use certain judgment strategies (Section 5.2.5). The subsequent subsection explores the least-studied procedural variable, which nonetheless could arguably have the greatest impact on judgments – namely, the presentation modality (spoken versus written). Closely tied up with this is the matter of register, since together these two factors define to a large degree the nature of the discourse situation, and hence how grammatically strict or permissive we are liable to be as listeners (Section 5.2.6). Finally, I take a brief look at speed of judgment (Section 5.2.7).

Section 5.3 takes a closer look at the properties of stimulus materials themselves. I begin with the role of the context in which the sentence is situated. I restrict the term *context* to the purely linguistic context, ignoring social factors

---

[2] I do not concern myself here with the much larger question of the range of tasks one might use to elicit information about acceptability. This was discussed to some degree in Section 3.2; further exploration is beyond the scope of this book, since my focus is on judgments.

[3] One feature of the task instructions not covered explicitly in this chapter is the type of judgment required: good/bad or numeric rating or relative ranking. This issue is discussed in Section 3.3.4. I also omit mention of certain standard confounding effects that psychologists typically seek to avoid but that do not seem to have any special impact in the domain of language judgments. Some of these are mentioned in conjunction with the methodological proposals in Section 6.3.

that obviously influence acceptability in the broader sense (see van Dijk (1977) for a discussion of social factors). Nevertheless, the term *context* is used in at least four different ways (Section 5.3.1). My next concern is the extent to which the meaning of a sentence, or the apparent lack of meaning, affects people's judgments of grammaticality, in cases where (we assume) it is an orthogonal issue (Section 5.3.2). I then ask the same question about how easily a sentence is parsed (Section 5.3.3) and the (perceived) frequency of occurrence of sentences of the same type (Section 5.3.4). The final two subsections concern the level of individual words: what happens when one word is replaced by another that is grammatically equivalent (Section 5.3.5), or with one that is grammatically identical (Section 5.3.6). Some potential stimulus variables do not have separate headings devoted to them in this chapter. Intonation is mentioned briefly in conjunction with modality in Section 5.2.6. Its written counterpart, punctuation, does not appear to have been studied for its effects on grammaticality judgments in general (but see Levelt (1974) for some discussion of its possible effects), although it is occasionally mentioned anecdotally in other types of psycholinguistic studies. The most detailed work I am aware of on the linguistic significance of punctuation is by Steegar (1975), who analyzes its relation to prosody. Finally, Section 5.4 summarizes the major implications of the reviewed research.

5.2 Procedural Factors

5.2.1 Instructions

Hill (1961) performed some of the earliest investigations into the nature of grammaticality judgments. He used 10 subjects, of which 3 were linguists and several others were English professors, which should immediately lead us to suspect that his results will not generalize to the population at large. They were instructed to "reject any sentences which were ungrammatical, and to accept those which were grammatical," but there was apparently no definition or explanation of these terms given, nor any examples of their application. The results and anecdotal comments he reports show that subjects had no clear notion of the concept of grammaticality. For instance, while all 10 subjects rejected *Those man left early*, 6 of them accepted *The child seems sleeping*. Even more troubling is the fact that two rejecters of the sentence *I never heard a green horse smoke a dozen oranges* changed their judgments to accept it once it was pointed out to them that the sentence was true.[4] Other subjects explained their acceptance of a sentence by saying that "it sounds like poetry"[5] or rejected a sentence because it did not start with a capital letter. The conclusion to be drawn from all this should be obvious: even subjects who are supposedly experts on language cannot be expected to know what linguists mean by *grammatical* (or *acceptable*, for that matter).[6] If you do not explain to subjects what you want, each one takes his or her own interpretation and the results are meaningless. This criticism was made in the same journal volume by Chomsky (1961); see Lees (1976) for another response to Hill, including an enlightening analogy to a chemistry experiment in which most informants fail to report that iron rusts in water, for various irrelevant reasons – a demonstration of the pitfalls of a naive research strategy. We will see in Section 5.3.2 that Maclay & Sleator (1960) encountered the same problem with linguistically naive subjects. Carden (1976a) was able to avoid contaminating his data with such cases because he used face-to-face interviews. He discovered that one of his subjects rejected all imperative sentences because he would have added *please* to them! In a very widely cited passage, Carden (1970a) states, "You must define 'grammatical' or 'acceptable,' words that naive informants use in widely varying ways. It is of no value to know that 13 informants consider a sentence acceptable unless you know that they mean the same thing by 'acceptable'." Bley-Vroman, Felix & Ioup (1988) found that minimal instructions led to highly inconsistent responses in their pilot studies, while more detailed instructions with examples led to 90% agreement among their experimental subjects. Coleman (1965), Quirk & Svartvik (1966), Schnitser (1973), Cohen (1981), Greenbaum (1977c), Newmeyer (1983), and Botha (1973) make similar points. Birdsong (1989) suggests that the problem is particularly acute when the forms in question occur in speech but are proscribed in writing.

Unfortunately, as we have seen in previous chapters and will continue to see in this one, many studies have fallen into exactly the same trap. In fact, if we were to ignore all studies in which we believe the instructions to subjects were inade-

---

[4] Quirk & Svartvik (1966) respond to this particular finding by disparaging the whole paradigm: "When the notion of what is grammatical is confounded with eternal verities, it is time to look for other techniques of investigation" (p. 12).

[5] This and other irrelevant reactions are taken by Lees (1976) as evidence that, contrary to Hill's conclusion, his subjects in fact demonstrated even greater knowledge of language than was attributed to them by Chomsky's claims, which Hill believed he had refuted.

[6] Actually, it is not even clear that linguists agree among themselves as to what exactly is supposed to count towards grammaticality. As mentioned in Chapter 2, the concept changes as the theory evolves. At the very least, researchers must clarify this point in their own minds before trying to design a set of instructions.

quate to convey the subtlety of a linguistic definition, the remaining studies could likely be counted on one hand. Thus, I will continue my practice of describing the experimenter's instructions in considerable detail, in order that the usefulness of the results can be assessed. But in order to make any progress, we will have to assume that the major findings would hold up under more careful procedures. (Therefore, some of Hill's other results will be reported in subsequent sections.) This is not meant to condone the existing practice or deny the need for replication, but merely to accept the fact that somewhat confounded data are better than none at all. By way of ending on a positive note, I also occasionally report instances of very well designed instructions, and proposals for how to test their effectiveness. For instance, Chaudron (1983) suggests asking subjects what they consider to be valid judgment criteria, and how they make use of these criteria in particular sentences. See Greenbaum & Quirk (1970) for an examination of the instructions surrounding performance tasks.

A recent experiment by (Cowart 1997: 55–59) suggests that as long as subjects are given *some* explicit set of instructions, the exact contents of those instructions might not matter a great deal, at least for some classes of sentence types. He contrasted the same judgment experiment (which involved *that*-trace effects) run with two different sets of directions regarding how subjects were to decide on their responses. One set appealed to their prescriptive sense by invoking English professors marking term papers, the other emphasized the absence of right or wrong answers and appealed to personal reactions. This manipulation turned out to have almost no effect on the pattern of responses. While such negative findings are notoriously hard to interpret, this may be an indication that when other factors are suitably controlled, instructions turn out to be fairly benign, perhaps because subjects really do not have multiple judgment routines they can invoke in such an experiment; regardless of the instructions, they will do the only kind of judging they know how to do. It is up to the experimenter to design stimuli that will not mislead them. My feeling is that due care is still advised in handling instructions, because Cowart's finding does not rule out the possibility that instructions could interact with the type of sentence being judged.

Another important factor, arguably part of the instructions of a judgment task, is the response scale required (Van Kleeck 1982), i.e., how many choices the subjects have and how those choices are described. The former issue is addressed at length in Section 3.3, where I show that little experimental work has looked directly at the differences induced by changes of response scale (but see Cowart (1997: 67–77) for a relevant experiment), and that graded behavior could be an artifact of the testing procedure. The issue of labeling the scale has received even less attention, so I attempt to bring it to the reader's attention whenever the details of an experimental response scale are published. Although some researchers have given advice on this topic (see Section 6.3.2), I am not aware of any research directed specifically at it. Bialystok (1979) did find that response bias among her subjects differed depending on the amount of detail required. When she asked for yes/no responses, subjects were biased toward saying "yes," but when she asked for specific kinds of errors to be identified, they were biased toward finding some error, i.e., toward judging a sentence ungrammatical. Such differences are expected under her theory since the various types of response place different demands on the subjects' analyzed knowledge and cognitive control (see Section 3.4).

5.2.2 Order of Presentation

Greenbaum (1973; 1976a) describes an experiment that looked at the effects of order of presentation of sentences on judgments. It required nonlinguist subjects to rate sentences containing participial *while* phrases attached in various places in a sentence:

(1)　a.　Sophia Loren was seen by the people while enjoying herself.

　　　b.　The people saw Sophia Loren while enjoying themselves.

　　　c.　Judy was seen by the people while enjoying themselves.

　　　d.　The people saw Karen while enjoying herself.

Subjects had a choice of four responses to each sentence: "acceptable," "uncertain, but probably acceptable," "uncertain, but probably unacceptable," and "unacceptable." Two subjects were assigned to each possible ordering of the four sentences, and statistical analysis showed that the first sentence for each group was rated significantly lower than the others. No significant effect was associated with any other position in the list. Clearly, then, sentence order should be controlled for, either by randomization or counterbalancing. The study was essentially a replication of one by Elliot, Legum & Thompson (1969), who apparently used the same order for all subjects, thus severely confounding their results. Problems remain with Greenbaum's procedure as well, however. First, he apparently gave his subjects no explanation of the term *acceptable*. Second, he ignored the standard psychological practice of using warm-up trials to get subjects comfortable with the procedure. If he had done so, the effect of first position might have been removed rather than just counterbalanced, thus reducing the amount of variability in the scores. See Labov (1975: 21) for a review of these two studies and ensuing work. Greenbaum & Quirk (1970) also reported order effects in their test batteries, both for judgment and performance tasks. In one case they found a significant difference between the two orders (between-subjects groups) in the number of subjects giving "grammatical" ratings for 5 out of 51 sentences tested. Interestingly, relative rankings showed almost no changes as a result of varied orders.

Certain effects of presentation order that arise due to relationships among stimulus sentences will be treated as context effects in Section 5.3.1.

5.2.3 Repetition

Nagata has performed a number of experiments investigating the effect of repeated exposure to sentences on judgments of their grammaticality, and the interaction of repetition with other manipulations. According to him, no previous experiments had examined this variable systematically (and I am not aware of any either), but it has important implications, because linguists, the most common producers of judgment data, often consider the grammaticality of sentences many times over the course of investigating some theoretical issue. (Spencer (1973) also speculates on the effects of repeated exposure to sentences on linguists.) Thus, if we have reason to suspect that their judgments are not stable, by the time they draw their conclusions their judgments might be quite different from their first impressions. (This issue comes up again in Section 5.2.7.) Nagata suggests a priori two possible outcomes of a repetition treatment, to which I will add a third. He proposes that judgments might become more lenient (sentences might be considered more grammatical) because subjects would construct additional linguistic or situational contexts for sentences, eventually finding cases where even fairly bad sentences would be reasonably acceptable. This would accord with the general psychological phenomenon of habituation, whereby repeated exposure to the same stimulus has diminishing effect (e.g., the same painful prod will evoke less and less reaction). On the other hand, Nagata postulates, we might expect judgments to become more *stringent* as people differentiate more syntactic or semantic properties of the sentence. That is, the more they look at a sentence, the more things they might find wrong with it. Graeme Hirst (personal communication) has suggested a third possible outcome, namely that repetition might just increase subjects' confidence in their original judgments. In that case, we would expect a polarization of judgments, i.e., good sentences would get better and bad sentences would get worse.

In his first study, Nagata (1988) performed three experiments to examine the basic effect of repetition and its interaction with the presence of context. The procedure was essentially the same for many subsequent experiments as well. His stimulus materials were pairs of grammatical and ungrammatical sentences drawn from the Japanese linguistics literature, matched as closely as possible, plus pairs of filler sentences. Whether the target sentences were considered good or bad was determined on the basis of whether or not they received any question marks or stars in the original source articles. Thus, the number of good and bad sentences would be roughly equal; the total number of sentences was 48. Subjects were asked to rate the extent to which the sentences were grammatical; i.e., "correctly expressed in Japanese," on a scale from 1 to 20. They were told that correct sentences should be rated as 1, while 2–20 indicated increasing degrees of badness. Subjects were also told to make use of the full scale.[7] First, the sentences were presented one at a time in random order on a CRT and the subjects were asked to give their numeric judgments of each, to be used as the baseline measure. In the second part of the procedure, each sentence in turn was presented in a repetition phase, followed immediately by another judgment. In the repetition phase, the sentence was displayed nine times in a row for 3 seconds each time, with a 1-second pause between presentations. During these repetitions, the subject was told to think of the grammaticality of the sentence. Then, upon the tenth presentation the subject was asked once again to rate the sentence. (The order of sentences in this part of the procedure was again random.) The first, unsurprising, result was that the supposedly good sentences received significantly better ratings than the bad ones both before and after repetition, confirming that the a priori division was reasonable. Wayne Cowart (personal communication) points out that this means the *pattern* of results, in terms of relative acceptability of sentences, was not affected by this manipulation. As for the effects of repetition itself, the grammaticality ratings of both kinds of sentence decreased significantly after repetition (i.e., the rating numbers were higher), as compared to before. Nagata concludes that subjects were engaged in differentiation rather than enrichment during the repetition phase. If this result is general, we must reexamine why the theory of mere exposure has been widely accepted in accounting for language change. It holds that as people hear a form more and

---

[7] The only justification given by Nagata for the unusually large rating scale and its asymmetric division (as opposed to making the best sentences 1, the worst 20, and the remainder evenly spread in between) is that the same scheme was used by Moore (1972). But Moore himself gives no justification for these choices. I can only speculate that they might have been inspired by the psychometric results mentioned in Section 3.3. I suggest that Nagata's results might profitably be replicated using a smaller, symmetrical rating scale, but it does not seem to me that his scale would have biased the results. If anything, the large scale should increase variability in the results and make it harder to find significant effects.

more, they like it more, deem it more acceptable, etc.: "familiarity breeds content."[8] To the extent that this is true in language change, why is it not true in Nagata's repetition paradigm? Is the time span involved too short, i.e., is repetition in quick succession different from repetition over a long period of time? Is the problem that all the repetitions come from the same source?

In the first follow-up experiment, the same sentences were used but the final judgments were made with the sentence preceded by a context string.[9] As compared to postrepetition ratings in the first experiment, the with-context condition showed that ungrammatical sentences were judged significantly more grammatical; they showed no significant change from the prerepetition ratings. Ratings for the grammatical sentences did not differ significantly from either the postrepetition ratings in Experiment 1 or the prerepetition ratings in Experiment 2. Nagata believes that this points to a change in encoding or organization of the bad sentences when embedded in context, somehow undoing the change induced by repetition. Apparently, context had some mitigating effect for the good sentences as well, since they failed to show the decrease in grammaticality found in the first experiment. A second follow-up, in which context preceded the target sentences before, during, and after repetition, confirmed the basic finding that context blocks the repetition effect, supposedly because it provides a stabilizing base for judgments.[10] The prerepetition ratings were also compared with those of the first experiment, allowing a direct analysis of the effect of context alone. No significant differences were found, apparently contradicting numerous other studies that found that context raises grammaticality ratings. Nagata suggests that the effect of context was somewhat masked by a ceiling effect, i.e., the sentences were already rated about as high as they could get. See Section 5.3.1 for further discussion of this point.

In two subsequent studies (Nagata 1987a; 1987b), two alternative accounts of the basic repetition finding were ruled out. First, one must consider the possibility that the subjects' use of the rating scale had changed, independent of repetition,

---

[8] Attributed in Bradac et al. (1980) to Walker (1973). Of course, in everyday situations, repeated exposure to a form is not accompanied by an instruction to ponder its grammaticality.

[9] Nagata provides translations of his target and context strings only for the grammatical sentences, of which I give two examples; the targets are italicized: (i) Look out of the window. *It is raining.* (ii) What's the matter with you? *If you don't eat, you'll be hungry.* Apparently the nature of the bad sentences was such that reasonable contexts could still be provided for them.

[10] Spencer (1973) cites several relevant background studies on repetition effects in word recognition, among them one by Taylor & Henning (1963) that reportedly shows a similar type of stabilizing effect: if subjects are told that they will hear only actual words, they do not report that some of the repetitions sound like nonsense syllables, whereas subjects who expect nonsense forms claim to hear them.

because the first set of ratings were made before all the sentences had been seen. Since subjects were told to use the full range of 20 values, and since they would only know which were the best and worst sentences after the first round of ratings, this is a distinct possibility. Thus, a new experiment was designed to seek out such a trend. Sentences were all judged once, then all judged a second time (in a different random order). Since no changes were found between first and second ratings, a "change in the modulus of judgmental scale" account, as Nagata calls it, is ruled out.[11] This result appears to contradict Carden's (1976b) survey of a number of studies that examined the internal consistency of their data by seeking a second rating from subjects some time after the initial data collection. Many of these studies found the second rating to be highly inconsistent with the first. However, Nagata was comparing *mean* ratings of all the good sentences pooled and all the bad sentences pooled, not ratings for individual sentences – a change could have been washed out by intersentence variability. A second potential confound is satiation: prolonged repetition of symbols (e.g., words) has been shown to lead to temporary loss of their meanings and concomitant illusory changes in their perception (see Pynte (1991) for some recent work and a review of the semantic satiation literature, and Section 7.2 on recent satiation research by Snyder). If Nagata's subjects reached satiation for the stimulus materials, the results do not necessarily bear on normal judgments. Since satiation is a short-term phenomenon, this possibility was tested by looking for long-term maintenance of the changes induced by repetition. The subjects from the original experiment were retested on the same sentences 4 months later. Their results were not significantly different from the original postrepetition judgments, and in most cases their ratings were still significantly higher than their original *prerepetition* judgments. That is, whatever had changed in their approach to these sentences still held long after any satiation effect would have worn off. But had they encoded something *specific* to these 48 sentences, something that was maintained in their minds for 4 months without reinforcement, or was it that their judgment process *in general* had changed as a result of greater experience with the task? Nagata does not consider the latter possibility, yet it strikes me as somewhat more plausible, and could be easily tested. For instance, 4 months after the repetition treatment one could give the same subjects novel sentences,

---

[11] Nagata does not discuss the possibility that subjects could have remembered their initial ratings and tried to be consistent by duplicating them the second time around. Since much less time intervened between first and second ratings as compared to conditions in the repetition experiment, the possibility is worth considering. However, given that there were 48 sentences and 20 possible scores for each, and the two presentations were in different orders, I doubt that accurate memory for one's ratings would be possible.

and compare their ratings to those of subjects who had never undergone repetition. If my interpretation is correct, the former group should show significantly more stringent ratings.

A fourth study (Nagata 1989d) was designed to assess the extent to which the repetition effect applies generally to sentence types other than those used earlier. Its first experiment factored out the differential effects of repetition on sentences marked with a question mark as opposed to a star in the original sources. Nagata's hypothesis was that the truly bad sentences could not get any worse through repetition, but in fact both groups of sentences were rated worse in postrepetition judgments. The second experiment used new stimulus materials altogether, instances of the three types of violation identified by Chomsky (see Section 3.3): incorrect lexical category, subcategorization violation, or selectional restriction violation. Here he found that repetition had no significant effect on any of the three types of badness. The latter two, in fact, did not show significant differences between them. His explanation is that these violations were all more blatant than those used in the earlier studies, which involved subtle uses of particles, reflexives, and honorifics. A more blatant violation might be easier for subjects to detect and explain, so they might tend to anchor more on initial judgments and resist change. Thus, at least for ungrammatical sentences, the repetition effect has limited external validity.

The only other study I am aware of that has involved repeated judgments of the same stimuli is one by Carroll (1979). The issue for Carroll was the extent to which complex compound nouns such as *girl that irons her clothes doll* (referring to a doll that looks like a girl and that irons her clothes) are judged acceptable in a sentential context as a function of the syntactic structure of the elements making up the compound. He was cognizant of the potential for a change in use of the (5-point) rating scale on the basis of the range of stimuli he was presenting, especially since subjects might never have seen such complex compounds before, and so he asked his subjects to make a second pass through the sentences, judging them again. While the mean ratings of several sentences did increase from the first to the second judgment, Carroll does not analyze the differences for statistical significance, so we cannot compare his results to those of Nagata. However, the statistical tests that *were* performed show that there were fewer significant differences *among* the 10 sentence types in the second set of judgments than in the first. Apparently, subjects see the range of sentences as more homogeneous the second time around. This study can also be held up as a rare example of one that took care to ensure that subjects had a strong understanding of the basis on which they were to make their judgments. Carroll gave example sentences with their ratings, discussed why the ratings had been chosen, and encouraged questions about the rating system (see Carroll 1979: 874–875).

5.2.4 Mental State

The next step in Nagata's project was to investigate the interaction of repetition with mental state, specifically the effect of objective versus subjective self-awareness. Before describing his study, I digress briefly to explore the nature and history of this manipulation and its application to language. There is a standard operational technique from social psychology that is used to manipulate the introspective set of subjects, inspired by the social facilitation effect: observation of yourself or others engaged in the same activity makes you do that activity more intensely. For example, people will ride a bike faster if they see other people riding bikes. Duval & Wicklund (1972) brought together a large number of findings in this area and unified them under the theoretical distinction of subjective versus objective self-awareness, states of consciousness directed at the external environment or at oneself, respectively. By their definitions, subjective self-awareness (SSA) is a state of consciousness in which attention is focused on events external to the individual's consciousness, personal history, or body; you are the *subject* of consciousness directed outward, the source of perception and action, but are not aware of yourself as experiencer. Objective self-awareness (OSA) is exactly the opposite state: your consciousness is focused on yourself, your own conscious state, personal history, or body: you are the *object* of your own consciousness, a state that often leads to self-evaluation and negative affect, by inducing self-comparison with external standards. SSA is humans' primary or default state; the environment normally draws your attention. OSA requires a reminder of your status as object in the world – stimuli that cause a shift of attention to yourself, such as looking in a mirror, hearing your voice on tape, seeing a photograph of yourself, or having a TV camera pointed at you. Once you are in the OSA state, attention shifts to your relevant features, regardless of which sort of stimulus induced the state.

One experiment that Duval & Wicklund used to demonstrate this manipulation went as follows. The experimenter described to the subject a hypothetical scenario involving him or her, such as a traffic accident. For each situation, subjects were asked to rate how responsible they were for the outcome, that is, how much of the causality was attributable to them. There were two conditions: the experimental room may have had a mirror in it, positioned so that subjects would see themselves in it (the OSA condition), or it may have had the nonreflective back of the mirror facing them (the SSA condition). The result was that OSA subjects attributed significantly more causality to themselves than SSA subjects. In another experiment, subjects were given an intelligence test. They were then told that they scored below average on it, left alone in a room with a clock, and instructed that if no one returned, they could leave after a certain number of minutes had passed. Again, self-awareness was manipulated by the presence or absence of a mirror. The OSA subjects tended to leave the room significantly sooner than the SSA subjects, supposedly because the mirror leads to negative feelings: subjects were constantly reminded of their "below-average intelligence." Note that in this case, unlike the previous experiment, there was no reporting involved. The manipulation affected the subjects' actions, not just their statements.

Carroll, Bever & Pollack (1981) conducted the first study I am aware of that applied self-awareness manipulations to linguistic intuitions. Their premise was quite similar to mine: since intuitions are produced by performance mechanisms, they wanted to control and study these mechanisms, specifically by manipulating mental state. They had a quasi-theoretical goal as well, which was to show that different mental states could produce intuitions that correspond to two competing theories of the relation between syntax and semantics, namely autonomous syntax and abstract syntax. Therefore, it was not a case of choosing one theory over another. Rather, both theories were correct, and they simply accounted for different kinds of intuitions.

Table 5.1: Mean Truth Ratings of Sentences as a Function of Self-Awareness (Carroll, Bever & Pollack 1981).

Sentence Type	SSA Condition	OSA Condition
A house is a building	9.55	9.60
A garage is a building.	7.60	8.60
A lean-to is a building.	**5.40**	**7.35**
A tent is a building.	3.25	4.50
OVERALL	6.45	7.51

Since this theoretical issue is not of concern to us here, and in fact is no longer much discussed, I will ignore the potential theoretical implications of the results and merely concern myself with the effects produced on judgments themselves. Carroll, Bever & Pollack suggested that linguists rendering intuitions need to be in something like the OSA state. Unlike a regular speaker, who is subjectively preoccupied and will tend to produce speech errors and ambiguities without noticing them (as Duval & Wicklund themselves suggest), linguists must cease being speaker-hearers to pause and reflect on the linguistic signal, to "objectify the sentence from all the specific potential functional contexts of its utterance." In a pilot study, they had subjects rate the truth of categorical statements like those listed in Table 5.1 on a scale of 1 (least true) to 10 (most true). In one condition, subjects had to use an answer key that was stuck to a mirror to fill out the questionnaire, but were not otherwise instructed to look at the mirror; the other condition had no mirror. The mean ratings for the two conditions are shown in Table 5.1 (from Carroll, Bever & Pollack 1981: 372). Overall, subjects in the OSA condition gave higher truth ratings. Furthermore, the greatest difference between the groups occurred on sentences like the one highlighted in the table – sentences that are technically true but pragmatically unlikely. The authors propose the explanation that OSA subjects consider more potential communicative situations than SSA subjects, and this is most important for the marginal cases. The false sentences are pragmatically appropriate in very few situations, and the paradigmatic ones require no contextualization to establish their truth. The more general conclusion is that self-awareness manipulation does make itself felt in linguistic tasks, although it is worth noting that the *relative* truth ratings were the same for both groups.

Thus, Carroll, Bever & Pollack proceeded to their central investigation. Since it does not concern grammaticality judgments, my summary will be rather brief, focusing on those aspects that are relevant to Nagata's study. The task was to rate the pair-wise similarity of sentences from the following sort of paradigm:[12]

Active:	The morning sun dried the sweet raisins.
Passive:	The sweet raisins were dried by the morning sun.
Inchoate:	The sweet raisins dried in the morning sun.
Were-Inchoate:	The sweet raisins were dried in the morning sun.
Cause:	The morning sun caused the sweet raisins to dry.
Because:	The sweet raisins dried because of the morning sun.

The relevant feature of this group of sentences is that they are semantically very close but syntactically quite different. The prediction was that OSA subjects, who are more aware of social interaction, would be more sensitive to communicative similarity, since they consider a wider range of potential situations for the utterances, and would thus differ from SSA subjects, who would focus on the surface form of sentences. This prediction was borne out. OSA subjects gave higher sim-

---

[12] Subjects were not told what to use as a basis for measuring similarity, so once again we have the potential for widely varying interpretations.

ilarity ratings overall; in addition, the multidimensional scaling plots come out quite different for the two groups. Carroll, Bever & Pollack take their results to show that people might use different *strategies for interpreting intuitions*, depending on the situation. Extrapolating from their statement, one could imagine that people have intuitions about *both* the structural and communicative properties of sentences, but how these are weighted in coming to an overall similarity measure would depend on whether the situation prompted communicative versus sentential assessment.[13]

Let us now return to the realm of grammaticality judgments, and specifically to the experiments reported by Nagata (1989a), which investigated the effects of self-awareness and its interaction with the repetition manipulation previously described. Nagata started from the assumption that in his earlier repetition studies, subjects were in an SSA state (since there was nothing to trigger OSA), and hence used sentential strategies like Carroll, Bever & Pollack's SSA subjects. Perhaps repetition would have a different effect on OSA subjects: over multiple repetitions they might consider more potential situations or contexts for the sentences and thus rate them more grammatical (recall this idea from Nagata's original experiment). The first test of this hypothesis involved the same repetition paradigm as before, except that in the OSA condition there were mirrors on either side of the CRT where sentences appeared, and the subjects were told to look at themselves in the mirror while making judgments and while thinking of the grammaticality of sentences during repetition. The SSA subjects showed a worsening of ratings, as in previous studies, but OSA subjects showed no change of ratings after repetition. Thus, it seems that the mirror manipulation did negate the effects of repetition, although it failed to induce greater leniency in judgments. Nagata was convinced that such a leniency effect should be demonstrable, and suggested that it was undermined by possible ceiling effects, unclear instructions, and overexposure to the mirror (that is, it might have begun to induce the communicative strategy on initial judgments, leaving less room for measurable change after repetition). A follow-up experiment tried to solve these problems by using only intermediately rated sentences (to avoid the ceiling, but in the process limiting the generality of the result), omitting mirrors from the initial judgment phase, and explicitly telling subjects to simultaneously look at themselves in the mirror and think about the sentences' grammaticality. Note that this

---

[13] If all that is involved is a communicative orientation, as opposed to seeing *oneself* objectified, one might expect other procedures to have the same effect, e.g., showing someone a photograph of another person instead of the mirror. To my knowledge, such an experiment has not been done.

is a much more explicit and forceful use of the mirror manipulation than the one used by Duval & Wicklund or Carroll, Bever & Pollack. Furthermore, no significant effect of self-awareness had been found for the before-repetition judgments in the first experiment. Apparently this particular procedure is not as susceptible to self-awareness manipulations as those others. This might be because judging grammaticality is more inherently a structural task, as compared to judging sentence similarity or truth. Despite all this emphasis, the OSA judgments came out only marginally more lenient after repetition. A second follow-up experiment was done to rule out a potential confounding variable: it is possible that the division of subjects' attention between mirror watching and sentence pondering could have created ratings different from those of the SSA subjects, independent of the fact that the competing activity was related to self-awareness. Thus, Nagata gave subjects a simple arithmetic problem to solve as a distractor during the repetition phase, instead of mirror gazing, to see whether division of processing resources could account for the previous finding. In this condition, there was no change in judgments after repetition as compared to before, so division of attention *can* nullify the repetition effect. However, there was no trend toward *increasing* ratings, so to the extent that such an effect is reliable, it cannot be explained by processing load alone: self-awareness must be considered.[14]

5.2.5 Judgment Strategy

Nagata concludes from the preceding three experiments that, in judging grammaticality, SSA subjects focus on syntactic and semantic structure, while OSA subjects look at pragmatic use. If this is so, then Carroll, Bever & Pollack's suggestion that linguists need to be in the OSA state seems misguided, at least for the purposes of judging grammaticality. But note that so far we have only circumstantial evidence concerning the actual strategies used. Nagata (1989c) wanted to explore this by explicitly telling subjects what sort of strategy to use in making their judgments, rather than inducing a strategy indirectly with mirrors and such. If the two explicit strategies show the same respective effects as the mirror versus no-mirror conditions, we have suggestive (though not conclusive) evidence that the interpretation of those effects is on the right track. This experiment again used sentences of intermediate grammaticality, where the leniency effect of OSA had shown up. One group of subjects was told to "analyze each sentential structure independently of sentential and/or situational contexts," and consider the

---

[14] This is not an airtight argument. Perhaps the arithmetic task, which involved subtracting 2 from an integer, was not as demanding as mirror gazing.

parts of speech involved, during the repetition phase. The other group had to "[supply] sentential and/or situational contexts to each sentence such that each sentence could be used in such contexts."[15] The standard repetition paradigm was used, except that after the repetition phase subjects had to describe what they had been thinking, so the experimenter could be sure they followed the desired strategy. Those who did not had their results discarded. While the differentiation condition produced significantly more ungrammatical ratings after repetition, the enrichment group showed only a nonsignificant tendency toward leniency. Again, Nagata tries to explain why the expected trend did not reach significance: apparently the enrichment strategy is hard to use, and even the subjects who seemed to describe the appropriate thoughts might not have used it as intended. But it is hard to see why subjects should use less of a strategy when explicitly told how to follow it than when it is induced indirectly by the mirror manipulation. This question casts some doubt on Nagata's interpretation of the OSA leniency effect. Perhaps the possibility that OSA affects reporting more than linguistic analysis is worth investigating further after all, if a more convincing demonstration of the change in judgment strategy cannot be made. As Bever's epigraph at the beginning of this chapter suggests, there certainly is a lot we don't know about mirrors.

Nonetheless, some more general conclusions can be unequivocally drawn from Nagata's studies. First, it is clear that the details of the process of intuitive judgment cannot be ignored when using intuitions for theoretical purposes. On that point, I agree with Carroll, Bever & Pollack as well as with Nagata. More specifically, we can conclude that it is easy to make sentences get worse in people's judgments, but hard to make them get better. Given the stringency effect of repetition, we should expect linguists' judgments to be more stringent than those of nonlinguists, at least on sentences that they have studied in detail. I am not aware of any studies that have been done specifically on sentences that linguists have worked on extensively (but see Snyder (1994), discussed in Section 7.2). More general studies have differed as to whether linguists are more or less lenient than normals (see Section 4.4.1). I would still maintain that the influence of repetition is another valid reason why linguists' judgments should not be used as crucial theoretical evidence. With regard to where the effects of self-awareness come from, they seem to transcend language and thus fit the general description of a cognitive manipulation whose effects carry over into linguistic judgments. The

---

[15] It is not evident from Nagata's description whether these are exact translations of the instructions, or whether subjects were given more explanation. Even knowing the purpose of the experiment, I do not find this wording particularly clear.

repetition effect is more problematic in this regard, however. It runs contrary to basic habituation effects. In fact, I have not been able to find any parallel manipulations in other cognitive domains. If Nagata's suggestion is right, then the effects stem essentially from discerning more fine-grained properties of the stimulus through repeated considerations. If the effects are limited to the particular sentences used rather than to overall ratings, then this is *not* a case of developing expertise, i.e., of increasing the ability to discriminate. Rather, a parallel effect would have to involve complex stimuli whose properties are not all apparent on first exposure, e.g., a complex geometric figure containing multiple subfigures that must be picked out. Finally, it is evident that psychological effects can interact in unpredictable ways, so that a complete understanding cannot be achieved merely by identifying each effect in isolation.

5.2.6 Modality and Register

Vetter, Volovecky & Howell (1979) were interested in the potential effects of modality of presentation and intonation on grammaticality judgments, although their main interest was with meaningfulness (see Section 5.3.2). They used five conditions for sentence presentation: visual presentation only, auditory presentation only, both presentations simultaneously, and the latter two modes with normal or monotone intonation. Interestingly, they found no overall effect of mode of presentation, although 16 of 60 particular conditions did show significant differences, which suggests to me that this variable is worth investigating more closely. But the basic result that intonation is not a factor echoes similar results in the domain of spoken surface-structure ambiguity resolution. Studies by Berkovits (1981; 1982) have shown that intonation plays a very limited role in disambiguating such sentences, being easily overridden by the inherent bias of the sentence or the surrounding context unless a subject's attention is explicitly drawn to prosodic cues. (On the other hand, Hill (1961) describes some cases where reading a sentence with normal intonation, as opposed to presenting it in written form, increased the number of acceptances. For reasons discussed in Section 5.2.1, his results should be taken very cautiously, however.)

The absence of any modality effect is at odds with the widely held belief that our judgment criteria are much stricter for written materials than for speech. (In line with this intuition, Bialystok & Ryan (1985) argue that oral presentation stresses meaning, whereas written presentation more naturally elicits attention to structure.) However, the issue of register is tied up in this as well. A formal speech would have to meet higher standards of grammaticality than a casual conversation. Greenbaum (1977b) suggests that written questionnaires present a fairly formal context for subjects, which might show up in sentence ratings as a preference for the more formal of two alternatives if they are compared side by side. He also suggests (Greenbaum 1977c) that the content of sentences could itself imply stylistic differences, e.g., scientific versus literary, which could evoke differential treatment from subjects. Yet another confounding factor could be the degree of preparation. Prepared text, whether spoken or written, can be freed of errors, whereas in spontaneous production speakers (or writers in certain circumstances) must be allowed some leeway in extricating themselves from grammatical culs-de-sac. Biber (1986) has done an extensive factor analysis of dimensions along which various kinds of written and spoken language differ, by analyzing 545 text samples of 16 different types, ranging from telephone conversations to government documents. He arrives at three major factors that account for much of the variation on 41 linguistic features that have been suggested to reflect spoken/written differences. None of these factors correlates entirely with speech versus writing. The first factor, interactive versus edited text, separates texts with high personal involvement and real-time constraints from those that have highly explicit lexical content and where much editing is possible. The second factor, abstract versus situated content, reflects the degree to which the style is detached and formal or concrete and colloquial. The third factor, reported versus immediate style, differentiates narrative about removed situations from present-tense description. Biber successfully uses these dimensions to reconcile the findings of numerous previous studies concerning spoken/written differences. One might approach the unraveling of these factors experimentally by using linked computer terminals that allow written communication with various speeds of transmission: instantaneous letter-by-letter, line-by-line, or complete messages (Graeme Hirst, personal communication). Whichever factor or factors determine one's degree of tolerance, we are then left with explaining how these various levels of grammaticality criteria are encoded in the mind: different grammars, different parsing rules, a reduced threshold on the same parsing rules, etc. I return to these issues in Chapter 6.

There are additional features of language that are related to register to some extent and that Ross (1979) speculates might have systematic effects on grammaticality judgments. These include clarity, awkwardness, slanginess, and floweriness. While these have likely been examined in a sociolinguistic context, I am not aware of any research looking for them as confounds where grammaticality was the property subjects were targeting. One might also expect that the modality of the subjects' response could show some effect of register. This idea was tested by Davy & Quirk (1969), replicating some of Quirk & Svartvik's (1966) testscompliance tests but using oral responses: subjects had to say the new version of the sentence, or answer judgment questions with "yes," "no," or "can't decide." The results of the judgment tests closely paralleled those of Quirk & Svartvik, with one notable exception. Davy & Quirk's subjects gave many fewer middle responses. The authors suspect that this is not a register effect, but rather is due to the fact that "can't decide" has negative connotations, suggesting indecision on the subject's part, which the corresponding written response "?" lacked. Thus, it seems that response modality does not much influence judgments. However, a positive conclusion to come out of this study is that much information can be gained from verbal responses. For instance, from the performance tasks the authors were able to gather data on subjects' hesitations, drawled segments, tempo, volume, pitch, and rhythm, which were useful in the analysis (although the interpretation is somewhat subjective), for instance, in finding the location of ungrammaticality within a sentence.

5.2.7 Speed of Judgment

Studies differ as to the amount of time subjects are given to make their judgments. In most cases, written questionnaires are self-paced, although they may also be speeded, i.e., subjects may be told to work quickly. Experiments using computer control (usually also measuring reaction time) may limit the amount of time a sentence is visible, and also limit the time available for judgment before the next sentence appears. This raises the issue of whether we want a subject's initial reactions to a sentence, or a carefully reasoned decision resulting from some amount of deliberation. Presumably these two kinds of judgments would differ, although the matter has not been much studied directly. Bialystok (1979) found that changing the response time in a yes/no grammaticality judgment task from 3 seconds to 15 seconds did not affect the accuracy of responses by her nonnative learners of French. Greenbaum (1977c) cites unpublished work by Legum, Elliot & Thompson (1974) as finding that different judgments resulted from timed versus self-paced tasks, but gives no further details. A study by Warner & Glass (1987), detailed in Section 5.3.1, found that context effects were attenuated by the delay in self-paced as opposed to on-line judgments. Also, I suggest in Section 5.2.3 that prolonged consideration of a sentence might induce effects similar to those found in Nagata's repetition treatment.

Obviously, if our goal is to examine the on-line processing of grammaticality, its effects on parsing, and so forth, then first reactions will be most useful. But if it is the status of sentences that concerns us, it is not clear which should be preferred. One advantage to first impressions is that there is little time for the subject to consider (potentially irrelevant) extrasentential factors. In fact, subjects might be able to go into a mode in which they ignore such factors. Mistler-Lachman (1972) found this to be the case in judgments of meaningfulness. Specifically, she argues that subjects can reach a kind of understanding that falls short of full interpretation, involving only "awareness of the potential for interpretation." In this mode, the time it takes subjects to give yes/no meaningfulness judgments does not increase with ambiguous sentences, and is not reduced by supporting context, although these factors are known to affect the time subjects take when reading for comprehension. Quick judgments are also useful because, given enough time, subjects might find structural analyses that we would not want them to find. Gleitman & Gleitman (1970) suggest an interpretation that someone with ingenuity could find for Maclay & Sleator's (1960) sentence *Label break to be calmed about and* (see Section 5.3.2), which leads them to make a distinction between "blithely accepts as grammatical" versus "after deep thought accepts as grammatical." In cases where initial reactions are desired, we need a methodology for getting them. The cost of computer-controlled experimentation can be prohibitive as compared to the cost of administering questionnaires, so some authors have tried to use the latter.[16] (In fact, Greenbaum (1977c) argues against the use of time-limited judgments anyway, since they fail to take account of individual differences in judgment speed.) For instance, the instructions in Heringer's (1970) study (discussed in Section 4.2) told subjects to refrain from changing their response after the initial judgment or rereading sentences that had already been judged; Greenbaum (1977b) told subjects not to turn back to previous pages in the questionnaire booklet, and to work as quickly as they could without being careless.

---

[16] Jim McCawley (personal communication) suggests that interesting effects might show up by using the inexpensive technology of videotape. His experience is that the discrepancies in time taken by different subjects to raise their hands in response to a sentence they are judging is large enough that frame-by-frame viewing would show clear differences.

5.3 Stimulus Factors

5.3.1 Context

> *Unhappily, the recurrent embarrass-*
> *ment of the generative grammarian*
> *is that his students and his critics*
> *are forever contriving situations in*
> *which the sentences he had needed to*
> *believe were ungrammatical turned*
> *out to be completely appropriate.*
>
> (Fillmore 1973)

I agree wholeheartedly with Bever (1970a) on the issue of context: "A science of the influence of context on acceptability judgements is as necessary in linguistic research as in every other area of psychology" (p. 347). First, however, we must set straight exactly what is meant by the term *context*, which tends to be bandied about rather casually. While the common folklore holds that sentences usually sound better in context, we shall see that this really only applies to one of the possible kinds of context. In this subsection I report on four types of context manipulation. First, I look at a few studies dealing with a context consisting of semantically or pragmatically related content. This is the most extensively studied of the four types, and I cannot hope to cover the entire literature here. One large subdomain that I systematically exclude is the area of discourse-dependent utterance forms such as ellipses, cross-sentential anaphora, etc. (see van Dijk (1977) for discussion). This seems a reasonable omission, because there do not appear to be too many interesting issues that bear on elicitation methodology. Obviously, if a sentence is dependent on prior sentences for coherence, they must be included when the sentence is judged. The second type of context I consider consists of paradigmatically related sentences; very little work has been done in this area. The same is true for the third type, which consists of the theoretical context under which linguists consider data. The fourth type of context, which seems to have the most insidious implications for grammaticality judging, is made up of structurally related sentences that can set up extraordinary contrasts or prepare us for later sentences.

Bolinger (1968) prefaces his discussion of context effects by saying, "it is worth a moment to consider how a normal sentence can come to be thought abnormal" (p. 35; see also Bolinger (1971)). By this he means that disembodying a sentence from its (semantico-pragmatic) context can make it appear unacceptable when in its original setting it was unexceptional. For the most part, the type of judgment he is concerned with is of semantic rather than syntactic well-formedness. For example, he assumes that *I'm the soup* is ungrammatical in isolation. Nonetheless, some of his observations have implications for our study as well. For instance, a sentence heard out of context will tend to trigger dominant senses of the words it contains. Once a situation for the sentence as a whole is derived from these meanings, secondary senses are not likely to come to mind, even if they would make the sentence grammatical.[17] Situating sentences within a larger discourse (possibly by expanding a single sentence) also improves their acceptability by providing the motivation for marked constructions, such as the clefts in the following examples:

(2)   ? It's a lawyer that he is.

(3)   It wasn't a lawyer that he wanted to be but a doctor.

The low-bias reading of an ambiguous word or phrase can sound bad out of context, as in the following sentence when spoken:

(4)   ? Never have too close friends.

Along similar lines, Bever, Carroll & Hurtig (1976) give the following example:

(5)   a. ? The owner of the horse's steps were rapid.
       b. Because he was in a hurry to place a bet, the owner of the horse's steps were rapid.

See Section 4.2 for the effect of this kind of context on quantifier-negative sentences.

This was the kind of context that Nagata (1988) looked at as well (see Section 5.2.3). Recall that while it did cancel the effects of repetition, it made no significant difference to prerepetition judgments. He points out that, unlike his own materials, experimenters often specifically design their stimuli to be good only under a fairly obscure interpretation, which the context is then designed to bring out (see also Gleitman & Gleitman (1970)). This assessment applies to some of the contexts used in Heringer's (1970) study. For instance, he compared reactions to sentences like (6) with and without the bracketed context:

(6)   John left until 6 pm. [John left earlier and is going to come back at 6.]

---

[17] The example Bolinger gives is not a particularly good one. He claims that *The girl was turned to* tends to be considered ungrammatical in isolation because the extended meaning of *turn to* does not come to mind, but I do not have any trouble with this sentence.

While none of Heringer's 20 subjects accepted (6) without the context, 15 of 39 accepted it with context.[18] It should not be surprising that context improves grammaticality under such conditions, but we cannot conclude from this that *any* semantically coherent context will improve ratings. This was certainly not true for Nagata's contexts, which were appropriate to the target sentence but did not bring out any abnormal readings. Under these conditions, context apparently has no effect, perhaps because some default context is assumed when none is directly supplied (Danks & Glucksberg 1971).

Snow (1975) refers to this type of context as paralinguistic context and suggests that it should always be supplied by the experimenter. We can reasonably expect that when subjects are asked to judge sentences in isolation, they might attempt to call up a suitable linguistic context. If we provide them with such a context instead of leaving them to their own devices, we will most likely find less variation in the resulting judgments. If we further assume that context cannot make a truly ungrammatical sentence seem acceptable (which is likely true for the vast majority of sentences), we are not biasing the outcome of the experiment by giving the sentence its best shot in this way (Householder (1973) concurs). Furthermore, by testing the same sentence in multiple contexts, we can examine the grammatical and discourse factors that distinguish various readings.

Along the same lines, Crain & Steedman (1985) make the important point that a null context is not the same as a neutral context. Rather, the effect of not presenting subjects with an explicit context is that the actual context envisioned by them is not under the experimenter's control. They go on to argue that certain grammatical constructions, notably restrictive modification, are infelicitous in the absence of context, and hence force subjects to do the work of constructing an appropriate context by adding necessary presuppositions to their discourse model in order to interpret the sentence. Their experiments involved a speeded grammaticality judgment task. One showed that reduced-relative garden path sentences are judged more grammatical when the subject is indefinite and hence (they argue) does not presuppose an already mentioned set from which certain members are being singled out. Sentences like (7b) below were judged grammatical significantly more often than their counterparts like (7a) in a yes/no task.

---

[18] These numbers represent a pooling of subjects who answered "acceptable" or "uncertain, but probably acceptable" on the four-choice questionnaire. In explaining this analysis, Heringer acknowledges that "some people apparently use a stricter interpretation of acceptability than others, while what is of interest here is not absolute acceptability but relative acceptability with respect to other sentences" (p. 291, fn. 5). There is also variability in the relative certainty of subjects, i.e., some will give many more "uncertain" responses than others. We must be extremely careful thinking about what information we are trying to extract from judgments, in choosing what to do with raw ratings.

(7)   a. The teachers taught by the Berlitz method passed the test.

   b. Teachers taught by the Berlitz method passed the test.

Crain & Steedman also showed that the grammaticality rating of a particular sentence varied dramatically depending on whether a preceding context supported the presuppositions of the correct versus the incorrect parse. Either completion of a temporarily ambiguous sentence could be judged ungrammatical by at least half the subjects if the context favored the wrong reading. Example (8) illustrates the possible contexts and target sentences.

(8)   a. *Complement-inducing context*
          A psychologist was counseling a married couple. One member of the pair was fighting with him but the other one was nice to him.

   b. *Relative-inducing context*
          A psychologist was counseling two married couples. One of the couples was fighting with him but the other one was nice to him.

   c. *Complement target*
          The psychologist told the wife that he was having trouble with her husband.

   d. *Relative target*
          The psychologist told the wife that he was having trouble with to leave her husband.

Pesetsky (1981) demonstrates how context can interact with grammar in especially intricate and insidious ways. In particular, he shows that Superiority violations can be made to go away, or at least become less severe, if they are presented in a context that encourages the reader to interpret *wh*-words as discourse-linked (D-linked), that is, constrained by some previously established set of alternatives. Thus, although *where* usually cannot follow *what* in a double question, the following setup makes that possible:

(9)   I know that we need to install transistor A, transistor B, and transistor C, and I know that these three holes are for transistors, but I'll be damned if I can figure out from the instructions *where what* goes!

In Pesetsky's account, D-linked *wh*-words have different LF movement requirements than non-D-linked ones have. The relevant point for us is that the grammar is (argued to be) sensitive to a distinction in interpretation that can only be made relative to surrounding context, so getting judgments to reflect the grammar in this respect requires careful control of context. Here, as with Crain & Steedman's examples, it is insufficient to control for or eliminate context effects on judgments. We must consider the effects of particular types of context that the grammar is sensitive to.

Let us turn now to paradigmatically related contexts, by which I mean sentences that fill a parallel role in a paradigm. This can best be seen with an example. One finding of Hill (1961) that probably would hold up under more controlled conditions is that a more structured design (as compared to individual sentence judgments) produces a reduction in interspeaker variation. Hill's experiment involved presenting several sentence groups following the same paradigm, as in (10) and (11):

(10)   The plate is hot. The plate seems hot. The plate seems very hot.

(11)   The child is sleeping. The child seems sleeping. The child seems very sleeping.

In this example, *The child seems sleeping* would presumably be the target sentence of interest. It is surrounded in (11) by two sentences that are related to it in a way that is parallel to the relations among the sentences in (10). This allows subjects to see where the sentence came from by analogy to an unequivocally good sentence. Apparently this procedure helps them to focus on the relevant features of the sentence. This type of parallel analysis is certainly common in linguistic argumentation, but no one else seems to have used it in studying the judgment process itself. In cases where it is feasible, it might prove to be a useful tool. (Recall a related finding by Scott & Mills (1973), reported in Section 3.3.3: viewing all the rearrangements of a sentence together increases grammaticality ratings.)

Spencer (1973) mentions a type of context made up of "the set of rules for which [a] sentence is an exemplar." Snow (1975) seems to mean something similar by the "context of discourse," which she defines as the linguistic issue on which a sentence bears. In both cases, such context is relevant only to linguists, and might actually be entirely implicit, without mention in the materials themselves. For instance, certain examples become closely associated with particular theoretical proposals or disputes by virtue of repeated discussion or published citations, e.g., Chomsky's *Colorless green ideas sleep furiously*. Spencer seems to suggest that when a linguist's initial intuitions about a sentence fail to conform to the context (presumably this means they contradict the theory), the sentence is reorganized to bring the intuition in line (see Section 4.4.1). Unfortunately, her experimental results do not show this in any direct way, and it is in fact hard to imagine a conclusive demonstration of this effect, so it must remain as intriguing speculation for the time being.

Now let us focus on the effects of the fourth kind of context, namely the neighboring stimulus sentences displayed for judgment. It has been common folklore among linguists that marginal sentences can be made to seem more acceptable when preceded by much worse examples and less acceptable when preceded by much better ones (see, e.g., Snow (1975), who calls this the context of judgment, and Levelt (1974: vol. 3)). Bever (1970a; 1974) might have been the first to make this explicit, in connection with the law of contrast from psychology:

> One's "absolute" judgement of a stimulus can be exaggerated by the difference between the stimulus and its context. This influence by contrast clearly can occur in "intuitions" about grammaticality. For example, [(12b)] preceded by [(12a)] may be judged ungrammatical, but contrasted with [(12c)] it will probably be judged as grammatical. (Bever 1970a: 346–47)

(12)   a. Who must telephone her?

      b. Who need telephone her?

      c. Who want telephone her?

Bever describes an analogous effect in color perception: a pale green spot might appear blue when surrounded by a yellow field, but appears green if surrounded by a red field. (Although the examples in (12) are very closed related, contrast effects can be found with unrelated stimuli; see the discussion of Snow (1975) below.) To test the hypothesis for linguistic context, Bever proposes taking a number of sentences from linguistics articles and presenting them in two different orders to two groups for judgment. One group would see them in their original order as they appeared in the source publications, while the other group w.ould see them in random order. Bever predicts that the former group would come much closer to the published judgments than would the latter group. Spencer (1973), as part of the study described in Section 4.4.1, did exactly that. In one condition the order of sentences was completely randomized, while in the other they appeared in their originally published order (the order of the articles was randomized). Unfortunately, the results are reported in the same vague manner as her comparison of naive and nonnaive subjects. We can see that the mean number of sentences accepted by the two groups differed by almost 6%, but we know nothing of the significance of this difference or to what extent the distribution of good and bad ratings differed for the two groups.

Greenbaum (1976a) performed an experiment that made the same point. The crucial sentences exemplified various uses of the verb *dare*:

(13)   We didn't dare answer him back.

(14)   We dared not answer him back.

(15)   We didn't dare to answer him back.

Two of the three sentences appeared together on one page of the experimental booklet, and subjects were implicitly encouraged to compare the two by having to rank which was better, in addition to rendering absolute judgments on the following scale: "perfectly natural and normal"; "wholly unnatural and abnormal"; "somewhere between"; and "not sure." Sentence (15) showed a significant change in absolute rating depending on which of the other two sentences it was paired with: it was judged much better alongside (14) than (13). Among the latter two sentences, (13) was rated significantly better overall. That is, greater contrast produced polarization of the results. Seeing the better alternative, subjects judged (15) even worse. This confirms the prediction made by Bever (1970a), although the results would be more convincing if they could be replicated without any explicit suggestion that subjects should compare the adjacent sentences. Greenbaum's conclusion is that closely related sentences should be presented for judgment as a group, with ordering counterbalanced across subjects, because he believes that in the absence of comparable sentences provided by the experimenter, subjects might try to think up their own related items, so that intersubject differences in ratings could be related to differences in their ability to make such inventions. (This parallels Bolinger's point for semantic contexts.)

Snow (1975) conducted an experiment that demonstrated contrast effects with unrelated sentences. Her test consisted of alternating target and filler sentences. In one condition all the fillers were clearly grammatical, in the other they were clearly awful. Subjects judged acceptability on a yes/no basis. Although no statistical analysis of the raw data is reported, there was clearly a substantial shift in judgments between the two groups: 18 of the 20 target sentences were accepted by more subjects when surrounded by bad fillers, showing a mean increase of 11.7% in the number of subjects who accepted them. The most dramatic example showed a 32% increase. Nagata (1992) reports a similar finding. As Carden & Dieterich (1981) put it, "'ungrammatical' often should be interpreted as 'clearly worse than the "good" examples [a sentence] is being compared to'" (p. 589). They describe a data disagreement over backwards coreference constructions such as *I knew him when Harvey was a little boy*, where *him* and *Harvey* are taken as coreferential (see Section 1.3). A linguist who claims the sentence is bad pairs it with a clearly good example, and vice versa. Carden & Dieterich argue that both good and bad related sentences should be presented for subjects' consideration. Beyond an absolute shift in assigned grammaticality, Cowart (1994, 1997: 22–27) designed a set of experiments to explore the question of whether this kind of context manipulation would affect the *relative* status of sentences. His two conditions involved interspersing among actual linguistically interesting examples a group of filler sentences that were either all quite good or in which one-third of the sentences were awful. As in the previous studies, with bad fillers around subjects gave significantly higher ratings overall to the experimental sentences. However, the *pattern* of results among these sentences was not affected at all by this manipulation. In particular, it was not true, as one might have expected, that those who saw very bad fillers would be less sensitive to subtle differences among the experimental sentences. Thus, if we limit ourselves to relative comparisons, the goodness or badness of filler sentences might not be very important.

The results of some experiments by Warner & Glass (1987) bear on the effects of context by both structural and semantic relatedness. Their main goal was to examine the processing of garden path sentences,[19] but what surfaces as well is a striking case of judgments not reflecting the underlying grammar, because a majority of subjects judged sentences bad that are uncontroversially grammatical. The authors' design allowed them to measure the effects of two kinds of context sentence: those that were structurally similar to the target garden paths and those that were semantically related. Since garden path sentences can mislead the reader by virtue of temporary ambiguities, context sentences could either help or hinder their parsing, by priming either the correct or the misleading choice at the point of ambiguity. Where positive bias was induced, we find examples of the type Nagata mentioned: sentences that would probably be judged bad unless subjects were directed toward the necessary situation or structural analysis. Below are examples of the four possible relations between context and target. In each pair, the first (context) sentence is unambiguously parsable and grammatical, while the second (target) sentence is a garden path:

(16)   *Syntactically related, positive bias:*
   a.   When the girl sleeps the cat eats.
   b.   When the boys strike the dog kills.

---

[19] The authors use the term *garden path* to refer to all sentences with temporary ambiguities, regardless of whether people actually tend to fail on their first parse of them.

(17)   *Syntactically related, negative bias:*

    a. If the girl pets the cat she sings.

    b. When the boys strike the dog kills.

(18)   *Semantically related, positive bias:*

    a. The cat attacks because the boy harms the man.

    b. While the boy kills the man the cat strikes.

(19)   *Semantically related, negative bias:*

    a. The boy attacks when the man is hurt by the cat.

    b. While the boy kills the man the cat strikes.

Their first experiment elicited speeded grammaticality judgments and found there was a significant main effect of context. Sentences preceded by positive-bias context received an average 87% rating, while those with negative-bias context received only a 65% grammaticality rating. There was no significant difference between syntactic and semantic contexts. However, a subsequent self-paced judgment task showed no context effects in most cases. The authors suggest that this change is attributable to the relative speed of judging. At their own pace, subjects would not be reaching final judgment decisions until much longer after reading the context sentences. Thus it appears that context-induced priming is a fleeting phenomenon, which might account for some of the discrepancies in the literature. Interestingly, in the absence of any biasing context, the class of garden paths that are hardest to process (namely, those requiring an intransitive reading of a transitive verb and with a delayed resolution of the ambiguity, such as *Before the boy kills the man the dog bites strikes*, were judged grammatical 25% of the time, or only as often as ungrammatical control sentences (e.g., *Who is strong killed that strike men*).[20] Apparently, people either are not very persistent or not very creative in looking for alternative parses, because this result held up in the self-paced experiment as well.

Milne (1982) presents both anecdotal and quantitative evidence corroborating this finding for other kinds of garden paths. For instance, when asked to judge

---

[20] Many of these potential garden path sentences normally require additional punctuation. Nonetheless, Warner & Glass did not include it in their materials. See Frazier & Rayner (1982) for an attempt to justify this common methodology. See Mitchell & Holmes (1985) for evidence that adding the appropriate punctuation significantly changes the processing of such sentences. The latter result does not invalidate the conclusion that context can affect parsing (interacting with other cues), but we must be cautious in our conclusions about the status of an incorrectly punctuated sentence.

whether *The prime number few* was a complete sentence or only a fragment, all 47 of his subjects thought it was a fragment. In a timed comprehension task, *The horse raced past the barn fell* took an average of 10.13 seconds to read, with many subjects still reporting they had not understood it after that period. Bever (1970b) hypothesizes that such reduced-relative sentences would be parsed much more readily if an example pair consisting of full and reduced versions of a sentence were presented first, and Matthews (1979) reports such a result on a judgment task, although he gives no quantitative data. Thus, methodological caution is advised. If we suspect that the specific reading of a sentence that we want to test is hard for human parsers to arrive at, independent of whether it is grammatical, we should make every effort to ensure that subjects think of the right reading. Otherwise, rejections on the basis of ungrammaticality are confounded with those based on never having "found" the sentence in question.

The main conclusion from these studies of context is that it does not make sense to speak of *the* effect of context on judgments, because the type of context and its relation to the sentences in question must be considered. Context can be used to make sentences look better or worse than they appear in isolation; whether this is desirable will depend on the goals of particular investigations.

5.3.2 Meaning

The earliest study that I am aware of that looked specifically at the nature of linguistic intuitions as expressed in judgments about sentences was done by Maclay & Sleator (1960). They were specifically interested in the extent to which subjects could judge grammaticality independent of meaningful content and likelihood of occurrence, so they asked subjects whether each stimulus sentence was grammatical, meaningful, and ordinary. (By the latter term they meant "occurring with high frequency," so that this portion of the study might belong in Section 5.3.4, which deals with frequency; but since it is not clear whether their subjects interpreted it this way, I keep the main discussion together.) Unfortunately, they apparently did not give subjects any further explanation as to the intended meanings of these terms, and some of their results clearly show that at least some subjects did not take the desired interpretation. One good feature of this procedure, however, is that it allows subjects to voice opinions on these issues separately. If people feel a sentence is meaningless or has no chance of occurring in natural speech, they will want to convey this opinion. If they are not asked specifically for the information, they will likely allow it to affect their responses on other matters, such as grammaticality (Elizabeth Cowper, personal communication). The experimenters had designed the sentences to represent various combinations of the three dimensions, e.g., grammatical but not meaningful and not ordinary. In addition, one group of grammatical sentences contained deliberate violations of "grammar school" rules, e.g., incorrect uses of *I/me*, that do occur in casual speech and ought (according to Maclay & Sleator) to be generated by a linguistic grammar.

Sentences were presented orally with normal intonation.[21] For sentences that were intended to be grammatical but not meaningful or ordinary (e.g., *Colorless green ideas sleep furiously*), significantly more subjects said "yes" to the grammaticality question than to the other two questions. Maclay & Sleator take this as evidence that subjects were making the intended distinctions and judging grammaticality independent of the other two variables (but see below). Across all the sentence types and all three rating criteria, the relative ratings conformed to prior classifications. Positive instances got a greater percentage of "yes" responses than noninstances. However, the absolute numbers were less convincing. The aforementioned grammatical-nonmeaningful-nonordinary sentences received only a 50% grammatical rating, as did those that violated only the prescriptive rules.[22] The other absolute numbers were similarly disappointing, often indicating approximately neutral ratings on average for all three criteria. From their lack of clear-cut outcomes, the authors conclude that there is no empirical basis on which to classify sentences as grammatical versus ungrammatical, or even into multiple discrete levels of grammaticality, and that we must be content with comparative rankings only. Why they discount the latter possibility without attempting to elicit multivalued ratings is not clear to me. But perhaps the most telling part of their conclusion is the admission that 3 of their 21 subjects said that *Label break to calmed about and* was grammatical. Furthermore, Quirk & Svartvik (1966) point out that this 14% acceptance rate compares with 19% acceptance for *Nor if I have anything to do with it*. Since these were all native speakers of English, they clearly were not applying grammaticality in the intended way, and so the experimental results do not represent a unitary phenomenon.

Vetter, Volovecky & Howell (1979) performed a follow-up to Maclay & Sleator's experiment, because they felt that the latter authors did not have statistical justification for the claim that grammaticality was being judged independently of the other two variables. Their new experimental design allowed for the direct assessment of such claims. They used the same 36 stimulus sentences as Maclay and

---

[21] It is not clear to me how the strings of word salad could be read with normal intonation; a standard contour would have to be placed arbitrarily over the words.

[22] Bradac et al. (1980) also looked at errors of "school grammar," but found most subjects oblivious to them.

Sleator, but made a small attempt to improve the instructions. For instance, in one condition subjects were asked, "Is this word sequence grammatical? In other words, is it acceptable English?" These instructions still leave a lot of room for interpretation and in this experiment we have direct evidence concerning how the subjects tried to perform the various discriminations. But first, let us look at their results. As in the previous study, an ANOVA showed a significant effect of type of sentence – grammatical versus meaningful versus ordinary – but Vetter, Volovecky & Howell correctly point out that such a finding is difficult to interpret because these do not represent values on a single dimension. Pair-wise chi-square tests of independence showed that in some of the conditions grammaticality and ordinariness were significantly related, whereas in other conditions meaningfulness and ordinariness were related. Thus, this study contradicts the earlier claim and suggests that these factors do influence each other. Other results largely replicated those of Maclay & Sleator. Sentence groups that were supposed to differ only on grammaticality did show a significant difference on that parameter, and similarly for the other variables. Once again, however, the most definite conclusion we can draw from this study is that much more work is needed on conveying to all subjects the same notion of grammaticality, as evidenced by the following remarks from the study's high-school-aged subjects regarding how they decided whether a sentence fit the criteria. For grammaticality, they considered punctuation, making sense, whether the sentence was "smooth," and "what I learned in elementary school about correct grammar"; for meaningfulness, they considered "pausing and verbalization," "if words could be rearranged to make sense," whether the "order of words seemed similar to reverse order in German," and whether it was "true or something that could happen"; for ordinariness, they considered that "word order inverted was ordinary, since it's natural in French," answered "yes" if the sentence "didn't make sense but had normal subject and verb order," and factored in "the way the words were typed."[23] From these reports it is clear that the ratings could not represent anything approaching a unitary phenomenon, a fact that might invalidate all the other conclusions of the experiment anyway.

Let me briefly review some other experiments on meaning and grammaticality. Danks & Glucksberg (1970) looked at grammaticality, meaningfulness, and ordinariness, plus familiarity, in conjunction with data used by Coleman (1965); see Section 3.3.3. They asked subjects to rate sentences on one of these dimensions using a 10-point scale; none of the terms was defined for them. They found that *fa-*

---

[23] There were also a few responses that seemed to bear some resemblance to the desired interpretation of the terms.

miliar and *ordinary* were treated the same by subjects. By principal components analysis, meaningfulness and familiarity were not independent, but meaningfulness and grammaticality were. Coleman (1965) performed a statistical analysis on Hill's (1961) data and found that 86.6% of his meaningless sentences were judged grammatical (significantly more than chance), from which Coleman infers that Hill's subjects were able to distinguish these two dimensions. Moore (1972) (see Section 3.3.2) reports a case where the existence of a metonymic or metaphoric reading of a literally ungrammatical sentence might have contributed to its being rated significantly higher than other structurally identical ones, which could be viewed as a meaning confound. The sentence in question was *College students read many professors,* which supposedly violates selectional restrictions on the verb *read.* But, as Moore correctly and humorously points out, "A college professor may be read in the sense that Plato is read; alternatively, professors may have such transparent neuroses that they are easily 'read' by their students" (p. 558). It might also be true that meaning and meaningfulness affect the difficulty of performing grammaticality-related tasks. For instance, Ryan & Ledger (1984) suggest that more cognitive control is required to correct a grammatical error in a false sentence than in a true one, in order to ignore its falsity. Bialystok (1986) claims that judging an ungrammatical meaningful sentence takes more analyzed knowledge, whereas judging a grammatical anomalous one takes more cognitive control. As evidence for the latter claim, she shows that bilingual children (who are claimed to have superior cognitive control skills) perform better than monolinguals on this kind of item.

5.3.3 Parsability

To the extent that the human parsing mechanism does not accept precisely the same set of sentences as the grammar, we should expect that cases where the parser fails might be taken as unacceptable, even if upon further consideration we feel that they are grammatical (Clark & Haviland 1974).[24] This is perhaps the most obvious case where speed of judgment would be expected to make a large difference in judgments, since the parser might take a while to process a difficult sentence, e.g., the garden paths used by Warner & Glass (1987); see Section 5.3.1. Once we discover their intended structure, we agree that they must be grammatical, but due to parsing failure our initial judgments tend to be negative. Van Kleeck (1982) suggests that sentence length and complexity will affect judgments.

---

[24] The reverse does not strike me as very likely, i.e., just because a string is easy to parse does not make us consider it grammatical; but see Section 2.2 for some pathological cases.

To this I would add any other factors that might make a sentence hard to parse, such as multiple center-embedding or the serial position of an error; on the latter, see Section 3.3.3 for a relevant experiment by Marks (1967). Finally, parsability is closely related to correctability, also discussed in Section 3.3.3: the closer a bad sentence is to satisfying all the parser's constraints, the easier it will generally be to correct.

5.3.4 Frequency

Another possible factor in judgments is the frequency of occurrence of the stimulus materials. This could be taken in at least two ways, to refer to the frequency of the lexical items in the sentences, or of the sentence structures themselves. I am not aware of the former having been studied, but Greenbaum (1976b; 1977b) looked at the latter.[25] His experiments involved judgments on closely related sentence pairs such as active/passive and dative movement contrasts. In the first phase, subjects (who were linguistically naive) had to judge the sentences' "overall frequency in the English Language" on a 5-tiered scale from "very rare" to "very frequent." In the second phase, which occurred a week later, the same subjects were asked to rate the *acceptability* of the same sentences, again on a 5-tiered scale, from "completely unacceptable" to "perfectly OK." Greenbaum compared mean numeric scores across 87 subjects and found that, for each sentence, the acceptability rating was within one point of the frequency rating. (In most cases, acceptability was rated higher than frequency.) On the surface, this suggests that the two ratings are highly correlated, but no statistical tests were carried out and there is a potential confound in the experimental procedure. We do not know if subjects were aware that they were supposed to be judging something completely different the second time. They might have taken the instructions as merely a variation in wording of the original procedure. (This possibility could easily be tested using a between-subjects design.) To the extent that the aforementioned results of Vetter, Volovecky & Howell (1979) have any validity, their finding that grammaticality was not independent of ordinariness points in the same direction. Greenbaum also examined the data on a subject-by-subject basis, finding that while identical ratings on the two scales were relatively rare, ratings within one point of each other occurred for 88% of the sentences among 65% of the subjects. By this measure there was also reasonable consistency in the relationships between the ratings for the members of a related pair of sentences.

---

[25] Note that his measure of frequency was subjective (i.e., people's judgments of it) rather than objective, as might be obtained by corpus analysis.

Whichever of the two was rated more frequent (e.g., the active version) would be rated more acceptable by half of the subjects in 64% of the cases. If Greenbaum's interpretation is correct, we must be wary of grammaticality judgments on very obscure types of sentence constructions, which might reflect their infrequent nature despite their grammaticality. Following one of my earlier suggestions, a way to reduce this effect might be to allow subjects a separate frequency rating when judging acceptability, so that they can express this intuition and perhaps factor it out of the other judgment. This is presumably what Maclay & Sleator were trying to do with their ordinariness scale, although the meaning of the term was probably obscure to most subjects. We must also keep in mind, however, that Greenbaum has only shown a correlation between perceived frequency and acceptability, with no evidence about causality.

Some other interesting results were by-products of the fact that sentences were presented in related pairs such as active/passive. In general, across various other constructions, actives are judged more acceptable than passives (no analysis of significance was done by Greenbaum). Such a bias must be taken into account in other analyses. In Chapter 2, for example, I cited an instance where the fact that the active and passive versions of a sentence were equally marginal formed part of a theoretical argument (example (8), Section 2.3.3). Of course, no experimental data had been used, but if they were, the general bias against passives would probably cause the result not to hold up, and yet this difference would have nothing to do with the particular theoretical issue involved. Other general biases were found as well, e.g., favoring present perfects over simple past tenses with both durative and iterative events, and subjunctives over indicatives and modals in subordinate clauses of demand or persuasion. The lesson for linguists is that whenever we rely on a nonminimal contrast, we should separately test each of the component minimal contrasts as well, to determine which one is responsible for the difference in acceptability.

5.3.5 Lexical Content

Levelt et al. (1977) wanted to bring home the point that the particular lexical items chosen to make up an example sentence could affect grammaticality ratings even when, from a normative point of view, the full range of words should all result in a grammatical utterance. The particular feature of lexical items they investigated was the imagery content of compound words in Dutch, by which they meant the extent to which they were concrete as opposed to abstract, and hence more easily imaginable. (This idea was inspired by phenomenological reports of subjects performing judgment tasks by trying to imagine a situation in which the phrase in question could be said.) Reaction time was measured as grammaticality ratings and paraphrases of novel Dutch compounds (not complete sentences) were elicited. The purpose of avoiding lexicalized compounds was to encourage computation of a rating, rather than the use of lexical look-up. The basic prediction of Levelt et al., that the facilitation effect of imagery would show up in these judgments, was confirmed. More easily imaginable compounds were rated significantly more grammatical and judged and paraphrased faster than ones that were harder to imagine,[26] supporting the notion of search for interpretation as (part of) the decision procedure. (The results for speed of judgment are confirmed by results in Grant et al. (1977).) The additional twist, however, was that imagery showed a much greater effect on reaction time for paraphrasing than for judging grammaticality. Levelt et al. considered two explanations. First, perhaps imagery is involved in the task of generating a paraphrase, as well as in comprehending the original sentence. They consider this unlikely, for reasons not given. Second, perhaps it is the grammaticality judgments that do not require full imagistic search. That is, once a preliminary check (involving some imagistic component) succeeds, the compound does not need to be fully processed or understood before being judged as good (see the discussion in Section 5.2.7). As the authors suggest, this could be tested by timing a task that requires full interpretation but does not involve paraphrase, such as verification (truth judgment). Whichever explanation is correct, we have another case of a supposedly irrelevant variable influencing judgments of grammaticality. McCawley (1985) views this as an instance of inaccurate *reporting* of judgments, i.e., the subjects think they are reporting on grammaticality, but really they are reporting their (degree of) success in imagining a context.

Another of Greenbaum's (1977) experiments examined the effects of lexical substitution by comparing acceptability ratings between two instances of the same sentence structure that differed only on certain lexical items. (He does not give a large range of examples, but the intent seems to have been that these substitutions could reasonably be expected to have no grammatical implications.) Again, judgments were on a 5-point scale. For 27 of 50 sentences at least half of the subjects gave identical ratings to the two variant sentences, and on 47 out of 50, 70% of subjects were within one position on the scale of their initial judgment. Variants were presented in separate parts of the questionnaire so that memory for the previous rating would be extremely unlikely, and subjects were explicitly told not to try to remember their earlier ratings. Thus, this effect seems to be fairly small.

---

[26] The imagery content of compounds was assessed in a pretest where other subjects reported how easily the expression lead to mental images of things or events.

5.3.6 Morphology and Spelling

Langendoen & Bever (1973: 407) claim that there are acceptability differences that depend on the transparency of morphology in cases where a pronoun later in the sentence refers to an implicit morphologically related word, e.g., in the contrast between (20) and (21):

(20)   ?Flutists are strange: *it* doesn't sound shrill to them.

(21)   *Flautists are strange: *it* doesn't sound shrill to them.

They claim that (20) is more acceptable than (21) because *flute*, the implicit antecedent of *it*, is more obviously part of *flutists* than of *flautists*. Unfortunately, they do not cite actual data on this point; they might simply be expressing their own intuitions. To my ear, both sentences are equally (quite) bad, but if such a result should be found systematically, it would constitute another factor to be taken into consideration. (See Smith 1981 for the argument that the pragmatic principles that Langendoen & Bever propose should not be able to save truly ungrammatical sentences from unacceptability.) Some researchers (e.g., Birdsong 1989) have cited this paper as showing that variant *spellings* cause changes in acceptability ratings, but Langendoen & Bever make no mention of spelling, which is confounded with pronunciation in this case. Still, it would not be surprising to find acceptability differences between alternate spellings of identically pronounced variants, e.g., *night* versus *nite*, triggered by relative frequency in the dialect of the subject. I am not aware of this issue ever having been studied. A complementary point is made by Hill (1961): before people can judge a sentence, they must first identify all the morphemes in it, but the presence of a normal intonation contour can lead one to interpret apparently familiar morphemes as novel ones. For instance, the sentence *I saw a fragile of*, read with declarative intonation, leads speakers to think that there is a novel noun *of*, rather than identifying *of* as the familiar preposition. This can lead them to judge bad sentences good unless they are informed that "all the words will be familiar," or some equivalent statement.

5.3.7 Rhetorical Structure

Langendoen (1972) claims that some apparent cases of ungrammaticality may be explained by what he calls rhetorical factors, such as particular readings of elliptical sentences:

(22)   a. Mary takes Nancy seriously, but Ollie lightly.

        b. Mary takes Nancy seriously, but Ollie takes Nancy lightly.

(23)   a. Mary takes life seriously, but Ollie lightly.

        b. Mary takes life seriously, but Ollie takes life lightly.

According to Langendoen, people judge that (22a) cannot have the meaning of (22b), while (23a) can have the meaning of (23b). If this judgment reflects speakers' grammars, one would have to find a grammatical difference to account for the asymmetry between the two (b) examples. However, Langendoen argues that there is a rhetorical principle at work that makes certain readings of grammatically ambiguous sentences more salient than others, to the point where the less salient reading cannot even be forced. The specific factors behind salience in this case are not particularly important, but Langendoen speculates that some parallelism preference is at work. An object interpretation of *Ollie* in (23a) would contrast him with *life*, so we prefer the subject interpretation in which he is contrasted with the human *Mary*, whereas in (22a) the object reading creates a comparison with *Nancy* that is more strictly parallel in some sense. What is relevant to us is that a grammatical reading might be judged ungrammatical due to a competing reading. The lesson to be drawn is that if one must work with potentially ambiguous structures, one had better consider a wide range of exemplars in order to rule out such possible confounds.

5.4 Conclusion

In this chapter, we have seen at least suggestive evidence for effects on grammaticality judgments of just about every stimulus and procedure variable one can think of. Serial order, repeated presentation, deliberate judgment strategies, modality, register, preparation, and judgment speed are all features of the elicitation task that might contribute systematically to variation in judgments. So might stimulus features, including the various types of contextual material, the meaningfulness of the sentence, the perceived frequency of the sentence structure, and idiosyncratic properties of its lexical items. We have also seen some unpredictable interactions between variables, such as context with repetition, and mental state with repetition. Interestingly, there has been relatively little work showing that these variables affect the overall *pattern* of acceptability results, e.g., by reversing the relative status of two classes of sentences. It would be encouraging for the field if this turned out not to happen in general. But perhaps the biggest lesson is the importance of the instructions we give to subjects.

In the face of all the disparity in subject interpretations of the intended tasks, there is a strong temptation to propose that the first order of business should be to replicate all these studies with much more carefully designed instructional procedures. There can no longer be any doubt of the importance of this experimental design feature with regard to the elusive definitions of grammaticality and acceptability, and until this knowledge is acted upon we cannot say much about the other experimental factors with any certainty. Nevertheless, I attempt to derive some methodological recommendations from the findings of this and the preceding chapters. These are presented in Section 6.3, following a speculative discussion of the kind of model one might use to account for them.

6 Theoretical and Methodological Implications

What sort of process underlies the formation of a grammaticality judgment? The only way to approach this question is to ignore all a priori *linguistic restrictions and to regard it as a problem in human information processing.*

(Levelt et al. 1977)

6.1 Introduction

The purpose of this chapter is to bring together many of the issues raised and results reviewed in the preceding chapters to consider what we can learn from them. I entertain two particular angles on that question, namely, what we can learn about what goes on in the mind to allow grammaticality judgments to be made, and what *should* go on in linguistic experimentation in order for those judgments to be useful.

In Section 6.2, I take up the idea proposed in Chapter 1 that a useful way to make sense of a large collection of diverse experimental results is to try to fit them into a single coherent model of the mental structures that underlie the behavior. That is, following the advice of the epigraph above, we should treat this like any other problem in human information processing. In Section 6.2.1, I review what very little previous work of this sort has been done. In Section 6.2.2, I propose a preliminary model that provides a way of picturing how the many mental components discussed so far might be brought together in the judgment process. Section 6.2.3 presents some examples of ways in which such a model, in conjunction with specific assumptions about how the underlying cognitive processes work, could account for some major findings. In Section 6.3, I move on to the applied issues. In light of the demonstration in Section 2.3 of the apparent necessity of using complex and fine-grained judgments in current theoretical argumentation, and the dismal record of "insufficient reporting of results or data, poorly elaborated stimulus materials, or ... lack of adequate controls" (Chaudron 1983: 367) evinced in experimental work to date, it should be obvious that considerable care and effort must be put into the elicitation of grammaticality judgments if we are to stand a chance of getting consistent, meaningful, and accurate results. This is not being done. I therefore make specific recommendations on how to improve almost every phase of the experimental process. I first examine the stimulus materials (Section 6.3.1), then the elicitation procedures themselves (Section 6.3.2), and finally the statistical analysis and interpretation of the results (Section 6.3.3). I conclude in Section 6.4 by exploring the potential benefits of the theoretical hypotheses and methodological proposals put forth in the chapter.

6.2 Modeling Grammaticality Judgments

6.2.1 Previous Work

Almost no work has been done to date by way of modeling the psychological representations and processes involved in making grammaticality judgments, despite the proliferation of models of other language behaviors, most notably sentence processing. The first attempt in this area that I am aware of was the work of Bialystok & Ryan (1985), described in Section 3.4. From my earlier description, it should be clear that this is a very high-level model, whose constructs are so abstract as to have almost no concrete content. This is not to say that they do not exhibit useful insights, but the details are left for others to work out. While the authors claim that the dimensions of analyzed knowledge and cognitive control underlie many of the more specific properties on which people differ (e.g., field dependence) nothing more specific is said. At the level of detail I wish to work at, they do not have much to offer. The same is unfortunately true of Van Kleeck's (1982) proposed model. Gombert (1992) proposes a model of metalinguistic development whose goals are rather different from mine.

Another line of work that could be considered a model of certain aspects of the grammaticality judgment process is that of Catt (1988; Catt & Hirst 1990), although this was not his main goal. Catt created a computer program for computer-assisted language instruction that was designed to perform automatic error diagnosis and correction of ungrammaticalities produced by second-language learners. In effect, the system was a model of a foreign-language instructor. It would classify the errors in a sentence as being due to phrase structure, transformations, morphology, verb subcategorization, or certain direct translations from the learner's native language. The heart of the system was a parser made up of constraints that could be selectively relaxed when an initial parse failed. Once a parse was eventually found in this way, the constraint(s) that had been relaxed indicated the nature and location of the ungrammaticality. (I will return to the idea of constraint relaxation in Section 6.2.3.) It is possible that people do something similar when they encounter ungrammaticality, and, if so, the nature and degree of constraint relaxation might be reflected in their grammaticality ratings. There is some evidence that people behave systematically and quite uniformly in interpreting and correcting ungrammatical sentences, e.g., Shanon's (1973) work on agreement rules in Hebrew. Unfortunately for us, Catt was not concerned with extragrammatical factors that could enter into this process, and Shanon's scope was very limited, so we shall have to go the rest of the way alone.

6.2.2 The Outlines of a Preliminary Model

> *If we take just a moment to reflect just a bit on our own linguistic performance, how implausible this whole "underlying generative grammar" concept seems in the first place. (Surely nobody but a linguist would ever have dreamed of such a thing!)*
>
> (Derwing 1979)

In this subsection I propose some high-level accounts of the phenomena discussed so far in this work, culminating in suggestions for what the relevant cognitive representations might be and what the steps in the grammaticality judgment process might be. The motivations for modeling this process are given in Chapters 1 and 2 and will not be repeated here. At this point it is important to stress the preliminary and speculative nature of these proposals. Much more experimental work is needed before we can begin to have any real confidence in our knowledge about the way the mind works in this regard. In addition, what the model should look like will depend in large measure on many larger unanswered questions in language processing that also display a lack of well-articulated, well-motivated models, since a major issue of interest to me is the interface between metalinguistic components and those related to regular processing. In these cases I can only adopt some fairly well-accepted assumptions and proceed.

To begin, I ask whether there is in fact a static representation of grammatical knowledge independent of production and comprehension mechanisms. Bever (Bever (1975b); Lachter & Bever (1988)), among many others, has argued for such a psychogrammar, "an internalized representation of the language, that is not necessarily a model of such behaviors as speech perception or production, but a representation of the structure used in those and other language behaviors" (p. 221). Bever's strongest argument for his position is based on the existence of two types of sentence that seem to presuppose mismatches between (psycho)grammatical status and processing status. Some sentences are unusable yet intuitively well-formed (e.g., multiply center-embedded ones), while others are usable or comprehensible but intuitively ill-formed. While acknowledging that psychogrammar is redundant for adults, since the production and perception mechanisms are fully capable of performing the mapping between ideas and utterances, Bever argues that the psychogrammar plays an important role in acquisition, namely to bootstrap the two performance systems, to keep them roughly consistent, and to record accumulated knowledge until it is incorporated in the processing procedures. When acquisition is far enough advanced, the psychogrammar may uncouple from everyday linguistic performance altogether, leading to the mismatches mentioned above. Although I do not find the arguments particularly convincing, I will adopt this assumption, in part for clarity of exposition, in part because it is such a deep-seated feature of the generative approach. At the same time we should accept that our concept of the grammar as a separable black box of static knowledge might eventually have to change. The next question is, what does the grammar look like? Here I assume a principles-and-parameters model of Universal Grammar (UG), only because it is the theory I am most familiar with. Now, what is the relationship between the principles and parameters, the grammar as a whole (including areas not covered by UG), and the parsing and processing mechanisms? Again mostly for expository ease, I shall assume that UG is part of the grammar that is separate from processing mechanisms, which are based on it in some unspecified way, but function independently. (See Gerken & Bever (1986) for discussion of the possible relations between linguistic universals, language-specific structures, and perceptual mechanisms.)

The major question we are attempting to answer by way of a psychological model is summed up by Klein (1979): "How much of acceptability, or what kind of acceptability, falls within the scope of grammar, and how much is to be accounted for by other parts of the linguistic description or by disciplines outside linguistics" (p. 8). This brings us back to two major issues touched on in Chapter 3: how does linguistic judgment differ from language use, and are any of the manipulations to which judgment is susceptible particular to language? In Section 3.4, I discuss the conceivable extremes in response to the first question: judgment involves all of the same components as conversation, or the two processes are entirely separate. Under either of these scenarios, the answer to the second question would be fairly uninteresting. If the mechanisms are identical, the only possible source of influence on judgments is the comprehension mechanism, so whatever we cannot attribute to that (linguistic) faculty cannot be accounted for. On that basis, we can probably rule out this model immediately. If the mechanisms are completely separate, there is no potential for normal language mechanisms to contribute to linguistic judgments, but since no other process relies on the judgment module, it can be a black box with arbitrary properties. Whatever effects we find can be dumped in there. However, if we make the reasonable assumption that reality lies somewhere between these extremes, then the question of how the various components contribute to the total process becomes more interesting. Figure 6.1 represents a first attempt at modeling this scenario. I explain below what I have in mind with the various pieces of the picture, but owing to its speculative nature I cannot justify the details in any rigorous way. (With reference to the discussion in Section 1.4 of whether nonlinguistic properties should be attributed to separate modules of the mind or to the underlying substrate, I have taken the former interpretation here mainly for diagrammatic convenience.)

The basic computational metaphor used in Figure 6.1 is that a program, procedure, or strategy uses static data or knowledge to process incoming information and yield information as output. The entire process is viewed as a computation. Thus, each computation symbol is connected by dashed lines to the program(s) that execute in order to perform that computation and to the data source(s) that must be referenced; the solid lines represent the processing flow. Let us first examine the upper portion of the diagram, implicated in the comprehension and production of language. Working from left to right, we see that the input to the system is a linguistic signal (in whatever modality), which undergoes a comprehension process to yield an understanding of the sentence (whatever that means). I take this understanding to be a *temporary* product of the computation, comprising information that might or might not subsequently be stored as part of one's long-term knowledge. Comprehension involves the use of parsing strategies, which I construe quite broadly here to include heuristics that do not involve assigning any hierarchical structure to the sentence string, such as interpreting a Noun-Verb-Noun sequence as Agent-Action-Patient. I certainly do not wish to claim that every sentence is assigned a complete constituent structure by the parser. Additionally, comprehension draws on information from compe-

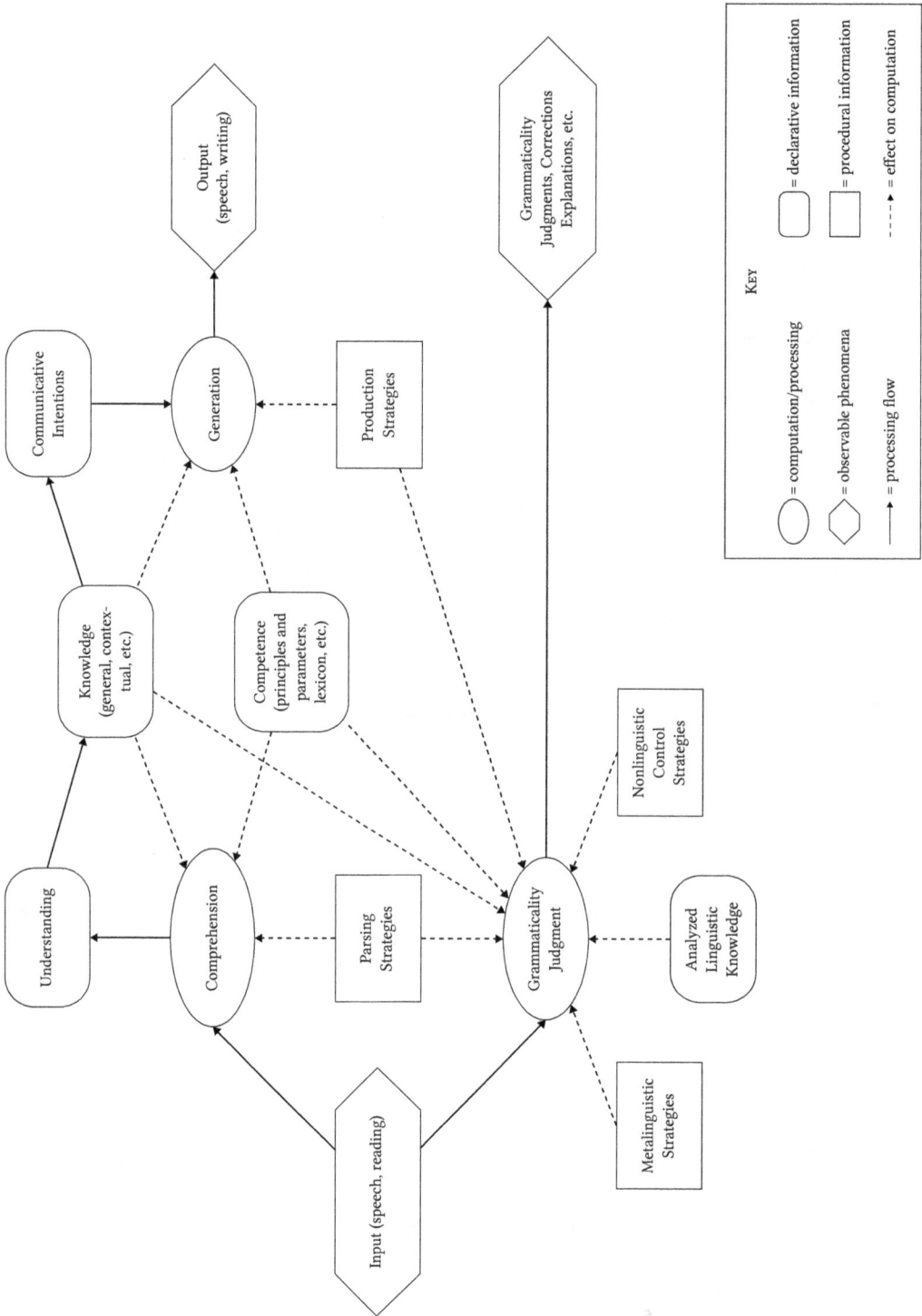

Figure 6.1: Model of Language Processing

tence (taken broadly here to include the lexicon); it also makes reference to general knowledge and specific memories to resolve ambiguities, etc. (See Berwick & Weinberg (1984) for a particular view of the interaction between the parser and the grammar.) On the production side, an utterance begins with the intention to communicate something. That message is used in the process of generation, which employs production strategies (whatever it takes to produce a sentence word by word) that also make use of linguistic competence and world knowledge (e.g., to decide which referential expressions are appropriate) and yields language output (in whatever modality).

Now let us examine the lower portion of Figure 6.1, which illustrates the grammaticality judgment process. The input to this process is the same sort of input as to the comprehension process, namely, utterances. The output will consist of judgments themselves, plus other related information that might be elicited in response to presentation of an utterance (for more examples, see Section 3.2). Since these need not be expressed through language (they could involve circling numbers on a questionnaire, for instance), no connection to the generation process is shown, although language generation will incidentally be required in some cases. The central question is, what processes or strategies are operative in generating these judgments, and what sources of knowledge do they draw upon? The answer provided in the diagram is in some sense a maximal one. I have included all the major components that *might* be involved. Perhaps not all of them are, and certainly they need not all be implicated in judging a particular sentence. The inherent danger here is that we will accomplish nothing in modeling if we merely supply a new component for each new experimental result we wish to account for. Therefore, we must hypothesize the minimal set of components that could reasonably capture the range of facts we are concerned with. (I do not claim to have struck the perfect balance between these criteria.) Let us consider these components in turn. On the assumption that one of the first things one does when processing a sentence for judgment is to simply try to understand it, the usual parsing strategies (in my broad sense) will be involved, and therefore by assumption so will the linguistic competence that they may draw on and the general cognitive resources they may use (e.g., short-term memory), with their incumbent limitations. "It is obvious that the processes of perception are involved to some extent in rendering acceptability intuitions, since a sentence must be apprehended in some sense in order to be adjudged acceptable, ambiguous, etc. We can expect there to be cases in which the perceptual processes themselves modify our apparent intuitions" (Bever & Carroll 1981: 229). If this step is exactly like normal comprehension, then general knowledge must also be involved, probably including strategies for handling conversational implicature. In reality, I suspect its role is somewhat smaller in the case of judgment, if concerns about plausibility, truth, etc., might be suspended. (See Bever, Carroll & Hurtig 1976 for a review of work on the components discussed so far.) An interesting question arises if the perception and production processes themselves encode grammatical information, rather than merely referring to the competence module. Bever, Carroll & Hurtig (1976) propose that these systems are substantially independent of the grammar (in adults), so that they may parse or generate sequences that the grammar does not include, e.g., by creative analogy. My model would allow for such sequences to be judged good or bad, depending on how much weight the various judgment sources carry.

The remaining influences are likely to be more controversial. The diagram suggests that production strategies might be involved, in two distinct ways. First, a yes/no judgment might be arrived at by attempting to generate the sentence in question. If our production mechanism cannot do so, then we judge the sentence ungrammatical, unless we have some relevant conscious knowledge about other dialects.[1] It seems that linguists may have better access to this kind of hypothetical production than untrained speakers, if Kroch (1981) is correct in his claim that resumptive pronouns can be generated by the production system despite being ungrammatical; linguists seem to find these more acceptable (see Section 2.2). Second, production strategies might be employed in the scalar rating, locating, explaining, and correcting of errors. Intuitively, it seems plausible that all of these activities involve comparison to a correct or predicted version of the sentence, and so it must be generated somehow. I am assuming that, while the parsing mechanism might embody some expectations about its input, it is not capable of generating a grammatical sentence from an intended meaning. In rating a marginal sentence, for example, one might first extract the intended meaning, then generate a grammatical sentence that is the expression of that meaning, then compare the two to decide how far off the original sentence was. But we cannot simply employ the regular generation process for this purpose, because we wish to follow the syntax of the original sentence insofar as it is correct; hence the use of production strategies referring to the input utterance.

Finally, let us consider those components implicated in grammaticality judgments but not in standard linguistic processing. The analyzed linguistic knowledge component is taken directly from Bialystok & Ryan (1985), and is meant to include consciously known rules of language such as the prescriptive rules one learns in school, which might be entirely independent of (unconscious) gram-

---

[1] I thank LouAnn Gerken for discussion of this idea.

matical knowledge. These would be responsible for labeling a sentence as ungrammatical if it ends with a preposition, for instance. Bialystok (1979) uses her experimental findings to argue that an initial good/bad decision is based mostly on implicit knowledge, while the explicit knowledge just described comes into play during subsequent error diagnosis. The control strategies are also inspired by Bialystok & Ryan's proposal. These strategies, which I take to be independent of language or any other particular cognitive function, are responsible for bringing the focus of attention to the form of an utterance, coordinating all the sources of information brought to bear in the process, and perhaps even coordinating the other sets of strategies. The latter might be required when, for instance, the parser fails on a sentence that one has been told is grammatical (e.g., a garden path). While many parsing models have been proposed to account for initial parsing failure on such sentences, very few have dealt with how one can eventually succeed in finding a valid structure for the sentence. One possibility is that control strategies intervene to prompt a search for obscure alternatives, such as verbs that could also be passive participles, as in *The horse <u>raced</u> past the barn fell*. Another possibility is that some sort of sentence frame matching takes place, so that while attempting to figure out *The prime number few*, one would try to think of other sentences that end in *number few*.

The final set of strategies has been simply labeled as metalinguistic, following the terminology we have seen in much of the literature. This module is meant to include any algorithm or heuristic used expressly for the purpose of making grammaticality judgments (in the broad sense). This is where we would find, for example, the strategy of trying to imagine a plausible context for some questionable sentence, or enriching the given context to make it seem more natural, as proposed by Nagata and discussed in Sections 5.2.3–5.2.5. It would also include procedures for interpreting the trace of execution of the parser (if this is possible) or the final state of the parser. For instance, failure with a certain set of conditions indicates that the parser could not find a suitable antecedent for some anaphor. Other possible strategies include thinking of a parallel construction to compare the given sentence to (e.g., *The child seems tired* for *The child seems sleeping*); considering the truth or plausibility of the situation described, by consulting world knowledge (to the extent that these criteria influence judgments); preliminary checking routines that would be run before parsing begins, as proposed by Levelt et al. (1977); and other strategies discussed in Section 3.4. Recall that in Section 1.4, it was hypothesized that there are no *language-specific* extragrammatical factors involved in the process of grammaticality judgment. It might appear that the presence of a set of metalinguistic strategies contradicts this hypothesis, but in fact it does not, unless the strategies contained in that module require language-specific means to be implemented. For example, the imagining of plausible contexts could be carried out in the same way as any other sort of imagination, (presumably) independent of language. The fact that such a strategy can be *employed* for the purpose of judging grammaticality must be a fact about language behavior, however. One possible component that I have not shown explicitly is a decision-making or judgment component for cognition in general, which might reflect, say, the tendency to use rating scales in a particular way. Obviously the mind must have a mechanism for decision making, and it will be implicated in judgments, but it is hard to conceive of this as a separable module of the mind, as opposed to an inherent feature of the low-level processes that underlie higher cognition. I also have not included any reference to general cognitive processes such as analogical reasoning, and the oft-mentioned but ill-defined perceptual strategies that are sometimes implicated in language processing. At this point I consider the evidence for their involvement to be marginal at best. A couple of other omissions are mostly for the sake of diagrammatic clarity. For instance, it is possible that some or all of the three components that are shown connected exclusively to the judgment computation could be used in everyday comprehension if some special need arose. Also, under certain circumstances, regular communicative output could be filtered through the judgment component as a means of quality control or self-monitoring; perhaps language teachers regularly do something like this, and everyone might do it to some extent.

If this picture is at all on the right track, then it is clear that we do not expect judgments to give all sentences the same status that linguistic performance does. The differences would be attributable to any or all of the components discussed in the previous two paragraphs. (The results of different metalinguistic tasks will differ as well, by virtue of how the contents of the modules are used, e.g., which metalinguistic strategies are employed under what conditions.) In fact, it might appear that grammaticality judgments are the *worst* way to get at linguistic competence, as compared to production and comprehension, because they involve the interaction of many more factors. This conclusion has been reached by others before: "Contrary to what has generally been claimed, the relations between explicit intuitions and underlying competence are *less* direct than those between phenomena of primary language use (speaking, listening) and competence" (Levelt, Sinclair & Jarvella 1978: 5–6). However, this by no means constitutes grounds for abandoning them as a source of data. Several arguments for their use were presented in Section 1.1; I can now provide two more. First, while more factors are involved in grammaticality judgments, they might be less mysterious than those that are connected to language use. For instance, what exactly is the understanding of a sentence, and how would we ever get at it and draw conclusions about grammaticality from it? The same goes for communicative intentions. Second, grammaticality judgments provide an *alternative path* to the grammar. To the extent that they are subject to *different* influences than language use is, we have a basis on which to search for the common core that underlies both kinds of behavior. This in turn might help us to factor out various nongrammatical contributions, so that each path by itself becomes more informative as well. (Of course, not nearly enough attention is paid to usage data by theoretical linguists for such a convergence to be applied at this time. While the above is an argument for not abandoning judgment data, it is also an argument for increasing the attention paid to other types of data.) Studying nonlinguistic judgment tasks in the framework of this model, as proposed in Section 1.4, will aid in this process by helping to clarify the role of its nonlinguistic elements.

One thing that is not reflected explicitly in the model presented in Figure 6.1 is the time course of the process of judging grammaticality. Would all the factors be assessed in parallel, or would some parts necessarily precede others? My hunch is that it can be usefully thought of in three main phases: parsing, decision, and diagnosis. The first is fairly uncontroversial, when taken to include the kinds of heuristics mentioned earlier. The second involves determining what the rating will be: yes/no, or a number on a scale, or whatever. This might involve an analysis of the remnants of the parsing process, for instance. The third, diagnosis, which might not always occur, involves *consciously* determining reasons for the particular ratings chosen, which could be used in explaining the error or correcting it. As we have discussed before, these might or might not bear any relation to the actual causes of the decision. This sketchy account will suffice for the rest of the discussion here; obviously many details remain to be worked out.

6.2.3 Applications of the Model

In order to see how my model might actually account for some interesting facts about grammaticality judgments, a bit more needs to be said about how the pieces of this picture are implemented. I will assume the widely used principle of spreading activation, together with the parallel-processing concept of competition.[2] That is, multiple processing paths might be active in parallel, and the first one to succeed will determine the outcome of the computation. This approach has already been used by McRoy & Hirst (1990) to implement so-called

---

[2] This is just one possibility that strikes me as promising, but certainly not the only one.

race-based parsing. In their model, each parsing rule takes a certain amount of time to execute, determined partially by its complexity but also influenced by the lexical content of the sentence, previously parsed sentences, etc. Multiple parse paths are tried in parallel, and whichever succeeds first is used to interpret the sentence. If none succeeds before a time-out deadline, the parse is considered to have failed. Thus, different readings of a structurally ambiguous sentence might be found on different occasions because the time weights associated with the relevant rules can change. Many order-of-presentation effects can be accounted for in this way. For instance, a sentence that could not be parsed at one time (e.g., a garden path) can be parsed at some other time if the required rules have been strengthened or sped up. This might be accomplished by employing them in parsing structurally similar non-garden-path sentences. More generally, context effects due to structural similarity or dissimilarity (see Section 5.3.1) can be derived as well. Bock (1986) provides experimental evidence suggesting that some mechanism of this sort is needed. Her paradigm involved having subjects repeat a sentence they had just heard, and then describe an unrelated picture they were shown, using a single sentence. The pictures were constructed so as to allow two natural types of sentence descriptions: either active versus passive or dative object versus double object. Bock found that the type of sentence that subjects had to repeat influenced their choice of a syntactic form used in describing the picture. She argues that this result cannot be attributed to lexical repetition effects, socially motivated matching of the form of another speaker's utterance, or persistent discourse strategies that trigger the same syntactic rules, but rather must be attributed to some purely syntactic decision process.

This scheme can be extended very naturally to deal with graded judgments of (un)grammaticality. I shall incorporate the idea of constraint relaxation from Catt's (1988)'s work, discussed in Section 6.2.1. While it is fairly clear that relaxing constraints will allow ill-formed input to be processed and the well-formed parts recovered, not all constraints can be of equal status if we are to get graded judgments based on grammatical properties (as opposed to imagery content of lexical items or other nongrammatical features). That is, it is not sufficient, as it was for Catt, to know *which* constraint must be relaxed in order to get through a sentence. We must know how much of a concession it was to relax that constraint. While one can imagine an ad hoc weighting function for this purpose, it is perhaps more naturally served using the race-based framework. The speed with which a parse path can be followed if its constraint is violated is inversely proportional to the importance of the constraint on that path. That is, a path with a very fundamental constraint (e.g., the lexical category of an input word) can be traversed only extremely slowly if the constraint is not satisfied, whereas a path with a lesser constraint (e.g., a semantic feature restriction on an input word) can be followed faster than the path with the greater constraint when *its* condition is not met, other things being equal.[3] Thus, degrees of grammaticality could be equated with parsing speed, where it is understood that speed is meant in a somewhat metaphorical sense that need not correspond to actual processing speed.[4]

This measure could yield both absolute and graded judgments. The absolute distinction is based on whether or not any constraints are violated, the graded measure is based on speed, so that a grammatical but hard-to-parse sentence (e.g., a garden path) would be rated the same as a truly ungrammatical sentence, which is exactly what Warner & Glass (1987) found (see Section 5.3.1). The relative leniency for ungrammaticality in spoken, as opposed to written, language could result from an across-the-board reduction in the time cost of traversing paths (including ones whose constraints are violated), in order to keep up with the real-time demands of continuous speech. Situationally related context could speed up parsing by decreasing the time required to access meanings and other properties of relevant words. In the same way, a processing advantage is predicted for frequently versus infrequently occurring words. The relative strengths of parse paths should also be reflected in corrections, i.e., how you change a bad sentence to make it good. Presumably, whatever was implicated in the constraint that got relaxed will be changed, since it is the only known locus of error. If you were to make a correction somewhere else, you could not be assured that it would be sufficient. Of course, we have seen that graded judgments can arise on a wide variety of nonlinguistic tasks as well. In my view, this occurs because race-based implementation is a feature of cognitive processing in general. I conclude this section by suggesting that the same competition principle can be applied at a macro level as well. Consider the situation where an ungrammatical but comprehensible sentence is encountered, e.g., *I just bought a CD for me.* Different knowledge components contribute to different views of this sentence. According to linguistic

---

[3] It seems that this approach could be applied quite directly to account for prototypicality effects of the kind discussed in Section 3.3.1. If an exemplar of a concept (e.g., bird) lacks a fundamental property (e.g., ability to fly), it will take longer to verify than one that lacks a less important property of the prototype.

[4] This scheme bears a certain resemblance to the concept of fuzzy grammar (see Mohan (1977) for a concise review). The idea is that each derivational rule that applies to generate a sentence rates its output on the basis of features of its input, eventually yielding a well-formedness rating between 0 and 1 for the sentence as a whole. But note that I am crucially *not* attributing this mechanism to the grammar itself.

competence, the sentence is ill-formed because it contains an improperly bound pronoun. Our knowledge of the world, and specifically the knowledge that Boris just walked in the door with a CD in hand (still in its factory shrinkwrap), allows us to interpret the sentence without any difficulty. Which component will be allowed to determine our reaction to the sentence – to ignore the error and take up the conversation, to make a mental note that Boris does not speak perfect English, to tell him he has made a mistake and see if he can discover it, or to blurt out the correct version of the sentence? This decision can be seen as the result of a competition, where the "speed" of each processing module is determined by the demands of the situation. Thus, teaching an ESL class primes grammatical competence and correction strategies, everyday conversation favors parsing, the current situation activates relevant knowledge of the world, seeing oneself in a mirror might strengthen the communicative over the structurally based strategies, and so forth. Of course, for speakers we know, this choice might have been made for good when we first got to know them. Under this interpretation, the control strategies themselves might not exist as strategies per se, but as the by-products of spreading activation and race-based competition.

6.3 Methodological Proposals

> *More and more subtle theory is now being constructed on less and less clear cases. In such a situation one would expect linguistics to turn to appropriate behavioral methods of data gathering and (statistical) analysis. Nothing of the sort occurs, however.*
>
> (Levelt et al. 1977)

6.3.1 Materials

There are basic precautions that could easily be taken in preparing materials for the elicitation of grammaticality judgments in order to avoid certain obvious kinds of bias.[5] One potential confound is the order in which sentences are presented to subjects. It has been shown experimentally (e.g., by Greenbaum (1973))

---

[5] Several of the suggestions in Section 6.3 have been synthesized from Birdsong (1989), Ray & Ravizza (1988), and Snow (1975).

that sentences will be rated differently depending on their order of presentation. A simple way to factor this effect out of results is to counterbalance orders across different subjects, thus controlling for nervousness at the beginning of the session, fatigue at the end, practice effects, the influence of surrounding test items, and any other serial position effects. (Of course, this requires that one consult more than one subject.) A second kind of bias is introduced if there are substantially more grammatical sentences in the test materials than ungrammatical sentences or vice versa. Subjects will tend to get into a yea-saying or nay-saying mode or will come to expect deviance. Thus, the numbers should be kept roughly equal. (We will need pilot trials to gather preliminary data for this purpose, since we presumably do not know the outcome of all the judgments in advance.) A third factor in our list of potential confounds in stimulus materials is the semantic content of the lexical items in the sentence.[6] As mentioned in Section 5.3.5 it is simply not true that people will rate all structurally identical sentences equally grammatical. For example, Levelt et al. (1977) found that different ratings could be induced by varying the imagery content of a sentence, i.e., the degree to which it represented an imaginable or concrete situation. With a good understanding of such a factor, one can reduce its effect by avoiding sentences at the extremes of imagistic content,[7] and by using several different exemplar sentences with the structure in question across subjects. That is, the lexical content of the sentences should be varied to guard against the influence of imagery, and any other potential biases of lexical items, such as word length, frequency, and semantic peculiarities. In light of the findings by Hill (1961), it might also be best to inform subjects that only common words will be used, or that if they are not sure about the status of a word, they should ask the experimenter. This would circumvent the possibility of subjects interpreting *of* as an unfamiliar noun, for instance.

More controversial than any of these issues in preparing materials is the surrounding contextual material, of all the various types. We have all had the experience of thinking at first that a sentence is totally ungrammatical, only to have someone suggest a real-world situation where it is quite plausible and sounds fine. As discussed in Section 5.3.1, there are numerous ways that context can influence grammaticality, from bringing out rare word meanings to priming certain

---

[6] Obviously, some semantic features of words are directly relevant to grammaticality; here, as in Section 5.3.2, I am concerned with properties not generally considered grammatically relevant.

[7] Alternatively, Birdsong (1989) proposes that only high-imagery content words should be used, so that all subjects can see the sentences as potentially referential and meaningful. Whether this is a good idea should probably be determined on the basis of experiments comparing the two methodologies; to my knowledge Birdsong's proposal has not yet been followed.

parsing procedures.[8] There is certainly no universally correct answer to the question of what sort of context, if any, is suitable for particular elicitation purposes, but it is a variable that cannot be ignored. Ratings of sentences in context cannot be compared with those made in isolation, for example. The consensus among the authors surveyed in the present work seems to be that a supporting pragmatically related context should always be provided, unless that would somehow defeat the purpose of the experiment. Since only structural well-formedness is at issue, not pragmatic appropriateness, if there exists a situation where the sentence would be appropriate, why should we not lead the subject to that situation? Furthermore, we will reduce between-subject variability by not leaving subjects to their own devices in imagining situations where the sentence might occur, which many researchers claim would otherwise be a major part of the judgment process. Of course, the question that then arises is what to do with sentences that seem to have no imaginable context. Householder (1973) claims that a sentence can be ungrammatical for that reason alone, i.e., that usability is not entirely separable from structural well-formedness. (The example he gives, which I do not find particularly problematic, is *Harry reminds me of himself.*)

Depending on the purpose of the experiment, one might wish to avoid choosing sentences whose rating is likely to be confounded by parsing difficulty. For instance, the garden paths studied by Warner & Glass (1987) showed extreme parsing difficulty. Since these researchers were interested in the parsing process, rather than in grammaticality per se, these were sensible choices, but if one wishes to know whether a sentence is accepted by the grammar, it does not make sense to confuse grammaticality with low parsability. Of course, the distinction might not always be obvious ahead of time, but one could call on a pilot study with a post-test questionnaire, where the intended interpretation of a sentence that was judged ungrammatical is stated, and the subject is asked whether the sentence is still bad under this reading.

If one wishes to detect very small differences between sentences, then it is crucial that they be matched as closely as possible on as many features as possible, including semantic plausibility (Carden & Dieterich 1981). That is, they should be minimal pairs at the sentence level. When the relative grammaticality of two or more related forms is at issue, it is best to allow subjects to see them side by side and draw their attention to the comparison. The order among the related sentences, and the order among the *sets* of such sentences, should still of course be counterbalanced. Judgment tests are likely to give misleading results if the

---

[8] For some striking demonstrations of how apparent word salad can be made plausible by context, see Hill (1961), especially fn. 4.

sentences used contain features that are unrepresentative of the whole range of sentences to which the results should generalize. Thus, Levelt (1974: vol. 3) and Bolinger (1971) plead for the avoidance of additional unnaturalness that has nothing to do with the crucial issue at stake but takes attention away from it. Levelt cites numerous cases where this seemingly obvious admonition has been violated, e.g., by what he views as unnecessary loading of short term memory (*That Tom's told everyone that he's staying proves that it's true that he's thinking that it would be a good idea for him to show that he likes it here*) or by the extra semantic load resulting from an unusual situation (*I dreamed that I was a proton and fell in love with a shapely green-and-orange-striped electron*), when these were not required for the issues under investigation (Levelt 1972). Again, to guard against unintentional distractions of this type, multiple sentence frames should be built around the same crucial construction wherever possible.

6.3.2 **Procedure**

> *Good practice in the more advanced sciences distrusts most of all the memory and impressions of the investigator himself.*
>
> (Labov 1978)

Once we have minimized potential confounds in the stimulus materials, the next logical step is to remove confounds from the process of gathering judgments. The first issue is the selection of subjects, perhaps the worst offense with regard to experimental method in linguistics to date. Here I would implore that these must be people with no linguistic training. If it is the competence of normal native speakers that we claim to be investigating, we need to study random samples of normal native speakers. This is almost never done by theoretical linguists. (Bolinger (1968), Greenbaum (1976a) and Derwing (1979) also make this point.) They first consult their own intuitions (one cannot find a more biased subject than the investigator), then their colleagues in the next office (almost as biased), and if they are really ambitious, perhaps a couple of their students (not exactly objective either, since students likely know which result their professors are hoping for and would like to gain their favor.) While striking differences between linguists and nonlinguists have not been convincingly demonstrated empirically due to poor experimental designs (see Section 4.4.1), we have enough reasons to *expect* them to be different that linguists simply ought to be excluded. Also, the small samples of linguists that are usually available are bound to lead to unreliabilities (Bradac et al. 1980). Nonetheless, linguists continue to insist that the ease of obtaining data is a reason for preferring oneself as a subject, ignoring the inferior quality of the data so obtained (Newmeyer 1983: 50) claims this justification is uncontroversial!). If linguists wish to live up to scientific standards of data validity, it is time for them to abandon the convenient fiction that data is never further away than their own minds.

Subjects must be sufficient in number in order for the assumptions of the required statistical tests to be met and to avoid distorting the results with atypical speakers. If there is any reason to suspect regional variation on the issue at hand, an effort should be made to find speakers of various dialects (this would usually be a good idea in any case). Snow (1975) and Ringen (1979) suggest that subjects be pretested and screened for their ability to judge reliably,[9] but such a procedure might systematically exclude a relevant class of judgments. A similar objection could be raised against the exclusive use of expert language users, e.g., prominent authors. Judgment tests should be carried out in a controlled setting, to decrease the chances that subjects will be "inebriated, inattentive, mendacious or whimsical" (Grandy 1981); the pub where everyone goes at the end of a conference is probably not an ideal locale. Individual differences on potentially relevant factors such as age, sex, and education should at least be noted on a personal questionnaire so that variability attributable to them can be examined in the analysis. If multiple conditions are being used (e.g., with context versus without), random assignment of subjects or counterbalancing on these factors is important.

The next problem linguists have is with the instructions to subjects. What exactly should one ask them to do? No two studies seem to agree. Certainly we have seen that one cannot hope for the terms *grammatical* or *acceptable* to have their intended meanings for naive subjects. Chaudron (1983) and many others point out the potentially nonunitary measure that would result. Experimenters must put considerable effort into designing an explanation for their subjects on how they want them to make their judgments, at least until such time as the field can agree on a standard set of instructions.[10] This will require linguists to make

---

[9] Reliability here means judging consistently on different occasions and under different circumstances, as well as giving reports that correlate as closely as possible with one's true intuitions, e.g., thinking carefully about possible contexts before deciding a sentence is impossible.

[10] Standardized instructions might seem unlikely ever to be adopted, given that there are apparently very few such cases in psychology, which is generally much more concerned with procedural matters than linguistics. I would argue that, unlike in psychology, large numbers of linguists are interested in asking exactly the same questions about their stimuli (sentences). At the very least, we can hope to make widely known what sorts of directives do and do not work. In fact, Bley-Vroman, Felix & Ioup (1988) reproduce their complete set of instructions and encourage other researchers to use it so that their results will be comparable. The instructions essentially ask the subjects to consider whether they feel the stimuli sound like possible English sentences for them, and to concentrate on structure.

explicit exactly what counts toward grammaticality, which perhaps can only be done with reference to particular types of theoretical issues being investigated. For this reason, I cannot propose a generally applicable set of instructions here, but I can suggest how to make them effective. Most experiments seem to have erred on the side of describing the task too briefly and vaguely. Instructions should be specific, should mention possible reasons why a sentence *should* be considered bad, and should also mention potential reasons that should *not* come into play. Asking subjects to say sentences out loud rather than just reading them silently may help to overcome some prescriptive compunctions associated with written norms. Give examples of sentences that you consider unequivocally good and unequivocally bad (but that do not contain the construction you wish to test) and explain why the good one is good, despite some irrelevant properties (e.g., meaninglessness) and why the bad one is bad, despite other irrelevant properties (e.g., interpretability). The examples should cover a wide enough range to avoid problems like the one Birdsong (1989) encountered. He reports that his subjects claimed a stimulus item was not a sentence because it was a question! Run some practice trials in which the subjects think aloud during the judgment process, so that you can point out if they are using inappropriate criteria. It is important to keep the statement of instructions itself down to a reasonable length. Otherwise it "becomes an essay on linguistics that only a sophisticated informant can understand, and only an unusually patient one will read" (Carden 1970a: 296).

If the field had a standard set of instructions, then at the very least everyone would be testing the same thing, even though considerable refinement would be required to make it the thing we are interested in. Results could be meaningfully compared across experiments, which is currently not possible.[11] This must become possible, however, if there is any chance of making linguistics a more objective endeavor. If the only people we can gather data from are other linguists, all hope is lost. (See Newmeyer (1983: 61) for the view that this state of affairs is unlikely to change anytime soon.) An alternative suggestion, made somewhat tongue-in-cheek by Hirst (1981: 101), is the establishment of a central sentence-testing service to which linguists would send their crucial sentences (and some money) and get back in the mail a standardized set of experimentally elicited ratings. This would eliminate the time and effort that would be required to set up appropriate testing facilities in each department, ensure consistent procedures, and reduce the overhead expense by dividing it among a larger user population. Of course, it would create a new set of problems, too.

---

[11] There is still an idealization here: while we can make instructions the same for all subjects, we cannot control for possible differences in the way they interpret those instructions.

Having dealt with how the concept of grammaticality is to be conveyed, we must now consider what to ask subjects to do with it. The biggest issue here is whether to use absolute ratings, and if so on what scale, or relative rankings, and if so on how many sentences at a time. If rankings are used, should we ask for a grammaticality threshold to be drawn, as some studies have done? The issues surrounding this choice are discussed in detail in Section 3.3.4, and will not be repeated here. The goals of the experiment will obviously play a role in this decision. All other things being equal, most researchers advocate comparative judgments, on the basis of their higher reliability. If a rating scale is used, I argue that it should be a balanced one. That is, unlike Nagata's scales (see Section 5.2.3) where 1 = grammatical, and $2-n$ are degrees of badness, it should range evenly from good to bad, with middling being in the middle. If verbal descriptions of the various positions on the scale are given, some care is called for.[12] Greenbaum & Quirk (1970) and Ellis (1991) advise against calling a middle rating "not sure," for instance, because this carries the potentially negative connotation that the subject is unable to make a decision, rather than labeling the sentence as intermediate in grammaticality. In fact, both answers should be available, so that cases where the subject truly *is* unsure can be treated separately. Greenbaum & Quirk also recommended against calling the middle category "marginal or dubious," as Quirk & Svartvik (1966) did, because this terminology sounds too technical. In fact, I believe the use of more than one rating criterion should be seriously considered. If one gives subjects a chance to rate grammaticality, stylistic felicity, likelihood of occurrence in conversation,[13] and their own (un)certainty separately, this should reduce the chances that the latter factors will play a role in subjects' ratings of the first. People seem to want to express their feelings about these other matters, so it is best to give them the opportunity to do so explicitly. The effectiveness of the rating scale(s) also depends on warm-up trials that encompass a representative range of sentences. At this stage (unlike the detailed examples advocated earlier) they probably *should* include sentences of the type that will occur in the experimental trials, otherwise there is a risk that novel stimuli will show a primacy effect. Using relevant sentences in practice trials is not a problem as long as experimenters do not bias the subjects with their own opinions of these sentences. In general, the purpose of warm-up trials is for subjects

---

[12] Wayne Cowart (personal communication) recommends anchoring only the endpoints of the scale with descriptions, because labeling intermediate points might induce subjects to use the scale unevenly.

[13] Householder (1973) lists numerous other questions that might be usefully posed, depending on the materials, e.g., Does the sentence sound low-class? Foreign? Rural? British/American? Old-fashioned? Bookish?

to arrive at the response strategy that works best for them, so that subsequent experimental trials will reflect a fairly stable process.

Carden (1970a) points out a problem with eliciting grammaticality judgments only on a questionnaire, rather than in an interview: "You often must focus on a particular reading or construction. It is of no value to know that speaker X considers a sentence ungrammatical if you do not know that his reason for rejecting it is unrelated to the construction you are studying" (p. 296). He thus argues for greater use of interviews, an issue to which I return below. I agree that asking for some sort of explanation is crucial to knowing that a sentence was rejected for the right reasons in many cases. However, there are ways of getting at which feature(s) of a sentence cause a subject to reject it, even with a written questionnaire. One can ask subjects to indicate the location of any errors they perceive, to explain why sentences are incorrect, and/or to correct them. If this is done, however, it is crucial to balance these tasks with corresponding ones to be performed if the sentence is good, otherwise subjects might be biased toward good ratings just to avoid the extra work. (Studies by Snow (1975) and Hakes (1980) had this problem.) As mentioned in Section 3.2, the most obvious candidate task is paraphrase: ask the subject to rewrite the sentences in a different way while preserving their meaning. This can additionally tell us how the sentence was interpreted, which could be useful information. (Of course, whether paraphrasing is as demanding as explaining errors is hard to assess, but it is a step in the right direction.) A similar kind of bias to that just discussed was exhibited by Rose's (1973) study, described in Section 4.4.1. His materials contained equal numbers of good and bad sentences (according to the sources they were drawn from), but subjects were divided by being asked to mark either the good or the bad sentences, while leaving the other kind unmarked. The groups differed significantly in the number of sentences accepted, with each group leaving more than half the sentences unmarked. This seems to be another instance of bias toward minimal action. To avoid it, subjects must be given the same amount of work to do no matter how they rate a sentence.

The issue of by what means judgments are to be elicited is another important question of methodology. The most detailed examination of this problem is found in Carden (1976b). His main concern was to find ways of increasing the *reliability* of elicited judgments, that is, the extent to which later ones by the same speakers or separate ones from other speakers of the same speech community will be consistent. Carden concurs with my own position that the major difficulties lie in explaining the task to naive subjects, particularly in noninteractive forms of data elicitation, such as (forced-choice) questionnaires. At the opposite end of the interactivity scale is the open-ended interview, which is rarely used systematically by linguists, but is claimed to yield considerably cleaner data than questionnaires. Carden cites two examples of interview studies that were later replicated with questionnaires. In both cases, the interview results showed clear patterns, whereas virtually no systematic patterns could be found in the questionnaire results. A plausible explanation for this is that interviews provide more opportunity for the experimenter's bias to influence the subjects (Newmeyer 1983), but Carden argues that there is evidence to suggest that interviews also allow real improvement in data quality, because the task can be explained in more detail, subjects' questions can be answered, and misunderstandings can be set straight. In follow-up interviews to the questionnaires, he found that much of the noise in the data was due to irrelevant readings of stimulus sentences, and in cases where statistical analysis was available, it did show significant patterns of the same sort found in interviews, although they were much less obvious from casual inspection of the unanalyzed data. Still, Carden acknowledges that until potential bias effects are studied in more detail, interviews remain suspect. In fact, he paints a gloomy overall picture that might not have improved much in the intervening years:

> The linguist's own intuitions are plainly untrustworthy. Direct observation of performance, while potentially important as a means of validating other methodologies is impractical as a primary technique. Performance tasks seem to be even less reliable than evaluation [judgment] tasks, and are difficult to adapt to the more interesting syntactic problems. Forced-choice questionnaires are also difficult to construct, and have at best marginal reliability and very noisy data. Open-ended interviews seem to produce clear results, but are very time-consuming and may have bias problems. (p. 103)

I suggest following the standard practice in social science of using interviews in the preliminary phases of an investigation only. Once potential ambiguities, misunderstandings, etc., have been discovered, the materials can be adjusted to deal with them and controlled experiments run, so that statistical analysis can legitimately be applied to the results. Another standard technique that could be useful in preliminary investigations is the focus group (Graeme Hirst, personal communication). Speakers could discuss test sentences among themselves, employ them in different contexts, point out problematic features, etc., while the experimenter observes surreptitiously. In this procedure, grammaticality judgment would be a group, as opposed to an individual, activity. Hirst believes this approach is valuable even beyond the preliminary stages. Citing the work of

Schober & Clark (1989), who argue that understanding in a conversation is a collaborative process wherein the participants work together moment by moment to achieve comprehension (which explains why overhearers do not understand as well as addressees), he proposes that judging grammaticality in a group setting could be profitably carried out in a parallel manner. I am not aware of this approach having been systematically tried.

Moving on now from the task itself, psychology has identified several kinds of experimenter effects, induced by the behavior of the experimenter, which can bias results (see also Labov (1975) and Greenbaum (1988)). In the linguistic case, there is great potential for the investigator to influence a subject's judgments, even if the experiment is not an interview per se. Experimenters might influence judgments by demonstrating the procedure using sample sentences that are related to the test materials; by the idiolect of their own speech, which might be different from the subject's; or by subtleties of their interaction with the subject, e.g., how they respond when the subject gives a judgment they do not expect. Heringer (1970) raised many of these issues over 20 years ago, in a passage that has been widely cited by psycholinguists, but that seems to have been ignored by most theoreticians: "In the casual interaction between linguist and informant, there are many opportunities for self-fulfilling prophesies to take effect, both ones conditioned by theoretical position and also ones conditioned by the linguist's own idiolect. This could occur even without the conscious knowledge of the linguist, especially if stress and intonation are not controlled" (p. 294; see also Bradac et al. 1980). These dangers are fairly easily removed, if one is aware of them, by not using the investigator as an experimenter and by scrutinizing the instruction and elicitation phases for potential influence. Carden (1970a) warns us that the linguist could also bias results by inconsistent coding of speakers' responses, so this should be done by disinterested parties as well. Typically, each set of responses would be coded independently by two judges, and consistency between them should be measured and reported.

Sentence judging is also particularly susceptible to what are known as maturation effects (also sometimes called order effects). These include the results of being asked for too many judgments at one sitting, such as boredom, frustration, and fatigue, which lead to inaccurate responses because the subject stops caring about the outcome. Satiation, whereby symbols lose their meaning after repeated exposure, strips subjects of their intuitions altogether (Quirk & Svartvik 1966). As Carden (1976a) puts it, "being an informant is very tiring; they find that after a while all sentences begin to sound alike" (p. 8). Short sessions and varied stimulus materials are the obvious remedies. Closely related to the effects just mentioned are testing effects. These include practice or training, whereby the subject gains skill in the judgment task over time, making early results not comparable with later ones. These can be controlled for across subjects by counterbalancing orders, as discussed in Section 6.3.1, but they will still distort within-subject comparisons. There is also potential for the subject to become aware of what particular issues the experimenter is interested in, which can cause the crucial sentences to be treated specially. Again, Carden (1976a) has recognized this danger: "If the informant hears similar constructions in quick succession, his remembered response to the previous sentence influences his response to the current one" (p. 8). For instance, subjects might identify parasitic gap constructions as the items of interest and decide that they ought to rate every one of these identically, regardless of their actual intuitions. (In Section 2.3.4, I suggest that linguists regularly do this.) This should be avoided by using enough filler or distractor sentences, i.e., ones that are unrelated to the crucial construction. These will also serve as anchors, to remind subjects of the range of potential goodness and badness; otherwise, after looking at marginal sentences for a long time, subjects might start spreading their ratings out farther on the scale.|israting scale, subjects' use of A more bizarre variable that can apparently affect subjects' perception of the purpose of the study is experimental setting. In a study by Greenbaum & Quirk (1970), performance tests were conducted on two groups of college students, one in a lecture hall with white-coated strangers as experimenters, the other in the investigators' own English department with familiar professors as experimenters. The test itself was tape recorded, so there could be no bias in the stimulus materials themselves, and yet the authors found significant differences between the two groups in the number of relevant noncompliances (RNCs):compliance tests the group with strangers showed fewer RNCs, i.e., they obeyed the instructions more strictly. Subsequent interviews showed the two groups of subjects had been put into different mental sets, thinking the test had a linguistic versus a psychological purpose. Those with the former opinion were more inclined to make their sentences into correct English, while the latter group was more concerned with remembering the stimulus sentence accurately. The authors conclude, "We have seen that opinions of the test's purpose can importantly affect RNC scores and that the opinions themselves can be easily affected to a significant degree by small changes in test (and pre-test) conditions" (p. 58). Greenbaum (1977c) recommends telling subjects what the experiment is really about, so that they will not introduce variability in the results by making differing guesses. A final procedural consideration is the mode of presentation of the sentences. It is common knowledge that spoken and written language have vastly differing norms (which might be attributable to the dimensions of interactivity and/or permanence of the communicative medium), so we should expect that judgments of sentences in the two modalities will reflect these differences (as discussed in Section 5.2.6); the two cannot be directly compared. If oral presentation is used, sentences should be read by a disinterested person, not the linguist, and audio recorded to ensure uniformity of intonation, and to edit out any speech errors; trained announcers serve this purpose well. If instructions are orally presented, these too should be recorded to ensure uniformity.

6.3.3 Analysis and Interpretation of Results

Levelt (1974) has complained that linguistics lacks a *theory of interpretation*, that is, a standard specification of how data are considered to bear on the theory. I conclude this section with some specific suggestions about the interpretation of grammaticality judgment data. The first seems almost too obvious to mention, and yet linguists consistently ignore it: without performing statistical tests of significance, we cannot know whether trends in our data are likely due to chance or to actual facts about grammars (or some other part of the mind), unless we truly have sledgehammer results. The more levels of grammaticality we try to distinguish, the less unanimity we find, and the more we need to rely on statistics. Hirst (1987: 157, fn. 31) cites a particularly serious example of this type of shortcoming. In an empirical study of ambiguity, Ford, Bresnan & Kaplan (1982) argue for a particular parsing theory on the basis of slight preferences of sentence readings among their subjects (e.g., an 11-to-9 majority in one case). Hirst shows that 12 of the 51 preferences they present as evidence are not statistically significant. (See Birdsong (1989) for other examples of spurious interpretations of experimental data.) Another problem of statistical ignorance, originally pointed out by Clark (1973), is the language-as-fixed-effect fallacy. Clark's point is that even when we find statistically significant results on a grammaticality test, we cannot necessarily generalize from the actual sentences used in the study to all sentences of the same form. The statistical analysis must treat the materials as a random rather than a fixed factor, which results in more stringent criteria for significance, but many studies have failed to do this. Additionally, the implications of the way the stimuli are gathered must be considered. It might not be crucial to do true random sampling of sentences (it is not entirely clear what that would mean), but, as suggested in Section 6.3.1, experimenters must consider the extent to which their materials are representative of the population of sentences to which they would like their results to generalize. (Clark also points out other common statistical problems with psycholinguistic experimentation.)

Simple statistical comparison of judgment ratings is not the only type of analysis that can be used to learn about grammaticality. Bradac et al. (1980) were motivated by the belief that looking at a single measure, such as grammaticality/acceptability, might conceal the "rich, multi-dimensional nature of language judgments." Thus, their technique was geared to multiple factor analysis. Their stimuli were broken down similarly to those of Maclay & Sleator (1960), by the various types of errors in sentences, including "school grammar" errors, typical foreign learner errors, and sentences that are supposedly grammatical although unacceptable. They asked 13 questions about each sentence that were answered on 7-point scales, including "Is this grammatical?"; "Is this English?"; "Is this clear?"; and "Is the speaker educated?". As usual, none of these terms were explained to the subjects, so it should not surprise us to see the authors conclude that "persons may be quite sensitive to the precise way in which such questions are asked," especially since half their subjects were linguists, the other half non-linguists. They also recorded various other attributes of the subjects. The experimental procedure was very carefully controlled. For instance, ratings on the various scales were elicited in different orders on different trials and the positions of the extremes of the scales were reversed for half the trials. The problem with this and most other multivariate studies is that it is very hard to draw any firm conclusions from them; what one is left with is a bunch of correlations among variables. For instance, the 13 rating scales were factored into four major dimensions, one of which was interpreted as grammaticality/acceptability.[14] Among the personal attributes, linguistic training or lack of it was a systematic source of variation in judgments, and so were the number of sisters the subject had and the subject's birth order, whereas sex and handedness accounted for very little variation. Still, this type of analysis can yield useful insights that might otherwise be overlooked.

One principle of interpretation that many researchers in this area have stressed (e.g., Chaudron (1983)) is that *any* conclusion on the basis of a single kind of experimental test is dubious. Wherever possible we should appeal to cross-methodology validation (Carden & Dieterich 1981). Even in cases where one kind of task (e.g., judgments) yields reliable results, its validity as an indicator of linguistic competence is suspect because of the numerous potential intervening factors, as discussed in Section 6.2. But if the same results show up reliably across additional types of task, such as unwarned judgments, performance tasks like those used by Quirk & Svartvik (1966), short-term memory measures, unintrusive reaction mea-

---

[14] The scales that comprised this dimension were "is grammatical/is ungrammatical," "is acceptable/is unacceptable," and "is correct/is incorrect."

sures such as event-related brain potentials, sentence completion tasks, or naturalistic observation of speech and writing, then the odds are much higher that the evidence does represent a convergence on fundamental underlying knowledge. In his review of early work, Carden (1976b) as showing that judgments *are* correlated with other performance measures.

This raises the more general question of replication. Following basic scientific principles, the elicitation of grammaticality judgments ought to be a replicable method of data gathering. Greenbaum (1977c) proposes four possible types of replication experiment. First, one can perform the same experiment on a different set of subjects. However, while the same outcome will support the original result, it is not so clear how to interpret a different outcome. Is the procedure flawed, were the first results a fluke, or do the new subjects actually have different grammars? Thus, one might prefer to repeat the experiment with the same subjects after some time has elapsed. Then interpreting the results is straightforward, but procedural problems might arise in getting subjects to attend a second session and there is the possibility that they will take a different approach to the task based on their first experience. A third possibility would be to keep the subjects, but replace the stimulus sentences with lexically varied but structurally equivalent ones. Of course, it is hard to know in advance which lexical items could actually be syntactically relevant, so once again negative results are problematic. The fourth possibility is essentially that discussed in the previous paragraph, namely, to keep the stimuli and subjects the same, but take a different measure of intuitions, e.g., change from a rating to a ranking task. Here the blame assignment problem is somewhat easier: differences are most likely caused by extragrammatical factors that differ across the two tasks. The problem is then to determine which set of judgments (if either) reflects the grammar more directly.

The final and perhaps most troubling problem I will comment on in interpreting grammaticality judgments is what to make of inconsistencies, be they changes in one subject's judgments over time or disagreements among subjects.[15] Fillmore (1979) points out that we must first rule out the possibilities that our data gathering was faulty, or that our subjects were uncooperative, insensitive, or unreliable, before concluding that different grammars are the cause. Generative linguists have often suggested that the between-speaker differences that are found represent minor disagreements on fringe data, but that the major sub-

---

[15] In Section 3.3.2, I raise the issue of what should count as an inconsistency. Different experimenters have used different criteria for deciding when two judgments are consistent. Some require them to be identical, while others allow a one-point variation on a scale of three or four values. Birdsong (1989) points out that a yea-saying bias, as found by Mohan (1977), reported in Section 3.3.4, can artificially inflate consistency scores.

stance of the grammar is the same for everyone, being a function of, say, UG plus parameter settings.[16] Others have disagreed, e.g., Grandy (1981) and Levelt (1972). Carden & Dieterich (1981) claim that "data disagreements, regrettably but perhaps not surprisingly, tend to center on theoretically crucial examples" (p. 584).[17] Under a principles-and-parameters approach, we might expect the periphery, that part of the grammar *not* specified by UG but somehow learned, to vary with people's learning abilities and experience, but we would presumably not expect variation on matters directly within the scope of innate universals. While it is hard to find data bearing directly on this point, my suspicion is that it is untrue.[18] My own experience is that Binding and Subjacency, conditions that are paradigmatic examples of the domain of UG, are two of the areas of greatest variation. (In fact, recent evidence suggests that Subjacency might not be a grammatical phenomenon after all; see Section 7.2.) As one example, see again the discussion of *that*-trace effects in Section 2.3.2. For another, see Kitagawa's (1991) paper on copying identity. With regard to sloppy versus strict identity interpretations of coreference in VP-Ellipsis, Kitagawa identifies five "dialects" among fifteen speakers.[19] Here one really cannot argue that the disagreements involve unimportant or fringe sentences. As rare as they might be in everyday speech, if they are governed by innate principles then this degree of variation is unexpected. The standard appeal to performance factors is also unconvincing here, at least in the usual narrow sense of the term, which typically refers to memory limitations or processing by analogy. While it is reasonable to suggest that people's ability to process multiply center-embedded sentences could be a function of their short-term memory capacity independent of their grammar, the same does not ring true for coreference constraints.

---

[16] Newmeyer (1983) explicitly argues that the vast majority of alleged data disagreements in generative grammar are actually disagreements about the role of the theory, not about judgments. My own experience has been that such a position is untenable, as exemplified by the cases discussed in Section 2.3.2.

[17] Newmeyer (1983) correctly points out that the particular example that Carden & Dieterich use to exemplify the situation (the debate between Chomsky on the one hand and Katz & Postal on the other over the interaction between passivization and quantifier scope) is probably not a true instance of data disagreement.

[18] This is not to deny that there is an (arguably very small) core of simple sentences that all speakers of a language will agree are grammatical. But this set is not identical to the core in Chomsky's technical sense; far from it.

[19] It should be noted that while coreference is in the domain of Binding Theory, the explanation that Kitagawa tentatively proposes for the range of dialects involves differences in feature-copying rules rather than in the conditions of Binding Theory per se. Still, these rules are presumably part of UG too.

Are we forced to conclude, then, that UG exhibits individual differences, that we are not all born with identical principles and parameters? This is certainly a possibility, and would not be a particularly surprising result – in general, people do exhibit individual differences on many, perhaps all, innately specified behaviors, while sharing the gross features. In fact, Chomsky (1991) takes it as a truism that genetically based UG will be subject to individual variation. It is merely a theoretically simplifying assumption that UG is invariant. Apparently this view has not been much stressed in the literature, since Lieberman (1991) believes that "until the past year, virtually all theoretical linguists working in the Chomskian tradition claimed that the Universal Grammar was *identical* in all humans" (p. 53, emphasis in original). One way to get at the extent to which inter-speaker variation in judgments can be traced to differences in UG might be to compare the degree of agreement on intuitions between identical versus fraternal twins. In principle, areas in which identical twins always agree but fraternal twins do not would be candidates for UG differences, while areas in which identical twins disagree would be candidates for a learning account. Whatever the source of individual differences, linguists must take responsibility for the range of variation that is actually found.[20]

An explanation in terms of extragrammatical factors seems more likely in the case of changes in one person's judgments from one elicitation to the next. (Either that or, as Snow (1975) suggests, poor experimental design could be to blame.) While grammars certainly do change in some aspects over the course of a lifetime, most linguists would probably not want to say that this happens on a day-to-day basis in adulthood. That is why Carden (1973) suggests that individual differences be attributed to the grammar only if they are reliable (he gives several ways of computing reliability indices) and if they correlate with other linguistic differences. Another alternative that has been bandied about occasionally is that grammars are probabilistically defined, so that some sentence will be judged good 90% of the time, bad the other 10%, based on variation in neural signal strength or some such factor. (In fact, the race-based approach predicts such a pattern of events, because the speed with which a given rule can be used depends in part on how recently it was used in the past, according to an activation function that decays over time.) The problem with this general line of probabilistic analysis is that it denies that there are any systematic causes behind the variation we find.

---

[20] Haj Ross seems to have felt that some linguists were not doing so; he paraphrased the standard research directive as "Write a grammar of what you find in your heart" (class lectures, MIT and Harvard University, 1966–67, attributed to Ross in Carden (1973)). In contrast, Noam Chomsky (personal communication) believes that variation has always been taken seriously in linguistic theory.

If instead we start with the assumption that it has a cause within the system of judgment performance, then as we understand more about that process we might eventually be in a position to say precisely what governs variation over time and predict it as a function of other cognitive and situational variables. Only after we have exhausted the search for such an explanation should we resort to random probabilities.

Labov (1975) has proposed a widely cited set of working principles for dealing with variation in grammaticality judgments and interpreting their relationship to the grammar:

I. The Consensus Principle: if there is no reason to think otherwise, assume that the judgments of any native speaker are characteristic of all speakers of the language.

II. The Experimenter Principle: if there is any disagreement on introspective judgments, the judgments of those who are familiar with the theoretical issues may not be counted as evidence.

III. The Clear Case' Principle: disputed judgments should be shown to include at least one consistent pattern in the speech community or be abandoned. If differing judgments are said to represent different dialects, enough investigation of each dialect should be carried out to show that each judgment is a clear case in that dialect. (p. 31)

IV. The Principle of Validity: when the use of language is shown to be more consistent than introspective judgments, a valid description of the language will agree with that use rather than introspections. (p. 40)

For the most part, these suggestions strike me as quite reasonable, although a note of caution is in order. Principle I is intended to allow the field to continue without having to resort to experimental verification of sentences whose (un)grammatical status no one has ever questioned. Principle II is intended to guard against experimenter effects; I suggest strengthening it so that the investigating linguists' own intuitions are *never* counted as evidence, even if their data have not been disputed.[21] Principle IV jibes well with my comments in Chapter 3 concerning the potential for differences between use and intuitions. Unfortunately, there is still no way of knowing when primary data from linguistic use

---

[21] Of course, linguists' intuitions will always be used to inspire theoretical work; I merely wish to exclude them from the verification of the data.

need to be sought out (since such relevant data are often not immediately available), and there is no obvious procedure for determining whether they are more consistent than judgment data. But the major problem comes with Principle III. Its wording (and that of Principle I) indicates that Labov is interested in accounting for the grammar of *groups* of speakers (as inferred also by Newmeyer (1983)), but I have argued that it is entirely possible for *individuals* to have unique grammars, so that discarding judgments that are not shared by other speakers could involve throwing away real data. As Ringen (1979) points out,

> Linguists frequently and publicly acknowledge that the reports of intuitions they are using provide data only about the dialect of a single speaker. ... Such acknowledgements characteristically come as responses to evidence of differences between informant intuitions. ... Where conflicting informant judgments indicate differences of idiolect or dialect, linguists do not conclude that the judgments are not judgments on which a [transformational generative grammar] should be based. Rather they conclude that the judgments must be taken into account by different grammars. (pp. 121–122)

Certainly, the more speakers we can find who share a set of intuitions, the more confident we can be of the legitimacy of those intuitions, but at a certain point we will have to hope that our methods have removed as many confounds as possible and treat the resulting data as significant, even if it applies only to a single speaker. While there might be little interest in studying individual idiolects for their own sake, the *range* of possibilities that are found is crucial to the construction of theories.

6.4 Conclusion

In this chapter I have presented two major proposals that assemble the information gleaned from the first five chapters of this work. The first is an initial attempt at a model of mental components of metalinguistic activity, with a focus on grammaticality judgments. There is clearly much more work that could be done in this vein. First, we might now go on to suggest specific experiments that could clarify aspects of the model or show where changes are required. Second, we could derive new empirical predictions regarding how certain effects should manifest themselves in tasks that implicate certain components of the mental structure, and run these tasks experimentally to see whether the predictions are borne out. Third, we might consider whether there is something to be gained from implementing a computer simulation of the model. Since it is highly parallel, and relies on very many microcopmutations, simulation could lead to better understanding and refinement, as it has for connectionism and race-based parsing. The second major proposal in this chapter takes the form of methodological guidelines for eliciting grammaticality judgments. I do not go so far as to propose a particular experimental design, since this must vary with the specific purpose of the experiment, but if even some of my suggestions are followed, significant strides toward a solid empirical foundation for linguistic research will have been made. Whether this is likely to occur will be the subject of part of the final chapter, after I propose some more general directions for future research.

7 Looking Back and Looking Ahead

Recent trends in linguistic research have placed increasing dependence on relatively subtle intuitions. ... Subtle intuitions are not to be trusted until we understand the nature of their interaction with factors that are irrelevant to grammaticality. If we depend too much on such intuitions without exploring their nature, linguistic research will perpetuate the defects of introspective mentalism as well as its virtues.

(Bever 1970b)

7.1 Introduction

The epigraph from Bever above concurs very well with my own findings in the preceding six chapters. By way of a response, it seems fair to say that the field has begun taking steps to explore the nature of grammaticality judgments, and I hope that the present work makes its own contribution to that exploration. In this final chapter I concentrate mostly on what lies ahead in this endeavor.

I will not attempt to summarize the discussion to this point in any detail, but will very briefly review the structure of the argumentation and illustrate that a major intention has been to provide substantive support for the views of grammaticality judgments that have been expressed succinctly and eloquently by previous researchers in this area. It might be hoped that their observations will carry more weight with the underpinnings of the extensive experimental and theoretical literature that this book has assembled.

In Chapters 1 and 2, I reviewed some of the history of how the concept of grammaticality has evolved since the 1950s, various opinions on its empirical status, and how it is used and misused today among theoretical linguists. On this basis I argued that theory is no longer being based on clear cases, and that detailed study of the judgment process is therefore required to establish how to deal with unclear cases. Botha (1973) extends the argument even further: "consider the status of the so-called clear cases of linguistic intuitions. Today, it can be seen that native speakers may make, concerning a particular linguistic property of some sentence, judgments which are at once, clear, decisive, and consistent without there necessarily being genuine linguistic intuitions at the basis of these judgments" (p. 205). I also pointed out that concern with these problems has been sorely lacking to date in linguistic work. As Pullum somewhat cynically puts it, "The median number of speakers on whom the entire corpus of examples in an English syntax paper is checked before publication, including its author, is zero" (Pullum 1987: 453). I made the specific proposal that the sources of the perturbations in grammaticality judgments exist independent of the language faculties of the mind. In retrospect, that position has probably turned out to be too strong. Some of them might be attributable specifically to the parser, for instance. Nonetheless, the more phenomena we can reduce to language-independent sources, the better, by Occam's razor, so I maintain that one should always seek evidence for this position first. Chapter 3 was devoted to pursuing the suggestion that grammaticality judgments be studied as an instance of (meta)linguistic performance: as part of a larger family of such tasks, as an instance of graded behavior, perhaps as an instance of introspective behavior, and as just one more source of evidence about grammars. By this point, it was already apparent that "in many ways, intuition is less regular and more difficult to interpret than speech" (Labov 1972a: 199).

Chapters 4 and 5 were devoted to detailed examinations of the range of causes for variability in judgments. Chapter 4 was concerned with the degree of variation between subjects and its attribution either to inherent characteristics or to life experiences. Chapter 5 examined task factors, which were broken down by being (mostly extragrammatical) features of the sentences being judged, or features of the procedure used to elicit judgments. It is clear that in neither case do we have a full understanding of the way these factors work, so that Birdsong's plea still stands: "thorough study of the psychological and epistemological intricacies of metalinguistic performance is necessary if we are to achieve an understanding of the linguistic knowledge it is often thought to reflect" (Birdsong 1989: 49). Finally, Chapter 6 was an attempt to integrate these findings in terms of an abstract view of the implied mental structures and a proposed methodology for more rigorous data collection among linguists. The componential view of the judgment process as involving many more pieces than language use lent credence to another of Birdsong's statements: "the hypocrisy of rejecting linguistic performance data as too noisy to study, while embracing metalinguistic performance data as proper input to theory, should be apparent to any thoughtful linguist" (p. 72). If it was not apparent before, it should be now!

The format of the remainder of this chapter is straightforward. In Section 7.2, I consider the sorts of research that naturally follow most directly from the present work, including both experimental and theoretical undertakings. I conclude in Section 7.3 with some speculation about the future in the field of linguistics, specifically about the role that grammaticality judgments are likely to play down the road, and the chances that attitudes toward their collection and application will change.

7.2 Directions for Further Research

As acknowledged in Section 1.5, what I have presented here is far from a complete picture of the state of the art in studying grammaticality judgments. There is great potential for elucidating many of the issues we have confronted by considering kinds of data that have been excluded here. For example, experiments involving people with amnesia could clarify the memory mechanisms underlying structural priming effects, repetition effects, context, etc. Research on the development of metalinguistic skills in children should tell us more about the interdependence of these skills and primary language skills. Work with second-language learners should help to establish the relationship between intuitions and use as skill in the language increases, while avoiding some of the methodological problems involved in eliciting judgments from children; experiments with aphasics could serve a similar purpose. Finally, more about the process of linguistic judgment in general could be learned by more detailed work on the nature of lexical, phonological, semantic, and pragmatic judgments, in comparison with syntactic ones. The larger open question of the existence of linguistic competence and its role in language processing remains a major unresolved issue in the psychological investigation of language processing.

As for specific lines of investigation that would follow more directly from the present work, many potentially informative experiments have been proposed in response to specific problems with published research; these will not be repeated here. One major area into which I have not delved deeply is the substantiation of the hypothesis proposed in Section 1.4, namely, that we can find a non-linguistic analog for all of the perturbations that grammaticality judgments are subject to. In many cases we have seen implicitly that this is true to a certain degree. For instance, individual differences correlated with field dependence, handedness, age, sex, creativity, and world knowledge are certainly not unique to linguistic intuitions. Neither are differences due to expertise, which parallel those of linguistic training and literacy. Likewise, most of the procedural factors considered in Section 5.2 are familiar from other branches of psychology, although the particular changes that some of them induce in grammaticality judgments (e.g., repetition and mental state effects) are not obviously analogous to those in other domains. Parallels to other cognitive spheres are hardest to draw in the area of stimulus factors, since many of these are closely tied to the nature of language itself. While at least some types of context effect have perceptual analogs, it is hard to think of a nonlinguistic equivalent of structural well-formedness being affected by meaning, lexical content, morphology, etc. It seems that the best we can do for the moment is to point to domains where supposedly orthogonal features of a stimulus affect judgments of the target feature. Thus, the first major hurdle in this line of work is to find suitable domains of cognition in which to look for such parallels to the manipulability of grammaticality judgments. By way of an example, in addition to possibilities discussed in Chapter 1, one intriguing area I have come across involves judgments in legal cases. Kaplan (1977) reports a number of phenomena that look promisingly parallel to the stimulus effects we have seen. For instance, it has been shown experimentally that jurors are influenced by factors totally irrelevant to the legal merits of a case in ways that depend on the nature of the crime. An attractive defendant will be judged less likely to be guilty of a burglary but more likely to be guilty in a confidence swindle. Personal traits such as race, sex, and marital status have been shown to affect outcomes of cases even when jurors are explicitly instructed not to pay attention to them. Even when jurors are told that a certain variable is or is not statistically a predictor of guilt, they do not use this information in deciding how to treat the data in question.

A second major area that cries out for follow-up is the methodology of judgment elicitation itself. The logical next step in the research program would be to design and run case study experiments incorporating the proposals made in Section 6.3, developing a specific set of instructions along the way. Such a study will undoubtedly point out problems with the proposals, suggest refinements, etc., and will allow the resulting data to be assessed for reliability and to be compared with results from more casual data collection. To the extent that the data are more reliable, one of the goals of the exercise will have been met. The third and perhaps most ethereal line of research to follow from the present work would involve finding independent motivation (outside linguistic judgments) for the components of the model proposed in Section 6.2, for instance the general control strategies. It is not at all obvious how to proceed here.

I would like to close this section by mentioning some excellent new experimental work that begins to address the three research areas just outlined, with very encouraging results. First I summarize the findings of several independent lines of investigation into the nature of Subjacency effects, all of which converge on the conclusion that these should not be attributed to the grammar, but rather to some extragrammatical component, perhaps the parser. Then I discuss work that shows the viability and benefits of taking judgment-gathering methodology seriously. Neville et al. (1991) present some event-related brain potential (ERP) results (see Section 3.2) that could be a step toward using this technology to confirm independently certain kinds of judgment data. They found, in addition to the frequently observed N400 response to semantic anomaly, distinct responses to certain types of syntactic ill-formedness. Neville et al. tested the following sort of paradigm, wherein the first four sentences are grammatical controls for the remaining ill-formed sentences:

(1) a. The man admired a sketch of the landscape.
   b. The man admired Don's sketch of the landscape.
   c. What did the man admire a sketch of?
   d. Was a sketch of the landscape admired by the man?
   e. The man admired Don's of sketch the landscape.
   f. The man admired Don's headache of the landscape.
   g. What did the man admire Don's sketch of?
   h. What was a sketch of admired by the man?

Sentence (1e) exemplifies a phrase structure violation in contrast with (1b), where *sketch* and *of* are in the correct order. Sentence (1f) supposedly instantiates semantic anomaly, in contrast with (1b), although it is not obvious that one could not just as well analyze it as a subcategorization failure, because *headache* cannot take an argument PP and that is the only function the following phrase can serve; hence, it might still embody a syntactic type of ill-formedness. The contrast between (1c), which is fine, and (1g), which is degraded, is attributed to the specificity of the NP from which the latter extraction has taken place (due to the genitive). Finally, the contrast between (1d) and (1h) illustrates the effect of a Subjacency violation in the latter. Neville et al.'s basic finding was that only the supposed semantic anomaly generated N400 responses. The Specificity violation generated an N125, which was similar to the effect of the phrase structure violation, while the Subjacency violation generated a substantially different pattern. The authors take these results as supporting the notion of a distinct syntactic type of ill-formedness not tied to meaning, and as suggesting that Subjacency may be of a different character from the other two types of syntactic violation, perhaps due to processing difficulty rather than grammatical prohibition. These conclusions are obviously speculative, but encouraging nonetheless. The weak link in this study is that it has not yet been shown that different sentence structure types that violate *the same* grammatical constraint yield the same type of ERP response. For instance, do Subjacency violations of the type (1h) (extraction from a complex NP) yield the same pattern as those of the type *What did you wonder who bought?* (extraction from a *wh*-island)? Until this is found, one cannot exclude the possibility that every sentence type simply yields a distinct pattern of activity. (See Kluender & Kutas (1993) for more evidence, from judgments as well as ERPs, bearing on the nature of Subjacency.)

Snyder (1994) has taken a different approach to the same question, conducting experiments into the nature of syntactic satiation effects on judgment tasks and what they might tell us about the nature of grammars and the extent of the problem of "linguists' disease," i.e., the possibility that linguists come to accept ill-formed structures due to repeated exposure. Snyder was able to experimentally induce some satiation effects that were specific to certain types of sentence, i.e., that did not involve an across-the-board change in the subjects' liberality of judgment, but did generalize somewhat across different lexical items within each type. He found that some classes of sentences were susceptible to satiation while others were not. The particular paradigm involved yes/no judgments of grammaticality of 58 sentences, where sentence types recurred over the course of the questionnaire. The measure of satiation was whether a particular subject judged a sentence type grammatical more often later on in the experiment. The types of ungrammaticality tested are exemplified in (2).

(2) a. Who does John want for Mary to meet? [*want-for*]
   b. What does John know that a bottle of fell on the floor? [subject island]
   c. Who does John wonder whether Mary likes? [*whether* island]
   d. Who does Mary think that likes John? [*that*-trace]
   e. Who does Mary believe the claim that John likes? [Complex NP Constraint]
   f. Who did John talk with Mary after seeing? [adjunct island]
   g. How many did John buy books? [Left Branch Constraint]

Sentence types (2c) and (2e) showed statistically significant satiation effects (with order of presentation counterbalanced), type (2b) tended towards such an effect, and no other sentence types showed any effect.

Somewhat surprisingly, those sentences that did satiate were not those among the sentence types that seem to show the greatest degree of interspeaker variation in general, namely, *that*-trace (see Section 2.3.3) and *want-for* violations. Snyder suggests that the sentences that *are* subject to satiation may be those whose ill-formedness has its roots in processing rather than in the grammar proper. Perhaps with repeated exposure, subjects develop alternate parsing strategies to deal with Subjacency violations, and having done so they do not find the sentences as bad. Conversely, violations that do not improve with repeated exposure are therefore less likely to be purely a result of parsing restrictions. This evidence converges with that of Neville et al. from ERP research as a compelling story in which judgments of badness involving Subjacency may not reflect the grammar at all. It is also interesting that Snyder did find two types of Subjacency violation that patterned the same way and differed from the other types of violation he looked at.

Turning more directly to issues of methodology, (Cowart 1997: 12–27) conducted a series of experiments to test the skeptics' claim that judgments from naive speakers would not be useful to linguists even if systematically collected. He focused on the question of whether their judgments were stable, i.e., whether the relative acceptability of a set of sentences stayed the same across different groups of subjects at different times under different conditions. With a careful experimental design involving counterbalanced orders and multiple instances of each crucial sentence type, several contrasts important to syntactic theory were shown to be highly statistically reliable. In each case, the amount of variability across subjects was much less than that across sentence types, i.e., there was a great deal of agreement on the relevant contrasts. One experiment tested *wh*-extraction from different kinds of *picture* NPs and found that four sentence types all showed significantly different judgments of grammaticality. In particular, in contrast to the standard judgment in the literature, an extraction like *Who did the Duchess sell a portrait of?*, while better than *Who did the Duchess sell Max's portrait of?*, is significantly worse than a simple adjunct question like *Why did the Duchess sell a portrait of Max?*, a result that was confirmed by comparison with other closely related sentence types. Cowart also demonstrates how these gradations of acceptability can be interpreted. A dialect-split interpretation can be excluded because of the very small amount of variation among subjects for the crucial sentence type, as compared to variation across sentence types. Thus, these sentences do seem to have an intermediate status for individual speakers. Another set of sentences studied by Cowart involves *that*-trace effects. Again, he found very stable results, with subject and object extractions ((3b) and (3d) below) being equally acceptable without *that*, but subject extractions being much worse in the presence of *that* ((3a) versus (3b)), confirming the standard judgments in the literature. However, object extraction is significantly worse with *that* than without it ((3c) versus (3d)), a fact that standard theories have not taken into account. (See Cowart (1997: 12–27) for some qualifications on this finding.)

(3)   a. I wonder who you think that likes John.
        b. I wonder who you think likes John.
        c. I wonder who you think that John likes.
        d. I wonder who you think John likes.

It remains to be argued whether the grammar should be responsible for these unexpected contrasts.

7.3 The Future in Linguistics

In Sections 1.3 and 7.2 I describe some recent work in the generative paradigm that I feel makes exemplary use of grammaticality judgments. Obviously if this trend of linguists basing their theories on experimental data is to continue and grow, linguists will have to be trained in areas that they traditionally have not been required to know anything about: statistics and experimental design in general, and the psychology of grammaticality judgments in particular. I would echo Greenbaum's (1977) recommendation that every linguistics department should offer a course in experimental linguistics. In addition to reasons internal to our own field, this would give students a leg up in joining the blossoming interdisciplinary enterprise of cognitive science. It would also seem to be a natural outgrowth of Chomsky's own suggestion that linguistics be viewed as a branch of cognitive psychology. Somehow, the focus on cognitive issues has not yet been accompanied by adoption of the scientific standards and concern with methodology of that discipline.[1] But even if only a small proportion of linguists were actually to carry out their own experimental data collection, all could benefit by

---

[1] Noam Chomsky (personal communication) believes that research practice in linguistics ought to follow that in the natural sciences, where (in contrast to the social sciences) "almost no one devotes attention to 'methodology'." Obviously, I disagree.

knowing more about problems of experimental bias, individual differences, introspection, etc. The question is whether theoretical linguists are likely to heed such advice. I suggest that part of the reason for linguists' lackadaisical attitude in this regard is not so much that they believe their data are clear-cut, but that there is little motivation for putting effort into a systematic approach because, unlike in most of the social sciences, there is no standard publication format requiring authors to describe how their data were gathered. (Grandy (1981) makes a similar point, and suggests other possible reasons why the deplorable state of lack of rigor continues.) Also, since linguists typically have no training in experimental design, they do not appreciate how useful and important it is. On this question, we can do little more than keep our fingers crossed. It does seem, based on my assessment of the literature, that more and more linguists are coming around.

Carden & Dieterich (1981), who make proposals similar to my own, give a typical response to their work, suggesting that many linguists will oppose such methodological changes. They cite Green (1978) as saying that if proposals like theirs were adopted, "research would come to a standstill." Certainly this would be true if *every* sentence had to be subjected to extensive experimental verification (Labov 1975), but that is unnecessary. If we adopt Labov's Clear Case Principle (see Section 6.3.3), this will only be required when we have reason to believe that there is disagreement. Green continues with a second objection: "I doubt if any experimental results, no matter how clean, would affect the status of crucial disputed examples. Linguists will still trust their own intuitions of grammaticality." A third objection that I have frequently heard is that much more money will be required to carry out linguistic research under these proposals (Elan Dresher, personal communication). Ringen (1979) believes that is only a rationalization for inaction: "The cost of data does not explain the traditional reliance on small numbers of informants since many linguistic research projects are extremely well-funded. One suspects that even if time and funds were unlimited, surveying large numbers of informants would be judged an unnecessary and indeed trivial endeavor" (p. 120, fn. 39). All I can say in response to the latter two objections is, I hope not.

Somewhat more optimistically, Labov suggests that introspective linguists are most likely to resort to experimentation on data that are crucial both ways, i.e., that can either clinch their argument or destroy it. This would be a reasonable first step. Certainly, intuitive judgments by native speakers (but, one hopes, fewer and fewer linguists) will not be replaced by other kinds of language behavior as the major source of data, at least on syntactic questions, in the foreseeable future. But it is perfectly legitimate to keep using judgment data while we attempt to understand them better. While their potential contamination by extraneous factors is an important concern, once we are willing to actively explore the nature of these factors the problem becomes manageable. They might add sufficient noise to obscure actual grammatical phenomena, but they cannot systematically change the pattern of results unless they too are stable. If so, they can be studied directly and then factored out, as people have attempted to do with Subjacency effects in the studies mentioned above. The key is that we must always ask ourselves whether a systematic effect we find might be attributable to a combination of grammatical and extragrammatical factors, rather than purely grammatical ones. If the best account we can find of a pattern of variance in judgment data involves some discrete grammatical construct, that is the closest we can come right now to knowing that the mind really embodies such a construct. One finding from the literature should leave us optimistic: relatively few experiments have shown that the *pattern* of results is changed by the various manipulations that have been tried. This should increase our confidence that judgments do tell us about something real and important. It is up to a critic who believes that even carefully collected systematic judgment evidence is distorted and not relevant to grammar to show that that is the case, by being explicit about what the confounding factor is and *how* it distorts the results.[2]

Linguistics has much to gain and nothing to lose by taking data collection, and particularly judgment collection, much more seriously, both with regard to the insights that will be gained and the theoretical issues that will be clarified, and with regard to the standing of the field as a scientific endeavor in the larger academic setting. The realization seems to be growing that the psychology of grammaticality judgments can no longer be ignored.

---

[2] I thank Wayne Cowart for discussion of issues raised in this section.

References

Andrews, Avery D. 1990. Case structures and control in Modern Icelandic. In Joan Maling & Annie Zaenen (eds.), *Modern Icelandic syntax* (Syntax and Semantics 24), 187–234. San Diego: Academic Press.

Aoun, Joseph, Norbert Hornstein, David Lightfoot & Amy Weinberg. 1987. Two types of locality. *Linguistic Inquiry* 18(4). 537–577.

Armstrong, Sharon Lee, Lila R. Gleitman & Henry Gleitman. 1983. What some concepts might not be. *Cognition* 13(3). 263–308.

Asquith, Peter D. & Ronald N. Giere (eds.). 1981. *PSA 1980: Proceedings of the 1980 biennial meeting of the Philosophy of Science Association. Volume 2: Symposia.* East Lansing, MI: Philosophy of Science Association.

Baker, Mark C. 1988. *Incorporation: A theory of grammatical function changing.* Chicago: University of Chicago Press.

Baltin, Mark. 1977. Quantifier-negative interaction. In Ralph W. Fasold & Roger W. Shuy (eds.), *Studies in language variation: Semantics, syntax, phonology, pragmatics, social situations, ethnographic approaches*, 30–36. Washington, D.C.: Georgetown University Press.

Bar-Hillel, Yehoshua. 1971. Out of the pragmatic wastebasket. *Linguistic Inquiry* 2(3). 401–407.

Barsalou, Lawrence W. 1987. The instability of graded structure: Implications for the nature of concepts. In Ulric Neisser (ed.), *Concepts and conceptual development: Ecological and intellectual factors in categorization*, 101–140. Cambridge: Cambridge University Press.

Becker, Joseph D. 1975. The phrasal lexicon. In Roger C. Schank & Bonnie L. Nash-Webber (eds.), *Theoretical issues in natural language processing: An interdisciplinary workshop in computational linguistics, psychology, linguistics, artificial intelligence, 10–13 June 1975, Cambridge, Massachusetts*, 70–73. Stroudsburg, PA: Association for Computational Linguistics.

Belletti, Adriana. 1988. The case of unaccusatives. *Linguistic Inquiry* 19(1). 1–34.

Belletti, Adriana & Luigi Rizzi. 1988. Psych-verbs and θ-theory. *Natural Language and Linguistic Theory* 6. 291–352.

Bergum, Bruce O. & Judith E. Bergum. 1979a. Creativity, perceptual stability, and self-perception. *Bulletin of the Psychonomic Society* 14(1). 61–63.

Bergum, Judith E. & Bruce O. Bergum. 1979b. Self-perceived creativity and ambiguous figure reversal rates. *Bulletin of the Psychonomic Society* 14(5). 373–374.

Berkovits, Rochele. 1981. Are spoken surface structure ambiguities perceptually unambiguous? *Journal of Psycholinguistic Research* 1(10). 41–56.

Berkovits, Rochele. 1982. On disambiguating surface-structure ambiguity. *Linguistics* 20. 713–726.

Berwick, Robert C. & Amy Weinberg. 1984. *The grammatical basis of linguistic performance: Language use and acquisition.* Cambridge, MA: MIT Press.

Bever, Thomas G. 1970a. The cognitive basis for linguistic structures. In John R. Hayes (ed.), *Cognition and the development of language*, 279–362. New York: John Wiley & Sons.

Bever, Thomas G. 1970b. The influence of speech performance on linguistic structure. In Giovanni B. Flores d'Arcais & Willem J.M. Levelt (eds.), *Advances in psycholinguistics*, 4–30. Amsterdam: North-Holland. Reprinted in Bever, Katz & Langendoen 1976, 65–88.

Bever, Thomas G. 1971. The integrated study of language behaviour. In John Morton (ed.), *Biological and social factors in psycholinguistics*, 158–209. Urbana: University of Illinois Press.

Bever, Thomas G. 1972. The limits of intuition. *Foundations of Language* 8. 411–412.

Bever, Thomas G. 1974. The ascent of the specious; or, There's a lot we don't know about mirrors. In David Cohen (ed.), *Explaining linguistic phenomena*, 173–200. Washington, D.C.: Hemisphere.

Bever, Thomas G. 1975a. Functional explanations require independently motivated functional theories. In Robin E. Grossman, L. James San & Timothy J. Vance (eds.), *Papers from the parasession on functionalism*, 580–609. Chicago: Chicago Linguistic Society.

Bever, Thomas G. 1975b. Psychologically real grammar emerges because of its role in language acquisition. In Daniel P. Dato (ed.), *Georgetown University round table in languages and linguistics 1975*, 63–75. Washington, D.C.: Georgetown University Press.

Bever, Thomas G. 1986. The aesthetic basis for cognitive structures. In Myles Brand & Robert M. Hamish (eds.), *The representation of knowledge and belief*, 314–356. Tucson: University of Arizona Press.

Bever, Thomas G. 1992. The logical and extrinsic sources of modularity. In Megan R. Gunnar & Michael Maratsos (eds.), *Modularity and constraints in language and cognition: The Minnesota symposia on child psychology*, vol. 25, 179–212. Hillsdale, N.J.: Erlbaum.

Bever, Thomas G., Caroline Carrithers, Wayne Cowart & David J. Townsend. 1989. Language processing and familial handedness. In Albert M. Galaburda (ed.), *From reading to neurons*, 331–360. Cambridge, MA: MIT Press.

Bever, Thomas G., Caroline Carrithers & David J. Townsend. 1987. A tale of two brains; or, The sinistral quasimodularity of language. In Cognitive Science Society (ed.), *Program of the ninth annual conference of the Cognitive Science Society*, 764–773. Hillsdale, N.J.: Erlbaum.

Bever, Thomas G. & John M. Carroll. 1981. On some continuous properties in language. In Terry Myers, John Laver & John Anderson (eds.), *The cognitive representation of speech*, 225–233. Amsterdam: North-Holland.

Bever, Thomas G., John M. Carroll & R. Hurtig. 1976. Analogy; or, Ungrammatical sequences that are utterable and comprehensible are the origins of new grammars in language acquisition and linguistic evolution. In Thomas G. Bever, Jerrold J. Katz & D. Terence Langendoen (eds.), *An integrated theory of linguistic ability*, 149–182. New York: Crowell.

Bever, Thomas G., Jerrold J. Katz & D. Terence Langendoen (eds.). 1976b. *An integrated theory of linguistic ability*. New York: Crowell.

Bever, Thomas G. & D. Terence Langendoen. 1971. A dynamic model of the evolution of language. *Linguistic Inquiry* 2. 433–463. Reprinted in Bever, Katz & Langendoen 1976, 115–147.

Bialystok, Ellen. 1979. Explicit and implicit judgements of L2 grammaticality. *Language Learning* 29. 81–103.

Bialystok, Ellen. 1986. Factors in the growth of linguistic awareness. *Child Development* 57. 498–510.

Bialystok, Ellen & Ellen Bouchard Ryan. 1985. A metacognitive framework for the development of first and second language skills. In Donna-Lynn Forrest-Presley, G.E. MacKinnon & T. Gary Waller (eds.), *Metacognition, cognition and human performance.* Volume 1: *Theoretical perspectives*, 207–252. Orlando: Academic Press.

Biber, Douglas. 1986. Spoken and written textual dimensions in English: Resolving the contradictory findings. *Language* 62(2). 384–414.

Birdsong, David. 1989. *Metalinguistic performance and interlinguistic competence.* New York: Springer.

Bley-Vroman, Robert W., Sascha W. Felix & Georgette L. Ioup. 1988. The accessibility of universal grammar in adult language learning. *Second Language Research* 4(1). 1–32.

Bock, J. Kathryn. 1986. Syntactic persistence in language production. *Cognitive Psychology* 18. 355–387.

Bolinger, Dwight L. 1961. *Generality, gradience, and the all-or-none.* The Hague: Mouton.

Bolinger, Dwight L. 1968. Judgments of grammaticality. *Lingua* 21. 34–40.

Bolinger, Dwight L. 1971. Semantic overloading: A restudy of the verb *remind. Language* 47(3). 522–547.

Boring, Edwin G. 1953. A history of introspection. *Psychological Bulletin* 50(3). 169–189.

Botha, Rudolph F. 1973. *The justification of linguistic hypotheses: A study of non-demonstrative inference in transformational grammar.* With the collaboration of Walter K. Winckler. The Hague: Mouton.

Botha, Rudolph F. 1981. *The conduct of linguistic inquiry: A systematic introduction to the methodology of generative grammar.* The Hague: Mouton.

Bradac, James J., Larry W. Martin, Norman D. Elliott & Charles H. Tardy. 1980. On the neglected side of linguistic science: Multivariate studies of sentence judgment. *Linguistics* 18(11/12). 967–995.

Browning, Marguerite A. 1987. Null operators and their antecedents. In Joyce McDonough & Bernadette Plunkett (eds.), *Proceedings of NELS 17*, vol. 1, 59–78. Amherst, MA: Graduate Linguistic Student Association, University of Massachusetts at Amherst.

Burzio, Luigi. 1981. *Intransitive verbs and Italian auxiliaries.* Cambridge, MA: MIT PhD dissertation.

Carden, Guy. 1970a. Discussion of Heringer 1970. In Chicago Linguistic Society (ed.), *Papers from the sixth regional meeting*, 296. Chicago: Chicago Linguistic Society.

Carden, Guy. 1970b. A note on conflicting idiolects. *Linguistic Inquiry* 1(3). 281–290.

Carden, Guy. 1973. Dialect variation and abstract syntax. In Roger W. Shuy (ed.), *Some new directions in linguistics*, 1–34. Washington, D.C.: Georgetown University Press.

Carden, Guy. 1976a. *English quantifiers: Logical structure and linguistic variation.* Corrected edition. New York: Academic Press.

Carden, Guy. 1976b. Syntactic and semantic data: Replication results. *Language in Society* 5(1). 99–104.

Carden, Guy & Thomas Dieterich. 1981. Introspection, observation, and experiment: An example where experiment pays off. In Peter D. Asquith & Ronald N. Giere (eds.), *PSA 1980: Proceedings of the 1980 biennial meeting of the Phi-*

losophy of Science Association. Volume 2: Symposia, 583–597. East Lansing, MI: Philosophy of Science Association.

Carr, Philip. 1990. *Linguistic realities: An autonomist metatheory for the generative enterprise.* Cambridge: Cambridge University Press.

Carroll, John M. 1979. Complex compounds: Phrasal embedding in lexical structures. *Linguistics* 17. 863–877.

Carroll, John M., Thomas G. Bever & Chava R. Pollack. 1981. The non-uniqueness of linguistic intuitions. *Language* 57(2). 368–383.

Catt, Mark. 1988. *Intelligent diagnosis of ungrammaticality in computer-assisted language instruction.* Department of Computer Science, University of Toronto MA thesis. Published as Technical Report CSRI-218, Computer Systems Research Institute, University of Toronto.

Catt, Mark & Graeme Hirst. 1990. An intelligent CALI system for grammatical error diagnosis. *Computer Assisted Language Learning* 3. 3–26.

Cazden, Courtney B. 1976. Play with language and meta-linguistic awareness: One dimension of language experience. In Jerome S. Bruner, Alison Jolly & Kathy Sylva (eds.), *Play – Its role in development and evolution*, 603–608. New York: Basic Books.

Chaudron, Craig. 1983. Research on metalinguistic judgments: A review of theory, methods and results. *Language Learning* 33(3). 343–377.

Chien, Yu-Chin & Kenneth Wexler. 1990. Children's knowledge of locality conditions in binding as evidence for the modularity of syntax and pragmatics. *Language Acquisition* 1(3). 225–295.

Chomsky, Noam. 1955. *The logical structure of linguistic theory.* Ms. Harvard University, Cambridge, MA. (Revised version published in part in Chomsky 1975).

Chomsky, Noam. 1957. *Syntactic structures.* The Hague: Mouton.

Chomsky, Noam. 1961. Some methodological remarks on generative grammar. *Word* 17. 219–239.

Chomsky, Noam. 1962. Various discussion sessions. In Archibald A. Hill (ed.), *Third Texas conference on problems of linguistic analysis in English*, 22–33. Austin: University of Texas.

Chomsky, Noam. 1964. *Current issues in linguistic theory.* The Hague: Mouton.

Chomsky, Noam. 1965. *Aspects of the theory of syntax.* Cambridge, MA: MIT Press.

Chomsky, Noam. 1969. Language and philosophy. In Sidney Hook (ed.), *Language and philosophy: A symposium*, 51–94. New York: New York University Press.

Chomsky, Noam. 1972. Some empirical issues in the theory of transformational grammar. In Stanley Peters (ed.), *Goals of linguistic theory*, 63–130. Englewood Cliffs, NJ: Prentice-Hall.

References

Chomsky, Noam. 1975. *The logical structure of linguistic theory.* New York: Plenum. (Contains part of the 1956 revision of Chomsky 1955, with a new introduction dated 1973.) Reprinted by University of Chicago Press, 1985.

Chomsky, Noam. 1981. *Lectures on government and binding.* Dordrecht: Foris.

Chomsky, Noam. 1982. *The generative enterprise: A discussion with Riny Huybregts and Henk van Riemsdijk.* Dordrecht: Foris.

Chomsky, Noam. 1986. *Knowledge of language: Its nature, origin, and use.* New York: Praeger.

Chomsky, Noam. 1991. Universal grammar. Letter to the editor. *The New York Review of Books* 38(21). In reply to Lieberman 1991, 82.

Clark, Herbert H. 1973. The language-as-fixed-effect fallacy: A critique of language statistics in psychological research. *Journal of Verbal Learning and Verbal Behavior* 12. 335–359.

Clark, Herbert H. & Susan E. Haviland. 1974. Psychological processes as linguistic explanation. In David Cohen (ed.), *Explaining linguistic phenomena*, 91–124. Washington, D.C.: Hemisphere.

Cohen, David (ed.). 1974. *Explaining linguistic phenomena.* Washington, D.C.: Hemisphere.

Cohen, L.J. 1981. Some remarks on the nature of linguistic theory. *Philosophical Transactions of the Royal Society of London. B: Biological Sciences* 295(1077). 235–243. Reprinted in Royal Society of London, *The psychological mechanisms of language: A joint symposium of the Royal Society and the British Academy.* London: The Royal Society and the British Academy, 1981.

Coleman, E.B. 1965. Responses to a scale of grammaticalness. *Journal of Verbal Learning and Verbal Behavior* 4(6). 521–527.

Connors, Kathleen & Benoît Ouellette. 1993. *Contrasts in meaning and grammaticality judgments among native speakers and advanced learners.* Ms., Université de Montréal.

Coppieters, René. 1987. Competence differences between native and near-native speakers. *Language* 63(3). 544–573.

Cowart, Wayne. 1989. Notes on the biology of syntactic processing. *Journal of Psycholinguistic Research* 18(1). 89–103.

Cowart, Wayne. 1994. Anchoring and grammar effects in judgments of sentence acceptability. *Perceptual and Motor Skills* 79. 1171–1182.

Cowart, Wayne. 1997. *Experimental syntax: Applying objective methods to sentence judgments.* Thousand Oaks, CA: SAGE Publications.

Crain, Stephen & Janet Dean Fodor. 1985. Rules and constraints in sentence processing. In Stephen Berman, Jae-Woong Choe & Joyce McDonough (eds.), *Pro-

ceedings of NELS 15, 87–104. Amherst, MA: Graduate Student Linguistic Association, University of Massachusetts at Amherst.

Crain, Stephen & Janet Dean Fodor. 1987. Sentence matching and overgeneration. *Cognition* 26(2). 123–169.

Crain, Stephen & Mark Steedman. 1985. On not being led up the garden path: The use of context by the psychological syntax processor. In David D. Dowty, Lauri Karttunen & Arnold M. Zwicky (eds.), *Natural language processing: Psychological, computational, and theoretical perspectives*, 320–358. Cambridge: Cambridge University Press.

Dahl, Östen. 1979. Is linguistics empirical? A critique of Esa Itkonen's *Linguistics and metascience*. In Thomas A. Perry (ed.), *Evidence and argumentation in linguistics*, 13–45. Berlin: de Gruyter.

Danks, Joseph H. 1969. Grammaticalness and meaningfulness in the comprehension of sentences. *Journal of Verbal Learning and Verbal Behavior* 8(6). 687–696.

Danks, Joseph H. & Sam Glucksberg. 1970. Psychological scaling of linguistic properties. *Language and Speech* 13(2). 118–138.

Danks, Joseph H. & Sam Glucksberg. 1971. Psychological scaling of adjective orders. *Journal of Verbal Learning and Verbal Behavior* 10(1). 63–67.

Davy, Derek & Randolph Quirk. 1969. An acceptability experiment with spoken output. *Journal of Linguistics* 5(1). 109–120.

Dellarosa, Denise. 1988. A history of thinking. In Robert J. Sternberg & Edward E. Smith (eds.), *The psychology of human thought*, 1–18. Cambridge: Cambridge University Press.

Derwing, Bruce L. 1973. *Transformational grammar as a theory of language acquisition: A study in the empirical, conceptual and methodological foundations of contemporary linguistics*. Cambridge: Cambridge University Press.

Derwing, Bruce L. 1979. Against autonomous linguistics. In Thomas A. Perry (ed.), *Evidence and argumentation in linguistics*, 163–189. Berlin: de Gruyter.

Downey, Ronald G. & David T. Hakes. 1968. Some psychological effects of violating linguistic rules. *Journal of Verbal Learning and Verbal Behavior* 7(1). 158–161.

Dowty, David D., Lauri Karttunen & Arnold M. Zwicky (eds.). 1985. *Natural language processing: Psychological, computational, and theoretical perspectives*. Cambridge: Cambridge University Press.

Duval, Shelley & Robert A. Wicklund. 1972. *A theory of objective self awareness*. New York: Academic Press.

Eckman, Fred R. (ed.). 1977. *Current themes in linguistics: Bilingualism, experimental linguistics, and language typologies*. Washington, D.C.: Hemisphere.

References

Einhorn, Hillel J. 1982. Learning from experience and suboptimal rules in decision making. In Daniel Kahneman, Paul Slovic & Amos Tversky (eds.), *Judgment under uncertainty: Heuristics and biases*, 268–283. Cambridge: Cambridge University Press.

Elliot, Dale, Stanley Legum & Sandra Annear Thompson. 1969. Syntactic variation as linguistic data. In Robert I. Binnick, Alice Davison, Georgia M. Green & Jerry L. Morgan (eds.), *Papers from the fifth regional meeting of the Chicago Linguistic Society*, 52–59. Chicago: Chicago Linguistic Society.

Ellis, Rod. 1991. Grammaticality judgments and second language acquisition. *Studies in Second Language Acquisition* 13(2). 161–186.

Ericsson, K. Anders & Herbert A. Simon. 1984. *Protocol analysis: Verbal reports as data*. Cambridge, MA: MIT Press.

Fillmore, Charles J. 1972. On generativity. In Stanley Peters (ed.), *Goals of linguistic theory*, 1–19. Englewood Cliffs, NJ: Prentice-Hall.

Fillmore, Charles J. 1973. A grammarian looks to sociolinguistics. In Roger W. Shuy (ed.), *Report of the Twenty-Third Annual Round Table Meeting on Linguistics and Language Studies*, 273–287. Washington, D.C.: Georgetown University Press.

Fillmore, Charles J. 1979. On fluency. In Charles J. Fillmore, Daniel Kempler & William S-Y. Wang (eds.), *Individual differences in language ability and language behavior*, 85–102. New York: Academic Press.

Fillmore, Charles J., Daniel Kempler & William S-Y. Wang (eds.). 1979a. *Individual differences in language ability and language behavior*. New York: Academic Press.

Fillmore, Charles J., Daniel Kempler & William S-Y. Wang. 1979b. Introduction. In Charles J. Fillmore, Daniel Kempler & William S-Y. Wang (eds.), *Individual differences in language ability and language behavior*, 1–10. New York: Academic Press.

Ford, Marilyn, Joan Bresnan & Ronald M. Kaplan. 1982. A competence-based theory of syntactic closure. In Joan Bresnan (ed.), *The mental representation of grammatical relations*, 727–796. Cambridge, MA: MIT Press.

Forster, Kenneth I. & B.J. Stevenson. 1987. Sentence matching and well-formedness. *Cognition* 26(2). 171–186.

Fowler, Roger. 1970. Against idealization: Some speculations on the theory of linguistic performance. *Linguistics* 63. 19–50.

Fraser, Bruce. 1971. An analysis of "even" in English. In Charles J. Fillmore & D. Terence Langendoen (eds.), *Studies in linguistic semantics*, 151–178. New York: Holt, Rinehart & Winston.

Frazier, Lyn. 1985. Syntactic complexity. In David D. Dowty, Lauri Karttunen & Arnold M. Zwicky (eds.), *Natural language processing: Psychological, computational, and theoretical perspectives*, 129–189. Cambridge: Cambridge University Press.

Frazier, Lyn & Keith Rayner. 1982. Making and correcting errors during sentence comprehension: Eye movements in the analysis of structurally ambiguous sentences. *Cognitive Psychology* 14. 178–210.

Gardner, Martin. 1974. On the paradoxical situations that arise from nontransitive relations. *Scientific American* 231(4). 120–125.

Garnsey, Susan M. 1993. Event-related brain potentials in the study of language: An introduction. *Language and Cognitive Processes* 8(4). 337–356.

Gerken, LouAnn & Thomas G. Bever. 1986. Linguistic intuitions are the result of interactions between perceptual processes and linguistic universals. *Cognitive Science* 10. 457–476.

Gethin, Amorey. 1990. *Antilinguistics: A critical assessment of modern linguistic theory and practice.* Oxford: Intellect.

Gleitman, Henry & Lila R. Gleitman. 1979. Language use and language judgment. In Charles J. Fillmore, Daniel Kempler & William S-Y. Wang (eds.), *Individual differences in language ability and language behavior*, 103–126. New York: Academic Press.

Gleitman, Lila R. & Henry Gleitman. 1970. *Phrase and paraphrase: Some innovative uses of language.* New York: W. W. Norton & Company.

Gleitman, Lila R., Henry Gleitman & Elizabeth F. Shipley. 1972. The emergence of the child as a grammarian. *Cognition* 1(2/3). 137–164.

Goldman, Susan R. 1982. Coincidence or causality in linguistic and cognitive skills: A reply to Van Kleeck. *Merrill-Palmer Quarterly* 28(2). 267–274.

Gombert, Jean Émile. 1992. *Metalinguistic development.* Chicago: University of Chicago Press.

Grandy, Richard E. 1981. Some thoughts on data and theory in linguistics. In Peter D. Asquith & Ronald N. Giere (eds.), *PSA 1980: Proceedings of the 1980 biennial meeting of the Philosophy of Science Association. Volume 2: Symposia*, 605–609. East Lansing, MI: Philosophy of Science Association.

Grant, David A., Jeffrey A. Kadlac, Marian Schwartz, Michael J. Zajano, Joseph B. Hellige, Louise C. Perry & Kenneth B. Solberg. 1977. The role of noun imagery in the speed of processing the grammaticality of adjective-noun phrases. *Memory and Cognition* 5(4). 491–498.

Green, Georgia. 1978. *Remarks on a proposal presented by Thomas Dieterich and Guy Carden at the NWAVE-VII Colloquium on the Validation of Introspective*

Judgments. Paper presented at the NWAVE-VII Conference, Georgetown University.

Greenbaum, Sidney. 1973. Informant elicitation of data on syntactic variation. *Lingua* 31. 201–212.

Greenbaum, Sidney. 1976a. Contextual influence on acceptability judgments. *Linguistics* 187. 5–11. Reprinted in *International Journal of Psycholinguistics* 6 (1977), 5–11.

Greenbaum, Sidney. 1976b. Syntactic frequency and acceptability. *Lingua* 40(2/3). 99–113. Reprinted in Perry (1979), 301–314.

Greenbaum, Sidney (ed.). 1977a. *Acceptability in language.* The Hague: Mouton.

Greenbaum, Sidney. 1977b. Judgments of syntactic acceptability and frequency. *Studia Linguistica* 31(2). 83–105.

Greenbaum, Sidney. 1977c. The linguist as experimenter. In Fred R. Eckman (ed.), *Current themes in linguistics: Bilingualism, experimental linguistics, and language typologies*, 125–144. Washington, D.C.: Hemisphere.

Greenbaum, Sidney. 1988. *Good English and the grammarian.* London: Longman.

Greenbaum, Sidney & Randolph Quirk. 1970. *Elicitation experiments in English: Linguistic studies in use and attitude.* Coral Gables, FL: University of Miami Press.

Grimshaw, Jane & Sara Thomas Rosen. 1990. Knowledge and obedience: The developmental status of the binding theory. *Linguistic Inquiry* 21(2). 187–222.

Hagège, Claude. 1981. *Critical reflections on generative grammar.* Lake Bluff, IL: Jupiter Press.

Hakes, David T. 1980. *The development of metalinguistic abilities in children.* New York: Springer.

Halpern, Diane F. 1992. *Sex differences in cognitive abilities.* 2nd edition. Hillsdale, NJ: Erlbaum.

Hardyck, Curtis, Hilary Naylor & Rebecca. M. Smith. 1979. How shall a thing-ummy be called? In Charles J. Fillmore, Daniel Kempler & William S-Y. Wang (eds.), *Individual differences in language ability and language behavior*, 261–276. New York: Academic Press.

Harris, Randy Allen. 1993. *The linguistics wars.* New York: Oxford University Press.

Heeschen, Volker. 1978. The metalinguistic vocabulary of a speech community in the highlands of Irian Jaya (West New Guinea). In Anne Sinclair, R.J. Jarvella & Willem J.M. Levelt (eds.), *The child's conception of language*, 155–187. Berlin: Springer.

Heringer, James T. 1970. Research on quantifier-negative idiolects. In Chicago Linguistic Society (ed.), *Papers from the sixth regional meeting*, 287–295. Chicago: Chicago Linguistic Society.

Hill, Archibald A. 1961. Grammaticality. *Word* 17(1). 1–10.

Hill, Archibald A. (ed.). 1962. *Third Texas conference on problems of linguistic analysis in English.* Austin: University of Texas.

Hindle, Donald & Ivan A. Sag. 1975. Some more on *anymore.* In Ralph W. Fasold & Roger W. Shuy (eds.), *Analyzing variation in language: Papers from the second colloquium on new ways of analyzing variation*, 89–110. Washington, D.C.: Georgetown University Press.

Hirsh-Pasek, Kathy, Lila R. Gleitman & Henry Gleitman. 1978. What did the brain say to the mind? A study of the detection and report of ambiguity by young children. In Anne Sinclair, R.J. Jarvella & Willem J.M. Levelt (eds.), *The child's conception of language*, 97–132. Berlin: Springer.

Hirst, Graeme. 1981. *Anaphora in natural language understanding: A survey.* Berlin: Springer.

Hirst, Graeme. 1987. *Semantic interpretation and the resolution of ambiguity.* Cambridge: Cambridge University Press.

Hockett, Charles F. 1955. *A manual of phonology.* Baltimore: Waverly Press.

Householder, Fred W. Jr. 1965. On some recent claims in phonological theory. *Journal of Linguistics* 1(1). 13–34.

Householder, Fred W. Jr. 1971. Review of D. Terence Langendoen, *The study of syntax. Language* 2(47). 453–465.

Householder, Fred W. Jr. 1973. On arguments from asterisks. *Foundations of Language* 3(10). 365–376.

Itkonen, Esa. 1979. Qualitative vs. quantitative analysis in linguistics. In Thomas A. Perry (ed.), *Evidence and argumentation in linguistics*, 334–366. Berlin: de Gruyter.

Kaplan, Martin F. 1977. Judgment by juries. In Martin F. Kaplan & Steven Schwartz (eds.), *Human judgment and decision processes in applied settings*, 31–55. New York: Academic Press.

Katz, Jerrold J. 1964. Semi-sentences. In Jerry A. Fodor & Jerrold J. Katz (eds.), *The structure of language: Readings in the philosophy of language*, 400–416. Englewood Cliffs, N.J.: Prentice-Hall.

Katz, Jerrold J. 1981. *Language and other abstract objects.* Totowa, NJ: Rowman & Littlefield.

Katz, Jerrold J. & Thomas G. Bever. 1976. The fall and rise of empiricism. In D. Terence Langendoen, Jerrold J. Katz & Thomas G. Bever (eds.), *An integrated theory of linguistic ability*, 11–64. New York: Crowell.

Kess, Joseph F. & Ronald A. Hoppe. 1983. Individual differences and meta-linguistic abilities. *Canadian Journal of Linguistics* 28(1). 47–53.

Kitagawa, Yoshihisa. 1991. Copying identity. *Natural Language and Linguistic Theory* 9(3). 497–536.

Klein, Eberhard. 1979. The role of syntactic and semantic factors in explaining degrees of acceptability of non-finite verbal complement structures in English. *Linguistische Berichte* 61. 1–20.

Kluender, Robert & Marta Kutas. 1993. Subjacency as a processing phenomenon. *Language and Cognitive Processes* 8(4). 573–633.

Kroch, Anthony S. 1981. On the role of resumptive pronouns in amnestying island constraint violations. In Roberta A. Hendrick, Carrie S. Masek & Mary Frances Miller (eds.), *Papers from the seventeenth regional meeting*, 125–135. Chicago: Chicago Linguistic Society.

Kutas, Marta & Steven A. Hillyard. 1983. Event-related brain potentials to grammatical errors and semantic anomalies. *Memory and Cognition* 15(11). 539–550.

Labov, William. 1972a. *Sociolinguistic patterns*. Philadelphia: University of Pennsylvania Press.

Labov, William. 1972b. Some principles of linguistic methodology. *Language in Society* 1(1). 97–120.

Labov, William. 1975. *What is a linguistic fact?* Lisse: Peter de Ridder. Also published as Empirical foundations of linguistic theory, in Robert Austerlitz (ed.), *The scope of American linguistics*, 77–133. Lisse: Peter de Ridder, 1975.

Labov, William. 1978. Sociolinguistics. In William Orr Dingwall (ed.), *A survey of linguistic science*, 339–372. Stamford, CT: Greylock.

Lachter, Joel & Thomas G. Bever. 1988. The relation between linguistic structure and associative theories of language learning – A constructive critique of some connectionist learning models. In Steven Pinker & Jacques Mehler (eds.), *Connections and symbols*, 195–247. Cambridge, MA: MIT Press.

Lakoff, George. 1971. Presupposition and relative well-formedness. In Danny D. Steinberg & Leon A. Jakobovits (eds.), *Semantics: An interdisciplinary reader in philosophy, linguistics and psychology*, 329–340. Cambridge: Cambridge University Press.

Lakoff, George. 1973. Fuzzy grammar and the performance/competence terminology game. In Claudia Corum, T. Cedric Smith-Stark & Ann Weiser (eds.),

Papers from the ninth regional meeting, 271–291. Chicago: Chicago Linguistic Society.

Lakoff, George. 1987. Cognitive models and prototype theory. In Ulric Neisser (ed.), *Concepts and conceptual development: Ecological and intellectual factors in categorization*, 63–100. Cambridge: Cambridge University Press.

Lakoff, Robin. 1977. You say what you are: Acceptability and gender-related language. In Sidney Greenbaum (ed.), *Acceptability in language*, 73–86. The Hague: Mouton.

Langacker, Ronald W. 1969. On pronominalization and the chain of command. In David A. Reibel & Sanford A. Schane (eds.), *Modern studies in English*, 160–186. Englewood Cliffs, NJ: Prentice-Hall.

Langendoen, D. Terence. 1972. The problem of grammaticality. *Peabody Journal of Education* 50(1). 20–23.

Langendoen, D. Terence. 1973. The problem of linguistic theory in relation to language behavior: a tribute and reply to Paul Goodman. *Daedalus* 102(3). 195–201.

Langendoen, D. Terence & Thomas G. Bever. 1973. Can a not unhappy person be called a not sad one? In Stephen R. Anderson & Paul Kiparsky (eds.), *A festschrift for Morris Halle*, 392–409. New York: Holt, Rinehart & Winston. Reprinted in Bever, Katz & Langendoen 1976, 239–260.

Lasnik, Howard. 1981. Learnability, restrictiveness, and the evaluation metric. In C.L. Baker & John J. McCarthy (eds.), *The logical problem of language acquisition*, 1–29. Cambridge, MA: MIT Press.

Lasnik, Howard & Mamoru Saito. 1984. On the nature of proper government. *Linguistic Inquiry* 15(2). 235–289.

Lees, Robert B. 1976. Optical illusions and grammar blindness. In James D. McCawley (ed.), *Notes from the linguistic underground* (Syntax and Semantics 7), 21–26. New York: Academic Press.

Lefever, Michael M. & Linnea C. Ehri. 1976. The relationship between field independence and sentence disambiguation ability. *Journal of Psycholinguistic Research* 5(2). 99–106.

Legum, Stanley, Dale Elliot & Sandra Annear Thompson. 1974. *Considerations in the analysis of syntactic variation*. Mimeographed. Los Alamitos, CA: SWRL Educational Research & Development.

Levelt, Willem J.M. 1972. Some psychological aspects of linguistic data. *Linguistische Berichte* 17. 18–30.

Levelt, Willem J.M. 1974. *Formal grammars in linguistics and psycholinguistics*. 3 volumes. The Hague: Mouton.

Levelt, Willem J.M., Anne Sinclair & R.J. Jarvella. 1978. Causes and functions of linguistic awareness in language acquisition: some introductory remarks. In Anne Sinclair, R.J. Jarvella & Willem J.M. Levelt (eds.), *The child's conception of language*, 1–14. Berlin: Springer.

Levelt, Willem J.M., J.A.W.M. van Gent, A.F.J. Haans & A.J.A. Meijers. 1977. Grammaticality, paraphrase, and imagery. In Sidney Greenbaum (ed.), *Acceptability in language*, 87–101. The Hague: Mouton.

Lieberman, Philip. 1991. Letter to the editor (under the heading Apes and us: An exchange). *The New York Review of Books* 38(16). 53. In reply to Lord Zuckerman, Apes R not us, *The New York Review of Books* 38(10) (1991), 43–49.

Liles, Betty Z., Martin D. Shulman & Susan Bartlett. 1977. Judgments of grammaticality by normal and language-disordered children. *Journal of Speech and Hearing Disorders* 42(2). 199–209.

Lyons, William. 1986. *The disappearance of introspection*. Cambridge, MA: MIT Press.

Maclay, Howard & Mary D. Sleator. 1960. Responses to language: Judgments of grammaticalness. *International Journal of American Linguistics* 26(4). 275–282.

Marks, Lawrence Edward. 1965. *Psychological investigations of semi-grammaticalness in English*. Cambridge, MA: Harvard University PhD dissertation.

Marks, Lawrence Edward. 1967. Judgments of grammaticalness of some English sentences and semi-sentences. *American Journal of Psychology* 80(2). 196–204.

Marks, Lawrence Edward. 1968. Scaling of grammaticalness of self-embedded English sentences. *Journal of Verbal Learning and Verbal Behavior* 7(5). 965–967.

Masny, Diana & Alison d'Anglejan. 1985. Language, cognition and second language grammaticality judgments. *Journal of Psycholinguistic Research* 14(2). 175–197.

Masny, Diana & Alison d'Anglejan. 1993. *Grammatical theory in the United States from Bloomfield to Chomsky*. Cambridge: Cambridge University Press.

Matthews, Robert J. 1979. Are the grammatical sentences of a language a recursive set? *Synthese* 40. 209–224.

Matthews, Robert J. 1993. *Grammatical theory in the United States from Bloomfield to Chomsky*. Cambridge: Cambridge University Press.

McCawley, James D. (ed.). 1976. *Notes from the linguistic underground* (Syntax and Semantics 7). New York: Academic Press.

McCawley, James D. 1979. Concerning a methodological pseudo-exorcism. *Linguistics* 17(1). 3–20.

McCawley, James D. 1982. How far can you trust a linguist? In Thomas W. Simon & Robert J. Scholes (eds.), *Language, mind, and brain*, 75–88. Hillsdale, NJ: Erlbaum.

McCawley, James D. 1985. Review of Newmeyer 1983. *Language* 61(3). 668–679.

McDaniel, Dana & Helen Smith Cairns. 1990. The child as informant: Eliciting linguistic intuitions from young children. *Journal of Psycholinguistic Research* 19(5). 331–344.

McNeill, David & Karen Lindig. 1973. The perceptual reality of phonemes, syllables, words and sentences. *Journal of Verbal Learning and Verbal Behavior* 12. 419–430.

McRoy, Susan Weber & Graeme Hirst. 1990. Race-based parsing and syntactic disambiguation. *Cognitive Science* 14(3). 313–353.

Miller, George A. & Stephen Isard. 1963. Some perceptual consequences of linguistic rules. *Journal of Verbal Learning and Verbal Behavior* 2(3). 217–228.

Milne, Robert William. 1982. Predicting garden path sentences. *Cognitive Science* 6. 349–373.

Mistler-Lachman, Janet L. 1972. Levels of comprehension in processing of normal and ambiguous sentences. *Journal of Verbal Learning and Verbal Behavior* 11. 614–623.

Mitchell, Don C. & Virginia M. Holmes. 1985. The role of specific information about the verb in parsing sentences with local structural ambiguity. *Journal of Memory and Language* 24. 542–559.

Mohan, B.A. 1977. Acceptability testing and fuzzy grammar. In Sidney Greenbaum (ed.), *Acceptability in language*, 133–148. The Hague: Mouton.

Moore, Timothy E. 1972. Speeded recognition of ungrammaticality. *Journal of Verbal Learning and Verbal Behavior* 11. 550–560.

Moore, Timothy E. & Irving Biederman. 1979. Speeded recognition of ungrammaticality: Double violations. *Cognition* 7(3). 285–299.

Morgan, J.L. 1972. Verb agreement as a rule of English. In Paul M. Peranteau, Judith N. Levi & Gloria C. Phares (eds.), *Papers from the eighth regional meeting*, 278–286. Chicago: Chicago Linguistic Society.

Nagata, Hiroshi. 1987a. Change in the modulus of judgmental scale: An inadequate explanation for the repetition effect in judgments of grammaticality. *Perceptual and Motor Skills* 65(3). 907–910.

Nagata, Hiroshi. 1987b. Long-term effect of repetition on judgments of grammaticality. *Perceptual and Motor Skills* 65(1). 295–299.

Nagata, Hiroshi. 1988. The relativity of linguistic intuition: The effect of repetition on grammaticality judgments. *Journal of Psycholinguistic Research* 17(1). 1–17.

Nagata, Hiroshi. 1989a. Effect of repetition on grammaticality judgments under objective and subjective self-awareness conditions. *Journal of Psycholinguistic Research* 18(3). 255–269.

Nagata, Hiroshi. 1989b. Judgments of sentence grammaticality and field-dependence of subjects. *Perceptual and Motor Skills* 69(3). 739–747.

Nagata, Hiroshi. 1989c. Judgments of sentence grammaticality with differentiation and enrichment strategies. *Perceptual and Motor Skills* 68(2). 463–469.

Nagata, Hiroshi. 1989d. Repetition effect in judgments of grammaticality of sentences: Examination with ungrammatical sentences. *Perceptual and Motor Skills* 68(1). 275–282.

Nagata, Hiroshi. 1990a. On-line judgments of grammaticality of sentences. *Perceptual and Motor Skills* 70(3). 987–994.

Nagata, Hiroshi. 1990b. Speaker's sensitivity to rule violations in sentences. *Psychologia* 33(3). 179–184.

Nagata, Hiroshi. 1992. Anchoring effects in judging grammaticality of sentences. *Perceptual and Motor Skills* 75. 159–164.

Neisser, Ulric (ed.). 1987. *Concepts and conceptual development: Ecological and intellectual factors in categorization.* Cambridge: Cambridge University Press.

Neubauer, Paul. 1976. The 2^3 verbs *pretend*. In James D. McCawley (ed.), *Notes from the linguistic underground* (Syntax and Semantics 7), 399–407. New York: Academic Press.

Neville, Helen, Janet L. Nicol, Andrew Barss, Kenneth I. Forster & Merrill F. Garrett. 1991. Syntactically-based sentence processing classes: Evidence from event-related brain potentials. *Journal of Cognitive Neuroscience* 3(2). 151–165.

Newmeyer, Frederick J. 1983. *Grammatical theory, its limits and its possibilities.* Chicago: University of Chicago Press.

Nisbett, Richard E. & Timothy Decamp Wilson. 1977. Telling more than we know: Verbal reports on mental processes. *Psychological Review* 84. 231–259.

Oller, John W. Jr., B. Dennis Sales & Ronald V. Harrington. 1970. Toward consistent definitions of some psycholinguistic terms. *Linguistics* 57. 48–59.

Osterhout, Lee & Phillip J. Holcomb. 1992. Event-related brain potentials elicited by syntactic anomaly. *Journal of Memory and Language* 31. 785–806.

Osterhout, Lee, Phillip J. Holcomb & David A. Swinney. 1994. Brain potentials elicited by garden-path sentences: Evidence of the application of verb information during parsing. *Journal of Experimental Psychology: Learning, Memory and Cognition* 20(4). 786–803.

Paikeday, Thomas M. 1985. *The native speaker is dead!* Toronto: Paikeday Publishing.

Pateman, Trevor. 1987. *Language in mind and language in society: Studies in linguistic reproduction.* Oxford: Clarendon Press.

Perry, Thomas A. (ed.). 1979. *Evidence and argumentation in linguistics.* Berlin: de Gruyter.

Pesetsky, David. 1981. *Wh*-in-situ: Movement and unselective binding. In Eric J. Reuland & Alice G.B. ter Meulen (eds.), *The representation of (in)definiteness*, 98–129. Cambridge, MA: MIT Press.

Peters, Stanley (ed.). 1972. *Goals of linguistic theory.* Englewood Cliffs, NJ: Prentice-Hall.

Philips, Susan U., Susan Steele & Christine Tanz (eds.). 1987. *Language, gender, and sex in comparative perspective.* Cambridge: Cambridge University Press.

Pollock, Jean-Yves. 1989. Verb movement, universal grammar and the structure of IP. *Linguistic Inquiry* 20(3). 365–424.

Postal, Paul M. 1976. Linguistic anarchy notes. In James D. McCawley (ed.), *Notes from the linguistic underground* (Syntax and Semantics 7), 201–225. New York: Academic Press.

Postal, Paul M. 1988. Advances in linguistic rhetoric. *Natural Language and Linguistic Theory* 6. 129–137.

Pullum, Geoffrey K. 1987. Seven deadly sins in journal publishing. *Natural Language and Linguistic Theory* 5. 453–459. Reprinted in Geoffrey K. Pullum, *The great Eskimo vocabulary hoax and other irreverent essays on the study of language* (1991), 84–91. Chicago: University of Chicago Press.

Pynte, Joel. 1991. The locus of semantic satiation in category membership decision and acceptability judgment. *Journal of Psycholinguistic Research* 20(4). 315–335.

Quirk, Randolph & Jan Svartvik. 1966. *Investigating linguistic acceptability.* The Hague: Mouton.

Ray, William J. & Richard Ravizza. 1988. *Methods toward a science of behavior and experience.* Belmont, CA: Wadsworth.

Reed, H.J. & Jean Lave. 1979. Arithmetic as a tool for investigating relations between culture and cognition. *American Ethnologist* 6(3). 568–582.

Reich, Peter A. 1969. The finiteness of natural language. *Language* 45(4). 831–843.

Reinhart, Tanya. 1976. *The syntactic domain of anaphora.* Cambridge, MA: MIT PhD dissertation.

Ringen, Jon D. 1977. On evaluating data concerning linguistic intuition. In Fred R. Eckman (ed.), *Current themes in linguistics: Bilingualism, experimental linguistics, and language typologies*, 145–160. Washington, D.C.: Hemisphere.

Ringen, Jon D. 1979. Linguistic facts: A study of the empirical scientific status of transformational generative grammars. In Thomas A. Perry (ed.), *Evidence and argumentation in linguistics*, 97–132. Berlin: de Gruyter. Originally published in David Cohen & Jessica R. Wirth (eds.), *Testing linguistic hypotheses*, 1–41. Washington, D.C.: Hemisphere, 1975.

Rosch, Eleanor. 1975. Cognitive representations of semantic categories. *Journal of Experimental Psychology: General* 104. 192–233.

Rose, Robert G. 1973. Linguist and nonlinguist agreement concerning surface structures. *The Journal of General Psychology* 89(2). 325–326.

Ross, John Robert. 1972. The category squish: Endstation Hauptwort. In Paul M. Peranteau, Judith N. Levi & Gloria C. Phares (eds.), *Papers from the eighth regional meeting*, 316–338. Chicago: Chicago Linguistic Society.

Ross, John Robert. 1979. Where's English? In Charles J. Fillmore, Daniel Kempler & William S-Y. Wang (eds.), *Individual differences in language ability and language behavior*, 127–163. New York: Academic Press.

Ryan, Ellen Bouchard & George W. Ledger. 1984. Learning to attend to sentence structure: Links between metalinguistic development and reading. In John Downing & Renate Valtin (eds.), *Language awareness and learning to read*, 149–171. New York: Springer.

Sachs, Jacqueline Strunk. 1967. Recognition memory for syntactic and semantic aspects of connected discourse. *Perception and Psychophysics* 2(9). 437–442.

Sampson, Geoffrey. 1975. *The form of language*. London: Weidenfeld & Nicolson.

Schmidt, Richard W. & Carol F. McCreary. 1977. Standard and super-standard English: Recognition and use of prescriptive rules by native and non-native speakers. *TESOL Quarterly* 11(4). 415–429.

Schnitser, Marc L. 1973. In search of an unproblematical notion of grammaticality. *Le Langage et l'Homme* 21. 27–38.

Schober, Michael F. & Herbert H. Clark. 1989. Understanding by addressees and overhearers. *Cognitive Psychology* 21(2). 211–232.

Scholes, Robert J. & Brenda J. Willis. 1987. Literacy and language. *Journal of Literary Semantics* 16(1). 3–11.

Schütze, Carson T. 1991. *Grammaticality judgements and linguistic methodology*. M.A. Forum paper, Department of Linguistics, University of Toronto.

Scott, Robert Ian. 1969. A permutational test of grammaticality. *Lingua* 24(1). 11–18.

Scott, Robert Ian & John A. Mills. 1973. Validating the permutational test of grammaticality. *Language and Speech* 16(2). 110–122.

Scribner, Sylvia & Michael Cole. 1981. *The psychology of literacy*. Cambridge, MA: Harvard University Press.

Shanon, Benny. 1973. Interpretation of ungrammatical sentences. *Journal of Verbal Learning and Verbal Behavior* 12(4). 389–400.

Simon, Thomas W. & Robert J. Scholes (eds.). 1982. *Language, mind, and brain.* Hillsdale, NJ: Erlbaum.

Sinclair, Anne, R.J. Jarvella & Willem J.M. Levelt (eds.). 1978. *The child's conception of language.* Berlin: Springer.

Sledd, James H. 1962. Prufrock among the syntacticians. In Archibald A. Hill (ed.), *Third Texas conference on problems of linguistic analysis in English*, 1–15. Austin: University of Texas.

Smith, Neil V. 1981. Grammaticality, time and tense. *Philosophical Transactions of the Royal Society of London. B: Biological Sciences* 295(1077). 253–265. Reprinted in Royal Society of London, *The psychological mechanisms of language: A joint symposium of the Royal Society and the British Academy.* London: The Royal Society and the British Academy, 1981.

Snow, Catherine E. 1975. Linguists as behavioral scientists: Towards a methodology for testing linguistic intuitions. In Albert Kraak (ed.), *Linguistics in the Netherlands 1972–1973*, 271–275. Assen: Van Gorcum.

Snow, Catherine E. & Guus Meijer. 1977. On the secondary nature of syntactic intuitions. In Sidney Greenbaum (ed.), *Acceptability in language*, 163–177. The Hague: Mouton.

Snyder, William. 1994. *A psycholinguistic investigation of weak crossover, scope, and syntactic satiation effects: implications for distinguishing competence from performance.* Paper presented at the CUNY Human Sentence Processing Conference Poster Session. Downloadable from the author's web page.

Sobin, Nicholas. 1987. The variable status of comp-trace phenomena. *Natural Language and Linguistic Theory* 5(1). 33–60.

Spencer, Nancy J. 1973. Differences between linguists and nonlinguists in intuitions of grammaticality-acceptability. *Journal of Psycholinguistic Research* 2(2). 83–98.

Steegar, David M. 1975. *Prosody and punctuation: A linguistic and experimental study.* Toronto: University of Toronto PhD dissertation.

Stokes, William. 1974. All of the work on quantifier-negation isn't convincing. In Michael W. La Galy, Robert A. Fox & Anthony Bruck (eds.), *Papers from the tenth regional meeting*, 692–700. Chicago: Chicago Linguistic Society.

Stolz, Walter S. 1969. Some experiments with queer sentences. *Language and Speech* 12. 203–219.

Svartvik, Jan & David Wright. 1977. The use of *ought* in teenage English. In Sidney Greenbaum (ed.), *Acceptability in language*, 179–201. The Hague: Mouton.

Taylor, M.M. & G.B. Henning. 1963. Verbal transformations and an effect of instructional bias on perception. *Canadian Journal of Psychology* 17. 210–223.

Taylor, Wilson L. 1953. "Cloze procedure": a new tool for measuring readability. *Journalism Quarterly* 30. 415–433.

Thráinsson, Höskuldur. 1979. *On complementation in Icelandic.* New York: Garland.

Tottie, Gunnel. 1977. Variation, acceptability and the advanced foreign learner: Towards a sociolinguistics without a social context. In Sidney Greenbaum (ed.), *Acceptability in language*, 203–213. The Hague: Mouton.

Valian, Virginia. 1982. Psycholinguistic experiment and linguistic intuition. In Thomas W. Simon & Robert J. Scholes (eds.), *Language, mind, and brain*, 179–188. Hillsdale, NJ: Erlbaum.

van Dijk, Teun A. 1977. Acceptability in context. In Sidney Greenbaum (ed.), *Acceptability in language*, 39–61. The Hague: Mouton.

Van Kleeck, Anne. 1982. The emergence of linguistic awareness: A cognitive framework. *Merrill-Palmer Quarterly* 28(2). 237–265.

Van Petten, Cyma & Marta Kutas. 1991. Influences of semantic and syntactic context on open- and closed-class words. *Memory and Cognition* 19(1). 95–112.

van Riemsdijk, Henk C. & Edwin Williams. 1986. *Introduction to the theory of grammar.* Cambridge, MA: MIT Press.

Vetter, Harold J., Jerry Volovecky & Richard W. Howell. 1979. Judgments of grammaticalness: A partial replication and extension. *Journal of Psycholinguistic Research* 8(6). 567–583.

Walker, Edward Lewis. 1973. Psychological complexity and preference: A hedgehog theory of behavior. In Daniel Ellis Berlyne & Kaj Berg Madsen (eds.), *Pleasure, reward, preference: Their nature, determinants, and role in behavior*, 65–91. New York: Academic Press.

Wardhaugh, Ronald. 1988. *An introduction to sociolinguistics.* Oxford: Blackwell.

Warner, John & Arnold L. Glass. 1987. Context and distance-to-disambiguation effects in ambiguity resolution: evidence from grammaticality judgments of garden path sentences. *Journal of Memory and Language* 26. 714–738.

Watt, W.C. 1975. The indiscreteness with which impenetrables are penetrated. *Lingua* 37. 95–128.

Weiner, Bernard, Willard Runquist, Peggy A. Runquist, Bertram H. Raven, William J. Meyer, Arnold Leiman, Charles L. Kutscher, Benjamin Kleinmuntz & Ralph Norman Haber. 1977. *Discovering psychology.* Chicago: Science Research Associates.

Wundt, Wilhelm. 1896. *Grundriss der Psychologie.* Leipzig: Engelmann.

Name index

Name index

Subject index

www.ingramcontent.com/pod-product-compliance
Lightning Source LLC
Chambersburg PA
CBHW080543110426
42813CB00006B/1197